15 $\frac{00}{n}$

THE EMPIRICAL ARGUMENT FOR GOD
IN LATE BRITISH THOUGHT

LONDON : HUMPHREY MILFORD

OXFORD UNIVERSITY PRESS

THE EMPIRICAL ARGUMENT FOR GOD IN LATE BRITISH THOUGHT

BY

PETER ANTHONY BERTOCCI

With a Foreword by
FREDERICK ROBERT TENNANT

CAMBRIDGE, MASSACHUSETTS

HARVARD UNIVERSITY PRESS

1938

KRAUS REPRINT CO.
New York
1970

BT 96
.B4
1970

Reprinted with the permission of the original publisher
KRAUS REPRINT CO.
A U.S. Division of Kraus-Thomson Organization Limited
Printed in U.S.A.

TO
MY MOTHER
AND
MY WIFE

TRUTH is the cry of all, but the game of a few. Certainly, where it is the chief passion, it doth not give way to vulgar cares and views; nor is it contented with a little ardour in the early time of life; active, perhaps, to pursue, but not so fit to weigh and revise. He that would make a real progress in knowledge must dedicate his age as well as youth, the later growth as well as first fruits, at the altar of Truth.

BERKELEY, *Siris*

FOREWORD

THERE are several types of theism and of theistic argument, distinguishable in themselves but more or less overlapping in the systems of individual writers, to be found in the philosophical and theological literature produced within the last few decades in Britain.

One mode of approach is to set out from religious experience in which there is considered to be an immediate apprehension of unique data, such as to constitute theology a science independent of other sciences and of philosophy, or else a peculiar kind of 'seeing things together as a whole.' This has kinship with Schleiermacher's endeavour to find a new basis for theology, and with Otto's theory of the numinous. It is best represented to-day by Dr. Oman, who has given an impressive exposition of it in his work *The Natural and the Supernatural*. Another approach is by means of a method having affinities with the dialectical, and by a more *a priori* procedure such as is evinced in neo-Hegelianism. Largely inspired by T. H. Green, Bradley, and Bosanquet, and using the coherence theory of truth, this approach issues in a predominantly immanentist kind of theism and in identification of God with The Absolute. A third type of approach is that which sets out from the knowledge furnished by the sciences and ethics, and professes to be empirical in method — at least up to a certain stage. Its arguments are, consequently, mainly of the teleological and moral kind. It is this last mode of approach which, almost exclusively, is illustrated and discussed in the essay of Mr. Bertocci. The writers of whose works he presents a comparative and critical study are representatives of it, whatever partial divergences from it in the direction of other modes of approach any of them may exhibit.

So far as I am able to judge, Mr. Bertocci has succeeded in getting to understand the systems with which he deals sufficiently to enable him to expound them without unconscious misrepresentation. The independence of his thought, and the critical ability which he evinces, should render his study a clarifying contribution to the department of theology with which it is concerned, and commend it to the attention of students such as are interested in any of the philosophical systems which he reviews.

F. R. TENNANT

PREFACE

THIS work is an essay in empirical philosophical theology. It proposes to accomplish two objectives. The first aim is to present an exposition and analysis of the main problems, with which any philosophically respectable theism must deal, as presented by five very significant English philosophers of the last hundred years. In order to present each philosopher's thought as a whole, a chapter has been devoted to the work of each thinker, though overlapping and repetition have been avoided by dealing with common ideas during the discussion of that philosopher who presented the clearest and most forceful analysis of the particular problem involved. Hence, Chapters V and VI, which between them include the discussion of almost all the problems in the scope of this essay, are longer than might seem advisable. Nevertheless, no chapter can be completely understood in itself, for each represents a phase of the development of the empirical argument for God, the delineation of which constitutes the main burden of this essay.

My trust in the fairness and accuracy of the exposition is based on the fact that the research for this work was done in England, at the University of Cambridge, with the guidance of Dr. F. R. Tennant, who read and discussed the whole manuscript with me when it was in a form substantially identical with what appears here. I was also exceedingly fortunate to have the needed suggestions and corrections of the late W. R. Sorley who read all but the first two chapters and was especially helpful in removing wrong emphases and inaccuracies in Chapter V, devoted to his own work. He also served as an expert critic of Chapter III, which deals with the thought of his highly esteemed friend, A. S. Pringle-Pattison. Both pupils of James Ward, Tennant and Sorley, served as invaluable critics of Chapter IV, which is devoted to Ward's theism. Without their help and encouragement this work would not dare to go beyond my own study.

The second aim of this essay, interwoven with the first, is

the evaluation and criticism of various contributions of these writers, with a view to the discovery and presentation of that argument for God which takes into account most adequately the various aspects of our human experience and knowledge. This leads to a detailed analysis of the moral argument for God and to its final rejection as such. It will be seen that in the argument finally approved, aspects of the thought of Dr. Tennant and Professor E. S. Brightman are most prominent, though there are points at which I cannot follow them. To the teaching and personal inspiration of Professor Brightman I am indebted in a measure incalculable, and for these same benefits am I grateful to Dr. Tennant.

I am indebted to the following publishers for permission to quote from their publications: The Abingdon Press, George Allen and Unwin Ltd., The British Academy, Wm. Blackwood and Sons Ltd., Librairie Bloud et Gay, The Cambridge University Press, The Macmillan Co., Macmillan and Company, and The Oxford University Press.

I wish that I might adequately express my gratitude to my father and mother and to the loyal friends who have helped to make this work possible. Immeasurable is my obligation to Mrs. Joseph Di Silva for her constant inspiration and unsparing efforts in my behalf. I am similarly indebted to my wife and to my brother Angelo for their continuous and painstaking helpfulness throughout the writing of this book.

P. A. B.

Bates College
Lewiston, Maine

CONTENTS

xiv CONTENTS

THE EMPIRICAL ARGUMENT FOR GOD
IN LATE BRITISH THOUGHT

CHAPTER I

INTRODUCTION

THE aim of this book is the exposition and evaluation of the reasons for belief in God advanced by five influential British philosophers since 1850.[1] These philosophers are: James Martineau, Andrew Seth Pringle-Pattison, James Ward, William R. Sorley, and Frederick R. Tennant. Though there are other points of agreement among these men, all are united in the contention that the argument for God must recognize and be based upon the known facts of experience. All reject any logical rationalism and sense-bound empiricism such as are most clearly exemplified in the philosophy of Spinoza and Hume respectively. All deny the validity of a priori arguments for theism and profess to proceed inductively to the conclusion that the existence of a certain kind of God is the best explanation of the whole of man's experience.

Hence the arguments of these men are called empirical. The empirical argument for God, then, is not a specific set of reasons but a generic name given to arguments which seek to show that the most reasonable interpretation of presumptive knowledge drawn from the various realms of human experience leads to belief in God. It will be seen that the contribution made by man's moral experience to the solution of the theistic problem is emphasized and carefully evaluated by each thinker, but in no instance does the argument pretend to rest solely on the moral life of man as separate from the rest of his experience.

A critical study of these arguments must first attempt a disinterested and thorough analysis of the most important elements in each. Consequently, whatever commentaries and reviews were available have been used only after a private

[1] The work of Alfred E. Taylor has also been studied, but since his contribution, though important, is not unique, it seemed wise to indicate the nature of his argument and include relevant parts at appropriate points in the discussion of these other philosophers.

analysis and evaluation had been made of the pertinent writings of each philosopher. In the exposition of the arguments special attention has been paid to the method of argument. Criticism has been focused on the extent to which each thinker faithfully employed the empirical method, as well as on the internal consistency of the arguments advanced and on their ability to explain experience coherently.

A few introductory remarks may be made on empirical method. Empiricism (used as a synonym for empirical method), as already indicated in the first paragraph, does not mean sensationism, not does it mean rationalism, though it *might* lead to either or any other "ism." The point is that, as a method of approach to truth, empiricism does not in itself favor any one aspect of experience. It is not a criterion of truth, but the basis for obtaining one. It influences the conclusions drawn through its use no more than the use of a pen determines the truth of what is written. To borrow a statement quoted approvingly by Tennant, empiricism means: "We must begin with experience, since otherwise there is no problem; and return to experience, since otherwise no solution is made good; and proceed on the analogy of experience, since otherwise there is failure of that continuity and resemblance in which explanation consists." [2] Empirical philosophy must start *in mediis rebus*, with commonsense knowledge (in some realms, fortunately, further refined by science, which itself uses this empirical method); and, as Tennant himself says: ". . . no analysis can stand, that is incompatible with the existence of any part of the analysandum itself; no theory of knowledge [or any other theory] can be approved which involves the impossibility of the data being forthcoming." [3]

That the empirical method should be used in the philosophy of religion no one of the men to be studied would deny, but the halting application of this method at critical points will be illustrated as the exposition proceeds. When applied

[2] F. R. Tennant, *Philosophical Theology* (1929–30), I, 216 n., quoting Carveth Read's *The Metaphysics of Nature* (2nd ed., 1908), p. 33.
[3] *Philosophical Theology*, p. 8.

to the problem of God, the empirical approach demands that all presumptive knowledge be analyzed and synthesized for the light it throws on the truth of the hypothesis of God. It does not mean the absurdity that the investigator must not previously have a conception of what he would prove, but it does imply that argument for such a conception proceeds not from the logical *implication* of an idea but from reasonable inferences based on the data as a whole. It does not mean that, for example, an idea of God conceived as a result of emotional experience may not be used as an hypothesis to be verified by an analysis of experience as a whole, but it does mean that every constituent of that complex idea (that is, the omnipotence, or goodness, or omniscience of God) be *freshly* verified by an appeal to the data, and not by deduction from any other constituent which has already been adequately verified. It is in the violation of this procedure that empiricism in the argument for God falters, as Hume and Kant showed. Aspects of their criticism will elucidate this fundamental point.

The reader of the *Dialogues On Natural Religion* will remember Hume's rejection of the traditional ontological argument (which, based on the analysis of a concept, disregards empirical method), and Hume's insistence that the argument for God's goodness, confronted with the problem of evil, be rooted in known facts only, and not proved by appealing to the unknown. The implication was that the existence of any attribute of God should be proved by reference to the facts of experience that particular attribute explained, and not by deductions from the rest of the idea of God. When Kant objected to the cosmological and the teleological arguments as in themselves the basis of a full-orbed conception of God (as omnipotent, for example), he was merely developing Hume's objection and exposing the subtle deception in the blending of a priori conclusions with those substantiated by empirical fact. A similar deception operates when the conclusion to be proved puts blinkers on the eyes of the investigator, so that only part of the facts come into his ken.

So much may be said by way of introduction. It must be

further noted, however, that though each chapter of this study stands as a relatively independent whole, comparison and criticism are cumulative, and that exposition and criticism of certain elements of one man's thought are combined or placed alongside of similar aspects of another's. The final chapter on the problem of evil is the complement of every chapter.

CHAPTER II

JAMES MARTINEAU'S REVOLT AGAINST SENSE–BOUND EMPIRICISM

A. Martineau's Background and Development

THE contribution of James Martineau to the religious thought of the nineteenth century is best understood in the light of the "winds of doctrine" current in the century which, with the exception of the first five years, his life spanned. F. E. Hutchinson says: "Religious thought has seldom been so stagnant in England as at the opening of the nineteenth century." [1] The French Revolution, with its rebellion against established notions, had served to put the English church on its guard against the invasion of traditional doctrines. Though religious fervor burned bright, there was so little speculative interest in ecclesiastical circles that it was left for the poet-philosopher, Samuel Coleridge, to plead that philosophy be given a hearing in the solution of religious problems. Martineau was one of those who helped to break the shackles which a priori theories of biblical inspiration had placed on religious discussion, and, as we shall see, when science threatened to invade the sphere of religion, he rose to defend its claims against the intruder.

In Martineau's college days (1822–27) German idealism had not yet been imported, and England was dominated by two schools of thought, the Hartleyan Empiricism, with its psychological determinism and ethical hedonism, and the Scottish Common Sense school. At Manchester College the former philosophy found favor with William Turner, who convinced his pupil, Martineau, of its truth. But during his post-college preaching and congregational teaching as a Unitarian clergyman in Liverpool, Martineau gradually changed his mind and by 1840, when he began his career as professor of philoso-

[1] "The Growth of Liberal Theology," *Cambridge History of English Literature*, XII, 279.

phy at Manchester New College he had given up the hedonism and determinism of his youth. His *Weltanschauung* took final form after a year of study (1848–49) in Germany, where, though dissatisfied with the treatment of man's ethical experience by contemporary thinkers, he did increase his knowledge of philosophical thought by studying its history and especially Plato, Kant, and Hegel. He dropped out of Lotze's lectures, which in the summer term of that year were very elementary. One is not impressed, however, with Martineau's understanding of the philosophical masters.

It is important to note the friendship which later developed between Martineau and T. H. Green (who, with the brothers Caird and Hutcheson Stirling, had introduced Hegel into England in the '60's), for Martineau's approval of Green's stress on God's immanence and his dissatisfaction with the absorption of the individual in Green's Absolute must have been the consequence of many a fireside discussion.

The results of Martineau's long years of thought found their maturest expression in his work, *A Study of Religion.* Though written late in life (1888), it might well be described in the same words with which W. R. Sorley characterizes his other main work, *Types of Ethical Theory:* "its style shows no marks of weariness: it is brilliant, pellucid, eloquent, rhetorical sometimes and coloured by emotion, but never falls below the dignity of his theme." [2]

Though Martineau is justly remembered mainly for his recognition of the light that man's moral life throws on the ultimate constitution of reality, the nature of this study demands that attention first be paid to the epistemology and metaphysics which lie at the basis of his "natural theism." In our own day the details of Martineau's thought may seem to some readers rather crude and his light darkness. Such persons may pass without great loss to Section C or to the next chapter. However, in order to trace the unity and contrasts in Martineau's basic thought, as well as to understand the evolution of important concepts within the period here studied, we must pause to inspect the treatment of problems so

[2] "Philosophers," in *Cambridge History*, XIV, 27.

essential to theism that they reappear in Martineau's successors less crudely, perhaps, but not always more convincingly expressed.

B. MARTINEAU'S NATURAL THEISM

1. THE KEY TO REALITY

Martineau is convinced of the "insufficiency of the empirical psychology as a base of metaphysic philosophy." [3] His approach to the existence and nature of God is, nevertheless, through the inspection and analysis of human experience, and we shall see that his objection is not to the method but to some of the conclusions of the empirical philosophy and psychology. Be the macrocosm what it may, man confronts it with a given intellectual and spiritual nature in the *hope* of knowing it and making it serve his interests, say some philosophers. The underlying conviction which breathes through every aspect of Martineau's philosophy is that man actually *holds* in his own experience the only clues to the macrocosm. Man is the measure of the world he knows in the sense that the fundamental deliverances of his consciousness reveal to him the nature of reality. This relativity of knowledge to the self does not mean, as idealists wrongly think, that the world has no independent existence, or that man, therefore, is deceived about its nature. It means solely that "not in religion only, but in every sphere of understanding, self-knowledge is the condition and limit of other knowledge. . . ." [4] The question is: What is knowledge and what are its conditions?

2. THE NATURE AND LIMITS OF KNOWLEDGE

Martineau holds that any attempt to discover the nature and limits of knowledge is doomed to scepticism unless it assumes that there can be objective knowledge until investigation has proved the contrary. To assume in the beginning that the faculty of knowledge is defective is to court the fatal

[3] James Martineau, *A Study of Religion* (2nd ed., 1889), I, 181. Unless otherwise stated, all further references in this chapter will be to Martineau's works.
[4] *The Seat of Authority in Religion* (1890), p. 3.

question: How, if the faculty is defective, can its limits, discovered through its use, be correctly known? We have to take something for granted before we can know anything, and to doubt the veracity of our faculties is to wreck the bark of knowledge before it sets out.

Now, for our faculties to give us the truth they must "reproduce in thought the relations which exist in reality." [5] To secure truth, he goes on, "we must have access to reality, and be able to compare its relations with their supposed reproduction in our affirming thought." [6] In one brief paragraph Martineau, having found that there is in all thinking an object, *there* and *then*, for a subject, *here* and *now*, concludes: "without Space and Time, therefore, no objectivity; without objectivity no thinking; without thinking, no knowing." [7] It is obvious that Martineau uses the word "objective" only when he means true awareness of a space-time object independent of the mind. Martineau also holds, however, that, as the possibility of imagination reveals, all thinking is not knowledge, for the imagination "can carry the semblance only until the real perceptions awake and withdraw the disguise." [8] But the complications which the existence of such a mental object introduces into a theory of knowledge do not trouble him, since his conviction is that, whatever the process of knowledge, our faculties correctly reproduce the relations existing in the world.

For Martineau, then, there are two alternatives; either subjective states give an "intuitive apprehension of what is," or they do not, and he rightly states that the acceptance of either conclusion is a postulate. Kant's psychology [9] is, on the whole,

[5] *Study of Religion*, I, 41.
[6] *Ibid.*
[7] *Ibid.*, I, 38.
[8] *Ibid.*, I, 40.
[9] Martineau holds, as against Kant, that the self knows its object as one from the first and does not construct it by adding properties which in truth are *analytica* of the object apprehended as single. Though he holds, with Kant, that space and time are a priori, for him they are not forms of a passive sensibility but are coördinate functions of a consciousness which, in its activity of willing, first discriminates the ego from the non-ego. See *Study of Religion*, I, 46, 61, 62, 70.

correct, but he fails to show that the subjectivity of space and time, for example, negates their independent existence as well. If we will rid ourselves of the arbitrary assumption that like can know like only, and trust the veracity of our faculties, a thing we must do sooner or later, we can justly hold that space and time are independent of our minds as well as subjectively a priori.[10]

Another curious aspect of Martineau's thought here is the assertion that this agreement of apprehension and fact does not demand the hypothesis of pre-established harmony, for this would be necessary only "if the order of knowing and the order of being were assumed to be two eternal series without possible contact or interaction; but not if relations of causality either subsist between them as they pass, or are prefixed to both in the unity of their source." [11] There is more reason for believing that our cognitive faculties should "be constituted in accordance with *things as they are*," than that they should be "conformable to *things as they are not*." [12] These passages indicate that for Martineau the veracity of our faculties may rest either on their interconnection with the environment or in the unity of the ultimate source of both (though it is hard to see the difference between *prefixed* and *pre-established* harmony). In any case, he does not further explicate these ideas, and they are mentioned here only because of their similarity to the views of Pringle-Pattison, whose justification for the validity of our intuition develops lines of thought implicit here.

Martineau's essential point is that there is no good reason for supposing that our faculties distort reality. He gains access to the external world by "natural trust," [13] what Santayana would call "animal faith." Planting his faith, as every "sound" mind must, "on all beliefs and feelings involved in the very exercise of the natural faculties," [14] Martineau is enabled to get beyond the "mere self-consistency" of his ideas and test

---

[10] That Martineau misunderstood Kant's thought and overemphasized the psychological at the expense of the logical is obvious.

[11] *Study of Religion*, I, 75.

[12] *Ibid.*

[13] *Ibid.*

[14] *Ibid.*, I, 76.

his judgments "by the agreement of their affirmed relations with the real one." [15] Even if we could carry out this test, why there should be need for testing and how error arises, are questions which this theory would have difficulty in answering, and to which we find no answer by Martineau. Martineau rejects any idealistic constructions of the universe, not because these may be incoherent or incomplete,[16] but because they do not satisfy certain human convictions. One's only answer can be: If we are to trust the veracity of our faculties, why should we not, then, also trust the veracity of reasoning? When one philosophy overthrows another by appealing to convictions and to the veracity of faculties, it does so only by destroying other convictions and distrusting other faculties.

The implications of Martineau's position for any kind of Berkeleyan idealism hardly need to be mentioned. Martineau accepts Mill's doctrine that other selves are known through analogy with self-experience, but he insists that this argument is valid only on the prior assumption that the selves are already given. If, with Mill, we start with phenomena of the Ego, "the difficulty is by no means to characterize and class *things other than self* when you get them; but to pass at all into *otherness*." [17] Martineau's incapability of allowing objectivity to mean anything other than space-time existence makes it impossible for him to acknowledge the objectivity Mill finds in the permanent possibility of sensation. Idealism may be good psychology, he feels, but it is bad metaphysics, since it makes one the prisoner of his skin. For Martineau, confidence in the objective existence of the world can be based only on the assurance that conscious states reproduce the space-time world.

3. THE SELF AND OBJECTIVE WILL

Having vindicated the belief in an external physical world, Martineau begins the construction of the argument for Theism by an analysis of the notion of cause. In the idea of cause he finds a certain "mustness" which no theory emphasizing

---

[15] *Study of Religion*, I, 75.   [16] *Ibid.*, I, 79.   [17] *Ibid.*, I, 102.

the fixity of the temporal order of events explains. What is to be explained is the change and not the order. The very fact that we do not doubt the existence of cause when we do not discover a particular cause indicates that the idea of cause is a priori, that, indeed, even if all order were lost, we should still believe in the dynamic origin of the existent state. Causality, then, is "an *a priori* law of thought brought by us to the interpretation of the world." [18] No adequate cause is found "till you go beyond the category of change, and instead of stepping from one member of it to another with endless beat, refer its whole contents, as such, to *that which is other than phenomenon.*" [19] As long as cause is sought on the surface of objects and defined in terms of Being or Time, it will not be found. It is only when we ask ourselves to conceive that all change has no origin that we find a basic conviction startled and unsatisfied. Thus, like Hume, Martineau now rests belief in necessary causation not on our rational nature but on psychological propensity. "It is only by reference to the psychological birth and history of the notion of causality, that we can detect its essence, and account for its modifications." [20]

But Martineau analyzes further the nature of that psychological origin. Unsatisfied with the abstract emptiness of words like *power* and *force*, he finds concrete meaning for them in terms of self-experience, within which he also discovers the clue to the more ultimate nature of the non-ego.

We have already referred to the birth-point of will in the very experience of resistance to impulse, but attention is now directed to the light thrown by similar passages on the nature of the self and the not-self.

We are born into self-consciousness in the moment of disputed spontaneity, and instantly assert ourselves by taking into our own hands the power which before was only passing through our nature. And as it is a shock of interrupted feeling that gives us notice to do this, the feeling must have the same owner as the power; and both are necessarily referred to one point and taken home to the Ego; henceforth known as the subject of both the sensory store and the forms of activity. . . . All else than these contents is embraced in the non-Ego.[21]

[18] *Ibid.*, I, 149.   [20] *Ibid.*, I, 132.
[19] *Ibid.*   [21] *Ibid.*, I, 187.

This spontaneous power which we take up and direct was really not without aim, but its previous aim was "given by Nature instead, and belongs to a counter-will in place of ours." [22] Thus, in our own experience of will we find the meaning of cause, and since our own self-consciousness originates in the experience of our resistance to a power which opposes our own spontaneous life, that power is intelligible only if conceived as Will. The knowledge of our causality rests upon the causality of the non-ego, but since our own causality is will, then that of the World also is Will.[23] Our "primary," "intellectual intuition" of the world's causality comes to us as we try to direct our own. This is "in truth the ground of that *fellow-feeling* with Nature which philosophy, deluded by its own abstractions, rashly surrendered to the poet. . . . To the world we are introduced . . . as to another self, just as causal as we, instinct with hidden Will. . . ." [24]

This is not all. In self-consciousness the ego is "introduced" to two related terms, namely, to an act or a feeling and to itself as owning [25] them, its phenomena. The difference between the two terms is that "while the act or feeling is a present change, the Ego is a *permanent* whence the change issues or whither it arrives, — which was there before and will be there after." [26] The self, then, is a "continuum" which *has* the phenomena, and is different from the substance to which we attribute qualities in that though physical substance "harbours the possibilities of *synchronous* phenomena," the self is restricted only to successive, though in both cases there is unity.[27] The self is noumenal, "a native habitat of phenomena," [28] which cannot be reduced to them.

Martineau is not clear, however, as to whether the noumenal self or object immanent in the phenomenal is permanent activity or not. To be sure, he uses the transitive verb *has* to denote the relation of the self or object to its attributes, but otherwise he speaks of substance as having *being* or *exist-*

[22] *Study of Religion*, I, 244.
[23] Cf. *ibid.*, I, 189, 190.
[24] *Ibid.*, I, 190.
[25] Cf. *ibid.*, I, 192.
[26] *Ibid.*
[27] *Ibid.*
[28] *Ibid.*

ence.[29] That he differentiates Being from activity, however, is indicated by the statement in another context: "without Being or existence, there is no possibility of Power." [30] The self *is* evidently the permanent source of activity but not the activity itself. What *being* might be apart from activity Martineau, despite his study of Plato, does not inquire, and one suspects on his part the hypostatization of logical distinctions. He seems to have forgotten his statement: "If I know myself at all it is in *trying* 'with all my might' to do something needed but difficult. . . ." [31] If external cause is Will, where is the place for static existence? Since we shall find a stronger defense of a similar position later,[32] further discussion is postponed until then.

We have seen that for Martineau cause is not, as it was for Kant, a category of the mind brought to, yet inapplicable beyond, experience. Rather is cause a subjective counterpart of objective reality. But, as A. W. Jackson says, though Martineau brings causality to the study of nature, "through the study of nature uniformity is found." [33] Hence we turn our attention to his treatment of Nature.

4. THE WORLD AND GOD

Martineau speaks of the changes of nature as willed by a power which, "like our own, is regarded as immanent in the objective nature, only available for possibilities indefinitely more numerous than ours." [34] One of the most confusing parts of Martineau's philosophy is his treatment of the relation of God to the world, and all that can be done is to show where the confusion lies.

This power immanent in nature is, of course, God, and if God means anything to Martineau He means Goodness. Hence Martineau proceeds in his investigation not with God meaning simply Will but with God as Good Will. There is

---

[29] *Ibid.*, I, 194, 195.   [30] *Ibid.*, I, 198.   [31] *Ibid.*, I, 188.
[32] Chapter VI, Section D, below.
[33] *James Martineau: A Biography and Study* (1900), p. 316.
[34] *Study of Religion*, I, 200.

no particular reason, at this stage in the argument, for holding that the cosmic Mind does not will every separate drop of rain, but Martineau cannot conceive of God's actions as separate fiats for every different event, for then God would be the immediate cause of the lightning which kills both the sinner and the saint. Every law of nature, therefore, must be construed "into a single thought or unit of volition," and we must replace "multifarious and fluctuating impulse *pro re nata* by a few great lines of purpose, each curving round and embracing innumerable particulars, and all forming sections of a universal plan." [35] In the same context Martineau speaks of every law as *"one thought,"* as the "unfolding of *one comprehensive and standing volition."* The origin of every law is "an act of Will, settling what was indeterminate before." [36] It is only as we disregard the source of these laws that we pass to scientific conceptions like "natural force" or "forces of nature" which can be depended upon for computation. Thus, what was given in intuitive apprehension as Will, has been developed under observation (prejudiced by a preconceived idea of God) into the notion of an Agent directing hitherto indeterminate streams of activity, a Will having the same relation to the world as we have to our bodies, whose automatic character we use to fulfill our purposes. The difference is that for God the mechanized media are self-adopted.

It is difficult to see what one of Martineau's standing volitions is, and it seems that Martineau, in rejecting "a volition for each drop of rain in a shower" for "a whole law at a sweep," [37] has hypostatized law. He is thinking of events as messengers whose private activities are directed and who abide by the rule of their monarch, and not of law as it is, a formulation by the observer of the way in which events take place. God is here [38] working on a datum of coexistent, indeterminate energy; yet Martineau, in another connection, avoids "resorting to a [Platonic] dualism which seems to involve the eternity of matter. . . ." [39] C. B. Upton, however, believes

<hr/>

[35] *Study of Religion*, I, 222.   [37] *Ibid.*, I, 236.
[36] *Ibid.*   [38] Cf. *ibid.*, I, 222.   [39] *Ibid.*, I, 223.

that in Martineau's cosmology "the sole causes in the universe are God and rational beings. The inorganic world results from the direct volitional action of God in all the so-called material elements which constitute the universe." [40]

Further light is shed on the relation between God and the world, as well as on Martineau's empiricism, when he is defending the teleological argument against the objections of Kant and E. Caird. Here Martineau is not distressed over the possibility of the eternal existence of matter. Insisting that, after all, signs of thought can only be found "amid a *scene of things*," [41] he holds that: "To ask for unconditioned mind is no less contradictory than to ask for an infinite ellipse." [42] Martineau's unwillingness to think of the cosmic Mind as transcending the conditions to which mind *as he knows it* is limited, is evidence of the basic empiricism [43] which pervades his thought as he tries to conceive the nature of God. His main point, however, is that the design argument is equally compatible with eternal or created matter. In any case, he believes that: "*Some* objective conditions, viz., those of Space and Time, everyone but the pure idealist must admit as present." [44]

That Martineau is not easily disposed to conceive God's intelligence as transcending the characteristics of intelligence *as experienced* is further illustrated by his answer to Caird's objection that it is arbitrary and unnecessary to think of God as first creating and then shaping a material world. The difficulty with Caird's objection is its implication that creation may be by fiat rather than by the use of means to an end. For intelligence as known is limited, in its pursuance of an end, to the use of means. Furthermore, for Martineau, matter need not oppose God's purpose; it is rather the ground for an indefinite number of purposes.[45] The whole spirit of the

[40] *Dr. Martineau's Philosophy* (1905), p. 179.
[41] *Study of Religion*, I, 308.
[42] *Ibid.*
[43] Of course the conclusions in any particular instance may not be justified by reference to the coherent interpretation of the rest of experience.
[44] *Study of Religion*, I, 311.
[45] Cf. *ibid.*, I, 310.

discussion, however, shows that Martineau was less concerned with the metaphysical solutions of the problems involved than with the insistence that the design argument does lend itself to satisfactory theistic conclusions. That he could accept the view of God creating the world in an independent Space and Time, which seems to be his ultimate conclusion, shows insufficient metaphysical insight perhaps, but the underlying reason for his insistence on objective conditions to God's willing is that "causality without conditions, agency with nothing to act out of or act upon, thought with no possibilities to define, are simply contradictory conceptions." [46] Here Martineau's approach is without doubt empirical.

And yet, that Martineau's empiricism operates between grooves carved out by his prior conviction of the goodness and supremacy of God is evident from the fact that even though he admits the possibility of another necessary existence, "it is admitted only to receive orders from the Divine Cause and afford the occasion for the victory of Thought." [47] Martineau is certain that the divine sway is limited by the "objective world" only as the sphere of a sovereign limits the area he rules. No attempt is made to correlate, as a Mill would, the existence of this uncreated world with the problem of evil, or to face the difficulties created by this ultimate dualism. He therefore holds that, after all, dualism "is a difficulty which equally besets every theory of the originating power." [48] Yet, since he now, strange to say,[49] sees no reason why intelligence needs to externalize its object in order to have one, Martineau holds that cosmical forces are "varieties of methods assumed by his [God's] conscious causality, and the whole of Nature . . . the evolution of his thought." [50] All one can say of this metaphysical maze is that Martineau held to the supremacy of God, as well as to his immanence,[51]

---

[46] *Study of Religion*, I, 311.   [47] *Ibid.*, I, 312.   [48] *Ibid.*, I, 329.
[49] In view of his insistence that natural knowledge must be of an independent space-time world.
[50] *Ibid.*, I, 328.
[51] Whether the world be external to God or not, immanence is possible, but the main reservation is that "it must not annex and absorb the faculties of created minds, but leave room for their personality. . . ." *Ibid.*, I, 329.

despite the existence of an uncreated world in addition to Space and Time. Yet the view of nature he favored was so close, actually, to the personalistic Berkeley-Lotzean conception of the world as the energizing of God's will, that his tight grip on the independent existence of Time and Space is astonishing. But we have leapt ahead of Martineau's argument and must now turn to the remaining grounds for his natural Theism.

5. THE PLEA FOR PHILOSOPHICAL THEOLOGY

Martineau's approach to religious truth is through an analysis of both man's cognitive and moral nature. We have noted his reaction against the philosophy of experience and its mental atomism, and we shall later study his protest against its analysis of conscience. But his equally great concern was to show that the conflict of religion and science came only when both misconstrued their functions.

Martineau characterized the science of his day as one which taught the student "to see the refinements of organism and exactitudes of adaptation disenchanted of their wonder; to watch the beauty of the flower fade into necessity. . . ." [52] It taught also "that man was never *intended* for his place upon this scene and has no commission to fulfill, but is simply flung hither by the competitive passions of the most gifted brutes. . . ." [53] The evolution of his day tended to make mind and its faculties ineffective bystanders in the cosmic process. To Martineau, who thought of man as "the crown of nature" and "the reflecting mirror of the world," [54] a view of human evolution which, having given man the "outfit" of an animal, later found him a product little lower than angels, was ludicrous. "In dealing with these three conceptions, — of Creation, Construction, Evolution, — there is one thing on which religion insists, viz., that *Mind is first, and rules forever,* and whatever the process be, is *its* process, moving toward congenial ends. . . ." [55]

[52] *Religion As Affected By Modern Materialism* (1874), p. 5.
[53] *Study of Religion,* I, 239.
[54] *The Place of Mind in Nature and Intuition in Man* (1872), p. 6.
[55] *Ibid.*

Thus Martineau insists again and again that the function of science is to classify phenomena and discover their laws, but not to deal with questions of ultimate origin. Theology may have gone too far in invoking a special act of God for inexplicables, but for science to fill the gaps by exhibiting the natural continuity of evolution as independent of Mind is to invoke another miracle from the great god Matter. In one of his earlier articles, therefore, Martineau pleads for a "scientific theology" which studies both nature and man in its search for God. But the word *scientific* is not used in the strict sense here, and in the latter part of this article Martineau implies that his is a "philosophical theology." [56] It is a happy coincidence that these very words should be used as the title of probably the most sustained attempt in empirical theology in contemporary British thought.[57] In demanding that man's moral and religious experience (as well as sense-experience) be taken into account in any thorough construction of experience, Martineau was fertilizing British soil for even greater attempts than his own to root theistic belief on experience *as a whole*. We are ready now to consider his own teleological argument for God.

6. THE FUNCTION OF THE TELEOLOGICAL ARGUMENT IN MARTINEAU'S THEISM

We have noted that Martineau's preconception of the goodness of God was the basis of deductions which constrained him to conceive of the expressions of the cosmic Will in such a way that the burden of natural evil would be lifted from him. But the point is that preconceptions, though allowable (indeed, indispensable and inevitable) in the study of reality, are misused when they constrict our gaze and make us insensitive to other suggestions the facts might produce. Martineau comes to this investigation of the nature of the cosmic Will with convictions arising from other aspects of his experience, and instead of patiently considering the different alternatives, as the careful, inductive, and thor-

---

[56] *Essays, Reviews and Addresses* (1890–91), IV, 143.
[57] Tennant's *Philosophical Theology*.

oughly empirical thinker would, he tends to fit the facts into a scheme consistent with conclusions arrived at independently of them.

The presence of a more inductive spirit has also been noted, however, and Martineau's use of the teleological argument illustrates it. Having arrived at the notion of a cosmic Will whose standing volitions represent the laws of Nature, Martineau realizes that he has proved no more than "a mathematical intelligence, whose faculties do the work of a calculating machine." [58] Such a will satisfies only one mark, selection or determinateness, of the will, which, *as we know it*, involves. also combination of independent activities to an end and the subordination of minor to major ends. It is to prove that the cosmic Will has these three experienced characteristics of will that Martineau turns to a consideration of nature and advances the teleological argument for God.

This view of the place of the teleological argument in Martineau's reasoning for God finds little corroboration by commentators on Martineau. Mr. Jackson, for example, believes that Martineau merely referred to adaptation in nature to give a posteriori illustrations of a God arrived at a priori in intuition, and he quotes a passage from Martineau to prove this contention. "His inquiry is to 'ascertain whether the world answers, in its constitution, to our *intuitive interpretation* of it as the manifestation of *intellectual purpose.*'" [59] On the same page he continues: "For the security of the primary postulate of his faith Dr. Martineau does not need Final Causes: like Descartes, he could have attained it, as he achieved it, by philosophic insight alone." Yet the very fact that Martineau, in justifying his interpretation of the Will as *intelligent* Purpose, appeals in his argument to empirical facts which opposing views do not treat adequately [60] shows that mere insight was not enough

[58] *Study of Religion*, I, 238; see also pp. 236, 308.
[59] Jackson, *James Martineau*, p. 338, quoting *Study of Religion*, I, 258. The italics are Jackson's.
[60] See *Study of Religion*, I, 242–258.

for his "natural Theism," [61] that though his own conviction might be solid, its defense demanded corroboration by
empirical data. And the passage cited above [62] indicates
dissatisfaction with the mere mathematical Intelligence
which the empirical argument thus far has produced. Mr.
Armstrong also slightly deviates from Jackson when he holds
that for Martineau, "although the strict scrutiny of our own
laws of thought . . . presents to us a mighty World-Maker
and World-Sustainer . . . , it is as well to check this argument from first principles by an argument from the actual
facts of the world, and to see whether these two arguments
tally." [63] Here, however, the word "check" conveys the impression that the teleological argument is a work of super-
erogation, as it were. No doubt the loose structure of
Martineau's argument, his reading the "Divine Causality"
into the primary intuition of the Will as mere resistance
long before he had defended his interpretation of the Will
as conscious purpose, his profound conviction of God as
found primarily in the moral and religious consciousness,
justify these views. But the appeal to the facts of experience to corroborate his insights is so constant that, though
one may declare Martineau's natural theism to be inspired
and sustained and even biased by his ethical and religious
theism, one may not deny that nevertheless its source was
in Martineau's desire to defend and justify his religious
conviction intellectually, especially in the face of the atheistic
interpretation placed by others in his day on the facts of
evolution. Professor Upton holds that though Martineau,
"like Kant, considered the argument to be a valuable *confirmation* to a belief in a Personal God independently obtained,
[he] never at any time thought that it was competent by
itself to establish such a belief." [64] The position which the

[61]*Study of Religion*, I, 242.   [62]*Ibid.*, I, 238.
[63]R. A. Armstrong, *Martineau's "Study of Religion": An Analysis and Appreciation* (1900). p. 53 Armstrong notes (pp. xiii, xiv) that in his last conversation with Martineau (in February 1897) the latter granted to the
emotional intuition of "Living Love" "parallel force and rank" in the arguments from causality and conscience.
[64] *Martineau's Philosophy*, p. 182.

Study of Religion seems to justify is that though a purposive, personal Will is demanded by the intuition of causality and the inspection of nature (Volume I), the *goodness* of that Will can be maintained only after an analysis of the moral life of man (Volume II). The rest of this chapter will help to justify this view. In relying on the moral nature of man, as apart from the rest of his nature and the world, Martineau not only follows Kant, but represents the main trend of the empirical argument for God in late British thought.

7. THE TELEOLOGICAL ARGUMENT

To give a complete summary of the mass of material Martineau introduces in his discussion of teleology is impossible, but the main strands of the argument may be brought together as follows. The problem is whether the selection in nature is owing to the automatic or chance working of natural forces or to an Intelligence fulfilling a preconceived purpose. Considering any definite set of organs, Martineau immediately insists: "It cannot be pretended that the medium [environment] itself can mould the organs committed to it into congenial shape," [65] for no amount of air that blows upon beating arms could develop them into wings. If we look into the organisms themselves for the explanation, then we either push the solutions back further by appealing to ultimate germ-constituents in which the keen eye might see the product "prefigured there," or we resort to epigenesis, which still does not explain the selection and is less easy to understand.[66] True, it is not impossible, Martineau continues, that Chance has simulated selection; but there is no more probability that the production of definite types of structure as well as their continuous creation were dependent on Chance than there is that Shakespeare's *Macbeth* could be produced and maintained by the same accidental variations which threw its constituent letters and none other together. There must have been, therefore, an original selection with a view to fitting one type of structure to the

[65] *Study of Religion*, I, 260.
[66] Cf. I, 261, 262.

environment, for it is inconceivable that *one* particular type with suitable variations for the medium could have been produced fortuitously. The summarizing paragraph of this whole section gives an insight into Martineau's approach.

> These few facts sufficiently indicate the presence of *selection* in nature, that is, the limitation of erratic possibilities to definitely chosen lines, and the steady production of these to the exclusion of the rest. In following them out, we have had to watch the divergence of one fundamental type of structure into several directions of variation, *computed mainly from the medium in* which the organism was to *subsist* [italics mine]; and the problem has been how *one idea* can obtain control over a *plurality of conditions.*[07]

We need to think of God here as an engineer who, knowing the force of the river, carefully calculates strains and stresses and wisely chooses the constituents for the bridge which is to span it.

But it does not occur to Martineau that nature itself, though it did not create them, might nevertheless be the partial and indirect cause of the existent structures and their particular modifications. Given a more or less constant nature, organisms bent on self-preservation might well have their plasticity and capabilities so tested that only one general type of structure persisted. Martineau thinks of nature as a house into whose conditions inhabitants must be fitted, and he consequently does not realize that organisms are a *joint*-product. Of course Shakespeare's *Macbeth* cannot be explained by the happy coincidence suggested, but neither are Shakespeare and *Macbeth* explicable apart from the development and modification that his native endowment received in contact with a more or less constant mental and physical environment. If we be asked: "How account for these characteristics of nature, for ultimate natural endowments and original plasticity?" we answer that *this* is the problem, that this is the ultimate adaptation to be accounted for by any philosophical theory. An elaboration of this view we shall meet in our consideration of F. R. Tennant.

A further implication of Martineau's view of teleology

[07] *Study of Religion,* I, 282.

leaves him open to the charge Bergson makes against some teleologies, namely that they are mechanistic even though determination is *a fronte* rather than *a tergo*. Martineau seems to think that the continuity of given species could not be accounted for except by a Mind which realized its pre-conceived plan. There is little or no place for creative evolution on Martineau's view, but this whole problem does not come up. We have not considered Martineau's justification for the second and third objective marks of will, combination, and gradation, but the argument is similar to that just noted, and no further value is gained from it.

8. THE NATURAL ATTRIBUTES OF GOD

Turning finally to the natural attributes of God, we may briefly indicate the empiricism expressed in Martineau's contention that when we attribute adjectives like *all*-wise and *all*-powerful to God, we are drawing "an unlimited conclusion from a partial experience," [68] but that this is no more a reflection against religious generalizations than it is against those of science. Nor can we argue from the finite phenomena of the world to an infinite God, but only to one indefinitely great. Yet, since Space, the other "self-existent condition" [69] of the cosmos, is infinite, we may conclude that there is nothing else to limit God in "planting out force *in any points of space whatsoever; or in only some.*" [70] Similarly, since God is always first cause of the phenomena and not himself a phenomenon, he must be eternal and self-existent. In each case the attributes are established inductively (regardless of the correctness of his inductions). Martineau concludes that the principle of Causality yields "one universal Cause, the infinite and eternal seat of all power, an omniscient Mind,[71] ordering all things for ends selected with perfect wisdom." [72] So much can be known through the study of Nature and man's intellect; for further knowledge we must go to the moral nature of man.

[68] *Ibid.*, I, 312.   [69] *Ibid.*, I, 389.   [70] *Ibid.*, I, 390.
[71] It may be stated here that Martineau does not hold that God can foreknow exactly the future of free spirits.   [72] *Study of Religion*, I, 391.

C. Martineau's Moral Argument for God

1. ITS IMPORTANCE

The teleological argument re-enforces and develops the original intuition of cosmic Will and gives adequate ground for belief in an intelligent Architect. Theism is safe against the onslaught of science in so far as God is conceived thus, but religion rests on the conviction that God is good. For Martineau, as we have already indicated, the stronghold of religion is the moral life. "It is not, I believe, through any physical aspect of things, if that were all, but through the human experiences of the conscience and affections that the living God comes to apprehension and communion with us." [73] The "purest and deepest" self-expression of God comes in the mutual contact of Spirit with spirit in the moral phenomena of life.[74] God must be more than an eternal Thinker; he must be a loving Father.

Since the roots of Martineau's argument for God lie in the nature of conscience, and since elements in his argument are to find favor and be developed by those who follow, a comprehensive study of Martineau's view of conscience will be valuable. We propose to distinguish three aspects of it: first, its psychological nature; second, its cognitive deliverance; third, its metaphysics. These three phases present different problems, and much confusion is avoided if they are distinguished.

2. THE PSYCHOLOGY OF CONSCIENCE

The essence of Martineau's psychology of conscience is found in the following quotation: "The rudest self-knowledge must own that the consciousness of *Moral Obligation* is an experience *sui generis*, separated by deep distinctions from *outward necessity* on the one hand, and *inward desire* upon the other." [75] Conscience is an irreducible element in human experience which can no more be deduced from heterogene-

[73] *Seat of Authority*, p. 17.
[74] *Ibid.*, p. 36.   [75] *Religion as Affected*, p. 29.

ous sources "than vision from hearing. If you have nothing
to work with but animal pleasures and pains, and unlimited
time for their experience and transmission, you can never
hope, through all eternity, to build up a conscience. . . ." [76]
Apart from conscience there is neither moral goodness nor
guilt, but only wisdom or folly. Martineau's revolt in the
moral realm, we begin to see, is against sensuousness, or, more
broadly, the reduction of moral obligation to desire. Two
further characteristics of conscience must be noted.

The peculiarity of the "visions of conscience," one which
"marks them off from other plays of ideality," is that in their
their very essence they are over-individual, non-egoistic commands applicable not only to ourselves but to every other
human being. No violation of the dictum of conscience destroys its imperative or its command over our allegiance. Even
though the *"de facto* sway" of conscience is in no two persons
the same, yet there is "universal consensus" with regard to its
"de jure power." [77] These, then, are the qualities which the
inspection of moral experience discovers.

Save for the important reservation that universality is not
confined to conscience, since whenever we think we have the
truth we believe it is "true for all," this on the whole is an
acceptable psychological analysis of conscience.[78] Before passing to the cognitive value of conscience, it will be well to
linger on Martineau's objection to alternative theories, for
here we begin to see the errors which result when the psychological status of the conscience is confused with its supposed
verdicts.

The theory that conscience is merely the product of the
approval and condemnation of others reduces conscience to
prudence, for conscience is now the means of securing and
reproducing advantages. But, objects Martineau, how can
the individual destitute of moral sense learn from a society
which is made up of individuals similarly destitute? To use
one of Martineau's own figures, a conscience can no more be

[76] *The Relation Between Ethics and Religion* (1881), p. 9.
[77] *Study of Religion*, II, 104.
[78] But consult Chapter V, Section E, below.

generated from individuals capable only of self-love than a
cedar of Lebanon can be grown from chalkstone. "I can
understand how 'Society,' taking an individual in hand, can
create a *Must* for him; but not how it can create an *Ought*." [79]
But surely what Martineau has in mind here is not the development of the *ought*, of moral obligation as such, but of a
particular obligation or verdict, namely, altruism. His whole
discussion is permeated by the confusion of the two (and we
shall see that he is not alone in this).[80]

The social theory of conscience described above, Martineau
continues, does not explain *self*-condemnation, for if our
standards are borrowed, how can we call this condemnation
by self? Beneath the verbal deception present, Martineau's
real point here is that conscience is *first* in the individual and,
indeed, not only anticipates the judgment of others but also
often clarifies itself as it draws away from the mere assent to
their voices. The unanimity of verdict in the agent and in the
spectator is impossible in a theory like Mill's, which begins
with the conflicting self-love of individuals. Leaving aside
the contradictions in Mill's thought, it must be said in fairness
to him, and against Martineau's criticism, that Martineau
minimizes too much the function of natural sympathy in a
theory like Mill's.

Turning to the alarm caused by the theory of evolution,
Martineau holds that it is false, for the authority *and validity*
of conscience are not dependent on its appearance at once in
ready-made perfection. It is indeed undeniable that even in
the evolution of a single person, "the rudiments of moral
goodness were as foreign to him as to the kitten or the calf." [81]
The development is very gradual, and conscience grows with
the help of disciplinary influences, but to distrust conscience
on this account is no more justified than to distrust Reason
because it develops. As Martineau humorously remarks, his
knowledge that five thousand years ago his ancestor had no
conscience does not persuade him to put out his "own light

[79] *Study of Religion*, II, 104.
[80] See below, Chapter VI, pp. 217 f.
[81] *Study of Religion*, II, 22.

in filial sympathy with his darkness." [82] "My protest, then, against James Mill's theory," he says, "is not that he evolves conscience, instead of treating it as innate; but that what he evolves is not conscience at all." Mill "is measuring the end by the beginning, and assuming that no new thing has risen between. . . ." Martineau, on the other hand, insists that "*conscience*, as compared with its antecedents, is a fact altogether fresh. . . ." [83] "In short, I admit that a new thing can come by degrees. I deny that what comes by degrees cannot be new." [84]

As selected and quoted, these passages do not clearly reveal the confusion which actually occurs again [85] between conscience as a faculty and its verdicts, but, disregarding this, we may notice that they attribute to the conscience as much validity as is permitted to our thinking. Now it would be ridiculous to say that our conclusions are correct every time we think, but, as we shall see, this is exactly what Martineau attributes to the verdicts of conscience. The point which may be granted here is that in the constitution of man there is a unique experience of moral obligation which can be reduced to no other type of experience.

Before moving on to the cognitive deliverances of conscience, it will be well to review the progress made. We now see that Martineau's essential position is that the authority and uniformity of conscience cannot be explained by evolution or by any theory of society as an aggregate of individuals motivated by love of pleasure. It is suggested, however, that the tempering of self-interest by natural sympathy plus the training of society could produce the unanimity of conscience's *verdict* when the latter concerns the social good: that, in any case, the authority of conscience has been wrongly confused with its verdicts. What Martineau really insists, against Mill, is that altruism cannot be explained by the play of self-love. This ethical question, however, has no logical connection with the psychological question as to the nature of moral obligation. In other words, if it be claimed that the

[82] *Ibid.*, II, 24.
[83] *Ibid.*, II, 25.
[84] *Ibid.*, II, 26.
[85] Cf. *ibid.*, II, 25.

conscience, as a faculty, is *sui generis*, then it must be proved
that neither feeling, will, nor reason, nor any combination of
them can be its entire constitution, and that, like each of
these, it cannot be reduced to the other. "Outward necessity"
or "inward desire" have nothing to do with the derivation of
conscience as a psychological capacity, but only with particular verdicts. In so far as Martineau holds that the sense of
guilt could never be explained if conscience were merely desire, or intelligence, he cannot, however, be gainsaid. More
light will be thrown on this theory of moral obligation as we
proceed.

3. THE COGNITIVE VALUE OF CONSCIENCE

Though an action may be analyzed into impulse, execution,
and effect, its moral character is to be judged only by the
initial intention. Consequences, Martineau agrees with Kant,
do not determine the merits of an action, but moral choice is
determined by the immediate intuition of the *relative* worth
of the qualities our conflicting impulses express.

> The moral faculty, therefore, is not any apprehension of invisible
> qualities in external action, not any partition of them into the abso-
> lutely good and the absolutely evil, not any *intellectual* [italics mine]
> testing of them by rules of congruity, or balances of utility, but a recog-
> nition, at their very source, of a scale of *relative* values lying within
> ourselves, and introducing a *preferential* character throughout the count-
> less combinations of our possible activity.[86]

Thus, if it be argued that moral judgments vary "in a race
which, by turns, has consecrated every wrong," and are therefore the "arbitrary creation of social necessity," [87] Martineau
answers that this objection has no weight against his theory but
only against one which sets up conscience as an "infallible
oracle, able to pronounce at sight on the ethical character of
external actions." [88] But if conscience is not a criticism of outward action, and "if it be taken simply for the sense we have
of better and worse among our inward springs of conduct,

[86] *Seat of Authority*, p. 46.
[87] *Ibid.*, p. 49.
[88] *Ibid.*

not only is its existence compatible with the conflicting judgments of mankind . . . but it affords the simplest key to these. . . ."[89]

As a matter of fact, the apparent discrepancies of ethical judgment disappear if we realize that in each case the inner motive, to do *right*, is the same. This evidently is what Martineau means by the universal *de jure* consensus which cannot be found *de facto*. The Greek's sacrifice of the weakly was right for him because he saw as its alternative the degeneration of the state, but it is wrong for the Christian who sees as its result the loss of respect for the individual; yet in both cases what was conceived as *the better* ruled. (Notice the unconscious reference to consequences.) The preferential character of conscience allows through its very nature for growth of moral discernment, as well as for degeneration.[90]

Martineau's account is complete if we note the nature of this preferential cognition in the following passage.

> It is the peculiarity of all properly moral verdicts that they are not the expression of individual opinions which we work out for ourselves by sifting of evidence; but the enunciation of what is given us ready-made and has only to pass through us into ready speech. We may indeed debate within ourselves the claims presented in this or that example of outward conduct, because the choice of action has to be determined not only by the principle that issues it, but by the effects that follow it: these are amenable to the calculus of the understanding, without resort to which the action cannot be *rational;* but so long as the prior problem is before us, of securing the right spring of conduct, we have nothing to seek by logical process, but only to give forth what we find. Here, where alone truly *moral* judgment resides, we are but organs of what is deposited with us. . . ."[91]

Just as he argued that definite structures were given man for his physical environment, so now Martineau has argued that moral information is given.

We may now turn to a criticism of this view.

Martineau holds that there is universal unanimity in the verdicts of conscience because each one chooses the *better than*. But since no one ever obeys or disobeys mere *better thans*, Martineau has unconsciously reified a universal class-characteristic which, like all universals, has lost the uniqueness of each particular. What has to be shown on this view, however, is that in all instances of relative value conscience dictates one particular choice, such as the salvation of the individual. Experience seems to foreclose the possibility of such a proof, and, furthermore, the belief in ready-made messages conflicts with Martineau's assertion [92] that our own ideals are clarified through our interaction with others.

But even granting the unanimity of conscience as thus described, can verdicts of conscience disregard consequences? Curiously enough, in the last-quoted passage Martineau allows that "the choice of action" must be influenced "by the effects that follow it," yet he insists that this intellectual calculation is not of the essence, but only a concomitant accident of the *morality* of the choice. The intellect, confined to the debate about the *wisdom* or *folly* of consequences, leaves the decision of its goodness to the non-intellectual and non-conative conscience. But if we are to obey conscience at all cost, why should consequences be considered, except for intellectual exercise?

The difficulty here arises from Martineau's anxiety to avoid the success-criterion of goodness. He is, as a result, forced both to separate the springs of an action from its consequences and to look for the morality of an action in the subjective source alone. However, even though the motive of an action can be distinguished from its results, can the subject guide his judgment in any *concrete* instance, except by the *foreseeable* consequences which now constitute his motive? Martineau, in other words, confuses the judgment of an action in *retrospect* (when the results may have been different from those intended, for which alone the person is morally responsible) and the judgment of it in *prospect* (when the motive can be none other than the production of certain foreseeable consequences). Without this confusion he might have seen that it is impossible to judge the moral quality of an action apart from its foreseeable consequences; and thus the intellect is brought back into the heart of the moral judgment, though

[92] *Seat of Authority*, p. 53.

not necessarily into the experience of moral obligation. Consequences alone do not qualify an act as morally good or bad, for some may not have been foreseen and intended, but to say that there can be moral judgment without consideration of consequences is to overlook the basis for moral action.

Another reason why Martineau overlooks the decisive part consequences play in moral choice is that, as we see, he conceives the conscience to be a moral eye, a perceptive faculty, parallel to the physical eye, as it were. Now the latter always has *direct* vision of an object, and its decision as to the quality (e.g., red) of the object does not follow on a calculation of consequences. Under the power of what shall be called the eye-analogy, the mind is easily led to suppose that moral qualities are also discerned apart from a consideration of consequences, especially since habit enables us to make most of our moral choices so quickly ("without a second thought") that we think we are reading off moral qualities as the eye reads off physical properties. This point is important, and it will be developed when other realistic theories of value are discussed. Martineau's view of moral judgment is called realistic because, in common with the others, it holds that human conation and intellect make no contribution to the constitution of value, and that moral perception is of an object independent of and unstained by the mind's cognition.

It is our contention, to be developed further, that though much can be said for the uniqueness of moral obligation as a *sui generis* fact of human experience, the transformation of this feeling of obligation into a faculty for moral perception has involved errors, similar to Martineau's, which consequently weaken the argument for ethical Theism based on them. We turn to the result in Martineau's case.

4. THE METAPHYSICS OF MORAL VALUE

Other pathways to the reality of God than the ethical are regarded by Martineau as "side-chapels." Schleiermacher's theory that religion arises in the feeling of dependence on the Infinite is an hypothesis which cannot be verified concretely. Reason, on the other hand, gives only a "thinking necessity." Yet, though there can be ethics without religion, Martineau complains: ". . . our age finds it easier to feel sure of what Religion *is* in man, than of what it *says* of God; and can treat it, therefore, with tenderness and respect as a subjective phenomenon, but hesitates to follow its daring launch-out to the ocean of real being." [93] That is, many men follow conscience without realizing that conscience may "act as human before it is discovered to be divine." [94] There are two fundamental arguments by which Martineau tries to show that the reality of conscience involves the reality of God. The first may be called the pragmatic argument, and the second the epistemological.

(a) The Pragmatic Argument

Conscience gives a commandment before which the personality kneels in reverence. "Here then is revealed not simply the thought of one mind, but the relation between two." [95] Up to the point where conscience issues into religion, it fills us with a realm of subjective "possibilities" and ideals which "oppress us with a *quasi-infinitude*," but beyond that, "the tremulous purpose has an infinite ally," [96] and conscience has real authority. Unless God is the ground of the authority of conscience, ethics degenerates into hedonism, for instead of having the assurance that "the requirements of perfection are no provincialism of this planet . . . [but] are known among the stars," [97] concience is now merely man's own subjective phenomenon, and there is no particular reason why (is the implication) it should be obeyed at all costs. Religion, therefore, transforms the empirical into the transcendent, "the subjective miniature into an objective infinitude. . . ." [98]

Developing this thought, Martineau states that moral ideas fail to produce greater reforms not because conscience is defective but because it is conceived as something only human, a subjective fact or a social product which has only human

[93] *Ideal Substitutes for God* (1878), p. 5.
[94] *Study of Religion*, I, 20.
[95] *Ibid.*, II, 22.
[96] *Ibid.*
[97] *Ibid.*, II, 26.
[98] *Ibid.*, II, 33.

authority behind it.[99] The moralist now "eviscerates Duty, and turns it into a mummy, and then expects it to get up and walk." [100] But if man keenly inspects his conscience, he finds that the tone of authority is personal, as all authority must be, and that there are two minds present in it, his own being subordinate to a command from a superior. "Thus in the ultimate penetralia of the conscience the Living Spirit of God himself is met, it may be unconsciously, or it may be consciously." [101] If one is unconscious of it, he issues forth with a proverb and uses logic in commending it to others, but if he is conscious of its indubitable command, he speaks with the voice of prophecy.

The fundamental argument here, apart from the epistemological considerations, we call *pragmatic* because the nerve of it is that unless there is a God, morality loses its power, and there is no reason why hedonism or mere prudence should not guide our actions. Here again we note that Martineau is thinking of particular verdicts of conscience, that there is no reason for self-sacrifice, for example, unless God commands it. Closely connected with this is the other conviction that unless the individual can feel that his ideals are also actualized realities, then all the drive and enthusiasm in morality is lost.

The thinking of A. E. Taylor endorses Martineau's argument here. He also believes that if the good will is only the individual's will and there is no more "profound" reason for his obedience, "absolute reverence for the good will and its laws of duty degenerate into self-worship." [102] Taylor would agree with Kant that the demands of morality are reasonable, but he adds "that they do not originate in a reason which is 'my' nature, that they come from a supreme and absolute reason into likeness with which I have to grow, but which remains always beyond me." Insisting that human reason imperfectly recognizes but never creates its obligations (moral realism), he continues: "It is just because the reason which is the source of the moral law is not originally mine, nor that of

[99] See *Ethics and Religion*, p. 17.
[100] *Ibid.*, p. 18.
[101] *Ibid.*, p. 19.　　　[102] *The Faith of a Moralist* (1932), I, 152.

any man or all men, that I can reverence it without reserva-
tions." [103] Taylor also holds that in concrete situations we,
are directed by the voice of conscience through which the
moral law is gradually revealed, but the only ground for "un-
qualified reverence" for the law is its realization in "a living,
spiritual, and personal God. . . ." [104]

In discussing this pragmatic argument we shall lead on to
Taylor's more specific argument by evaluating Martineau's
practical argument for theism. According to Martineau, if it
be granted that the possibilities conscience reveals are actualized in God, man will derive therefrom an enthusiasm in his
moral life impossible without the assurance of his partnership
with a cosmic Righteousness. Now we do not doubt that this
assurance is a basis for enthusiasm in many people, but we
hold it to be a mistaken and undeserved enthusiasm. We do
not mean that it is not good or just to be enthusiastic about
the realization by another of what one has not himself attained, but this is not the kind of enthusiasm meant by Martineau. What he really means is that it *helps* to know that the
universe does have One in it who is actually what we are
striving for.

Let us consider in what ways the assurance of a cosmic
Mind, wherein values are realized, may be a source of moral
encouragement.

(a) If we mean that it is encouraging to know that another
overcame difficulties similar to ours and thereby strengthened
our faith in our own possibilities, such encouragement is
impossible either on Martineau's or Taylor's idea of God
(who needs not strive to maintain His goodness) or on any
idea of God as ready-made Goodness.

(b) If we mean that it aids morale in the struggle for goodness to know that One sympathizes with us and wishes us well,
then the idea of a compassionate God is indeed helpful. But
it is questionable whether the blank sympathy of a God who
was not tempted as we are is preferable to the encouragement
of friends who in all things were like unto us and yet sinned
not.

[103] *The Faith of a Moralist*, I, 152.   [104] *Ibid.*, I, 159.

(c) But if this partnership helps in the sense (which we believe is surreptitiously introduced) that God will help us to be good, then this assurance, though it foster enthusiasm in some, may well dampen enthusiasm in others. For we remember that, if we really are to possess the dignity of free will and moral autonomy, God may not aid us even though he would. The real cause for our enthusiasm would be the assurance that *we* could control *ourselves* to realize the *possibilities* we approve. Merely the knowledge that our ideals are realized in Another does not make us any more enthusiastic about ourselves. It does seem to us, however, that a good God would in a number of ways be legitimately helpful and the source of a worthy enthusiasm.

Thus, even though he cannot help directly in the moral struggle and indeed must never interfere with *our* fight, God can yet see to it that the conditions for a fair moral struggle are not withdrawn. And this would mean, first, that, as far as it lies in his power, he must keep the physical world in such order as to provide a fair chance for us to make a "come-back" or improve our moral status. Second, he can grant life after death for a continuation of the struggle. If these conditions are fulfilled, then we may be as enthusiastic as the knowledge of ourselves allows us to be. (Whether, however, the satisfaction of these two conditions needs a perfectly good and omnipotent God, we are not prepared to say at present.) The whole idea of a morality conditional on the cards' being stacked in our favor (for otherwise Hedonism should logically follow) is utterly repugnant to us and takes every bit of manhood out of morality. We become little children not willing to do our best because we cannot win. Too many ideas of the Absolute have been born in man when he has not been willing to play the game to the last.

But Taylor, who is ever concerned with the motivation of human conduct, would not accept a view which limits God's relation to man's moral struggle to that of a Moral Referee. His question is: "What is to supply the driving force which will fan languid and faint desire [note the words!] for the best into a flame? How are we to be made to care enough for the highest?" [105] Though men like Socrates seem to need no more than "intellectual discernment" of a better to arouse passion for it, ordinary mortals need more than the vision, and the problem (reminiscent of Martineau) is: Can this motivation be found in the human or infra-human sphere, or must it be the result of contact with the superhuman source? [106]

In reply Taylor devotes many pages to variations on the theme that since the moral life demands the transformation and regeneration of *ourselves*, *we* cannot be the sole source of our amelioration. If man were a Leibnizian monad with no moral windows open to the eternal, moral progress would be impossible.

> To be quite plain, in all moral advance the *ultimate* "efficient cause" must be the real eternal source of both becoming and value. The initiative in the process of "assimilation to God" must come from the side of the eternal; it must be God who first comes to meet us, and who, all through the moral life itself, "works in us," in a sense which is more than metaphorical. Our moral endeavours must be genuinely ours, but they must be responses to intimate actual contacts in which a real God moves outward to meet His creatures, and by the contact at once sustains and inspires the appropriate response on the creature's part.[107]

God is not simply an ideal of personality, nor simply the source of our insight into the Good, but he also provides the moral environment without which morality "would amount to a prolonged attempt to breathe *in vacuo*, or to feed one's body on its own fat." [108] We cannot lift ourselves by our own hair. Thus, just as Taylor holds elsewhere that motion in the physical world needs an eternal Prime Mover, so now all moral activity finds its initiative in a realized Good.

One looks in vain, however, for an explanation of how this divine initiative as conceived by Taylor can be consistent with the free will of man. It may be answered that man may refuse to welcome the divine, but this is not adequate to explain either the *increase* of strength, which on Taylor's view is owing directly to God, or the initial desire for the Good as

---

[105] Taylor, *op. cit.*, I, 213.
[106] *Ibid.*, I, 215.

[107] *Ibid.*, I, 223.
[108] *Ibid.*, I, 231.

well as its cognition, which the divine initiative *makes pos-sible*. The human will seems ultimately to be reduced to a mere Spinozistic intellectual assent. On the other hand, if we should ask what it is which makes man desire or know evil we should probably be told that it was his own free will. But if man can *create* his evil, why can he not create his good?

The real difficulty is that Taylor [109] and Martineau think that man without God would degenerate into a complete victim of his desires. Man without the divine breath returns to the clay. Now of course if man is earth-born, he naturally cannot be a denizen of heaven without the efficient causality of the divine; but once this notion is introduced, man's free will vanishes. The *mystery* of life is its growth, but it loses its *meaning* unless free will is granted. The one great mystery of the creation of selves dominated by the *conatus* for self-preservation and capable of their own development in a restricted number of ways is the nearest we can come to a noncontradictory solution of moral growth. If we assume that the self as such does not desire goodness, we are lost, and the Creator of such selves must be judged accordingly.

(b) The Epistemological Argument

We saw that Martineau could not justify the validity of (the verdicts of) conscience by any consideration of it as the product of society. Its source cannot be in our springs of action, for not only do we share these with the animals who have no moral knowledge, but we are conscious of their competitive worth as well. In conscience we have an immediate intuition we can neither escape nor explain, and the mystery involved is no different from that we find in the similar communications of sense.

In the act of Perception, we are immediately introduced to an *other than ourselves that gives us what we feel:* in the act of Conscience, we are immediately introduced to a *Higher than ourselves that gives us what*

[109] A more complete study of A. E. Taylor's argument for God may be found in a forthcoming issue of the *Review of Religion* under the title: "The Perplexing Faith of a Moralist."

we feel: the externality in the one case, the authority in the other, the causality in both, are known upon exactly the same terms, and carry the same guarantee of their validity.[110]

This guarantee, we saw, was the postulate of the veracity of our faculties. Our highest ideals "lay claim to our will with an authority that is above us and that presents them as mere delegates of itself." [111] The moral faculty is different from the aesthetic faculty, through which we are given a scale of beauty and remain "on the level of ideal facts," for in it we are subject to "imperative law" and a transcendent relation which demands the sacrifice of ourselves. "In other words, the Moral Law first reaches its integral meaning when seen as impersonated in a Perfect Mind, which communicates it to us, and lends it power over our affections, sufficient to draw us into Divine communion." [112]

There is no need to repeat the objections already made to Martineau's realistic theory of knowledge. The problem of error did not bother him in connection with the physical world, and now, when there is even less hope of comparing ideas with the actual object, he resorts to faith in the veracity of the conscience. We have already pointed out the difficulties in his view of moral knowledge. The additional point may be made that if we distinguish carefully, as Martineau does not, between any particular verdict of a faculty and the faculty itself, though we *may* then be forced to have faith in the *general* veracity of that faculty, the presence of moral and physical mirages prevents us from trusting any particular verdict, even that God is present to us, without further verification.

5. A GENERAL ESTIMATE OF MARTINEAU'S PHILOSOPHY

In the foregoing the attempt has been made to delineate the strands of empiricism in the philosophical theology of Martineau. One may disagree with the findings of Martineau, but one cannot deny that at every point his analysis starts with experience and proceeds, with not enough philosophical

---

[110] *Study of Religion,* II, 27.   [111] *Ibid.*   [112] *Ibid.*

patience perhaps, to its explanation. Martineau's importance lies not in new philosophical insights but in his insistence that philosophy take account of every aspect of experience. If anything, the intensity of his moral convictions made it impossible for him to face epistemological and metaphysical problems with sufficient open-mindedness, and this detracted from his empiricism. His moral experience loomed so large that he tended to identify it with religious experience and underestimated the importance of the aesthetic. Nevertheless, in demanding that philosophy study the whole of man's experience, he laid in place of the narrow, sense-bound Empiricism of his day the foundations for a new and broader philosophical structure which should save the individual from disintegration in the analysis of the Empiricists and from absorption in the Absolute of the Rationalists. Martineau's ethical theism may seem crude, but the analysis of the work of other British philosophers since 1850 reveals refinements and developments of the general argument, if insufficient insight into fundamental errors. In closing this chapter with part of a quotation from Dr. Alfred Caldecott, we profit by Upton's example, who used it to bring his book to an end.

But when these deficiencies are noted and allowed for, the student of the philosophy of religion will still feel that in Martineau we have one of the great masters of the subject, one of the men who have made contributions of permanent value to its literature in Great Britain. His treatment of Causality made the intelligent interpretation of the cosmos *sauter aux yeux* once more in an age when mechanical theory was enveloping men with mist. His emphasis on the authority of conscience marks him as the truest successor of Butler in the history of English Ethics. . . .[113]

The following theses represent the main points in this chapter:

1. All knowledge of the space-time world is based on an initial trust in the veracity of our faculties. But this assumes that thought can be compared with thing, confuses the mean-

[113] *The Philosophy of Religion in England and America* (1901), p. 352, cited by Upton, *Martineau's Philosophy*, p. 229.

ings of objectivity, does not explain error, and, finally, distrusts the faculty of reason.

2. The resistance of the independent world to spontaneous impulses is interpreted, on analogy with human will, as owing to Cosmic Will, and the self is declared to be noumenal, though its nature is not adequately described.

3. The laws of nature are comprehensive volitions of God, but Martineau is not clear whether, in addition to space and time, there is a pre-existent datum for God, though he favors a Berkeley-Lotzean view. But his empiricism is vitiated by his preconceptions of God's goodness and supremacy.

4. There is a conflict of the empirical and the a priori in Martineau's thought, but Martineau uses the teleological argument to establish empirically the existence of a purposive, personal Will whose Goodness can be argued from the moral nature of man. Here Martineau represents the main trend of the argument for God in late British thought.

5. Martineau finds that the existence of definite types of structure can be explained only by supposing that they were created for their environment. But this mechanistic teleology must be set aside, for the structure may be the joint-product of the environment and the self-conserving organisms.

6. The authority, uniformity, and universality of conscience cannot be explained by evolution or by social influence of egoistic individuals, for conscience is an irreducible and unique faculty which is not invalidated because it grows. But though we grant that conscience is *sui generis*, Martineau confuses the verdicts of conscience with moral obligation, and even then overlooks the function of natural sympathy.

7. The moral merits of an action are not determined by the intellectual consideration of consequences, for conscience always demands the *right* and has infallible intuitions of the better, though the particular values chosen at various times or by different people conflict. But we do not choose mere *better thans*, consequences and the intellect cannot be disregarded in moral choice, and the conscience is misconceived when considered as a moral eye.

8. Unless God is the source of the moral law which conscience reveals, the latter has no authority; but in conscience we are immediately introduced to a Perfect God. But this argument rests on a theory of moral knowledge which is inadequate and on a confusion of particular verdicts with moral obligation.

CHAPTER III

THE CONFLICT OF THE EMPIRICAL AND NON–EMPIRICAL IN ANDREW PRINGLE–PATTISON'S THEISM

A. PRINGLE-PATTISON'S INTELLECTUAL DEVELOPMENT

ANDREW SETH (1856–1931), in later life Andrew Seth Pringle-Pattison, as a junior at the University of Edinburgh, went to the classes of the Berkeleyan theist, Campbell Fraser, "with a mind opening perhaps to literature." [1] In fact, it may well be said that his later philosophical thinking was to be influenced by a blend of Carlyle and Wordsworth; nor did George Eliot and Matthew Arnold leave Pringle-Pattison unmoved. But the study of philosophy at Edinburgh, including the discussion in the Philosophical Society (of which D. G. Ritchie, R. B. Haldane, and W. R. Sorley were co-members), was followed by graduate work in Germany in 1878–80. There Pringle-Pattison studied under Zeller and Paulsen at Berlin, became engrossed in the works of Fichte and Hegel at Jena, and at Göttingen he found "sober profit" from most of Lotze's *Metaphysics*. These years meanwhile had supplemented an earlier summer course in 1876 at Heidelberg, where Kuno Fischer was lecturing on modern philosophy. It is interesting that James Martineau should be instrumental in Pringle-Pattison's appointment to the Hibbert Travelling Scholarship providing for those two years in Germany which resulted in the Hibbert thesis, "The Permanent Results of the Kantio-Hegelian Philosophy," in 1881.

On his return from Germany, Pringle-Pattison accepted Fraser's offer to succeed W. R. Sorley as class assistant in logic and metaphysics. In 1883 Pringle-Pattison appeared as the editor, with R. B. Haldane, of an "epoch-making book," [2]

---

[1] A. S. Pringle-Pattison, *Man's Place in the Cosmos* (2nd ed., 1902), p. 25; cf. *Balfour Lectures on Realism* (1933), p. 10. Unless otherwise indicated all references will be to the works of Pringle-Pattison.

[2] J. H. Muirhead, *The Platonic Tradition in Anglo-Saxon Philosophy* (1931), pp. 175 ff.

Essays in Philosophical Criticism, in which a group of young writers, including Sorley, Henry Jones, and Bernard Bosanquet, joined in the attack on the narrow empiricism of *Mind* at that time. The volume was dedicated to T. H. Green, who had died the year before, and, as E. Caird said in the Introduction, the writers believed that philosophy should follow the Kantian lead as developed by Hegel. Yet, as Muirhead rightly says, four years later Pringle-Pattison "was to come forward as the leader of the revolt from the metaphysical conclusions which his colleagues sought to found upon that [Neo-Kantian] theory" of knowledge.[3] This revolt, especially in Pringle-Pattison, was no doubt inspired by Lotze who, thanks to the translations by Green and Bosanquet, was making himself felt in the later eighties, even in the thought of the Hegelians. Muirhead once more pertinently asserts that the difference between F. H. Bradley and Pringle-Pattison was that

. . . while the contradictions, to which the attempt to adhere to Lotze's view of thought led, roused Bradley to suspect its adequacy, and in the end to substitute another for it much more allied to Hegel's Absolutism, Seth was borne by the Lotzean reaction to suspect the whole idea of the Absolute as a menace to individual reality in general and human personality in particular.[4]

The influence of Hegel and the English Hegelians, Bradley and Bosanquet, on Pringle-Pattison is even greater, we suspect, than he himself realized. The many references to his friend, S. S. Laurie, show the latter's influence, and Martineau was not without effect. It was through Pringle-Pattison's efforts that both William James and Henri Bergson were brought to England to deliver Gifford Lectures. His own opportunity for writing was greatly enhanced by the establishment of the Balfour Lectureship, to which he was appointed twice by A. J. Balfour, who instituted them mainly for the sake of Pringle-Pattison's development.

Commenting correctly that the result of Pringle-Pattison's thinking is a transcendental Idealism based on the ethical

[3] *Ibid.,* p. 175.
[4] *Ibid.,* pp. 203, 204. Cf. this Chapter, Section H.

and religious life (though Pringle-Pattison always means to include the aesthetic), Alfred Caldecott contrasts Pringle-Pattison and his teacher strikingly as follows: "If Dr Fraser's lectures are somewhat of the nature of a farewell message from a veteran philosopher, Professor Seth's essays may be taken as the precursors of more massive and solidly compacted work yet to come." [5] Whether this evaluation is true is not to be decided now, but it does allude to what ultimately is a defect in Pringle-Pattison's exposition. His method in all his writings is that of "construction through criticism," a method which he "instinctively followed," and which does have the merit of producing common understanding in philosophy, as he suggests. Nevertheless, though his criticism is usually distinct, the *grounds* for his own constructions are far from clear, and therein lies the source of much difficulty. In the absence of an orderly presentation of arguments, the student who attempts to set forth Pringle-Pattison's views systematically is confronted with the task of unifying scattered statements, the premises of which are not always evident.

B.   The Nature of Philosophical Truth

In the introductory sections of the second part of Pringle-Pattison's Hibbert essay,[6] published in *The Development from Kant to Hegel* in 1882, the need is expressed for a philosophy "which should give a wider scope to reason and a more inward meaning to revelation," [7] in order to overcome "the abstract opposition of reason and revelation." [8] The contributions of Kant and Hegel to such a philosophy are discussed in this essay, but in these words the underlying motive of Pringle-Pattison's philosophy of religion may be found. His attempt to effect the right compromise between reason and revelation is expressed in Pringle-Pattison's criterion of truth, for the most explicit statement of which we must turn

---

[5] A. Caldecott, *The Philosophy of Religion in England and America* (1901), p. 187.

[6] "Philosophy of Religion in Kant and Hegel" in the thesis entitled "The Permanent Results of the Kantio-Hegelian Philosophy" (1881).

[7] *The Philosophical Radicals* (1907), p. 218.   [8] *Ibid.*, p. 217.

to the criticism of Bradley and Bosanquet in the second set of Gifford Lectures.

Pringle-Pattison holds that Bradley misuses the principle of non-contradiction and inclusive harmony, for, "except when applied to specific experience," this becomes, as it does in Bradley's hands (but less so in Bosanquet's), an "empty formula." The abstract use of the principle of coherence results in the Absolute from which Bradley reasons *"down"* to our actual experience and condemns "its most characteristic features." [9] Though Pringle-Pattison exaggerates Bradley's rationalism, our own study of Bradley seems to confirm this criticism in its essentials. But his indictment of Bradley is especially interesting in view of the fact that we shall in turn accuse Pringle-Pattison himself of denying some of the most characteristic features of human experience in his own description of God. His objections to Bradley do indicate, however, that the wedge between Pringle-Pattison and the English Hegelians was driven by the former's conviction that it is the function of reason to clarify *experience* and not to impose upon experience a logical strait jacket of its own making. It is Pringle-Pattison's penetrating insight into the consequences of this court-martial and expatriation of experience that accounts for his protest and for his insistence that the coherence-criterion must explain our experience, and not explain it away, that coherence must receive its character "from the concrete material in which it works itself out." [10] Accordingly, Pringle-Pattison agrees with Bosanquet that the path of knowledge is from the finite to the infinite. And the empirical method, concentrating on the "concrete material of life," is well described in the following words: "It is surely by this *experimental* and *tentative* method alone that we are likely to reach results of any value." [11] Beginning from what we *know*, *not* "from the bare idea of a systematic whole, but from the amount of system and *kind of system* which we are able to point to as realized in experience," we argue to *"more* of the

[9] *The Idea of God: in the Light of Recent Philosophy* (2nd ed., 1920), p. 230.
[10] *Ibid.*
[11] *Ibid.*, p. 231. (My italics.)

same kind, or at least on the same general lines," even though it may be "on an ampler and diviner scale." [12]

This insistence that philosophy should proceed from and consider carefully all the aspects of known experience takes a specific form, however, in the philosophical approach of Pringle-Pattison. Philosophical reasoning, he insists, is systematic; it must aim for a coherent whole. But the systematization of experience and knowledge is impossible apart from some ultimate value-judgment which forms a pivot, as it were, around which the facts may be organized. Reasoning about phenomena must be directed by some ultimate and supreme value, for if every phenomenon were as good as the rest there would be no hope of system, and the unity would be that of a "mere collection." Degrees of value are found in experience, and systematic reasoning is insignificant unless directed by some judgment of value. Pringle-Pattison finds ultimate value in human personality, and his system, therefore, is focused (his word is "founding") on "the verities of the spiritual life." [13] He frankly says:

. . . I would admit that there is an assumption in this philosophical theory, an assumption woven into its very texture, and without which, perhaps, the theory would never have been arrived at — I mean the conviction of the essential greatness of man and the infinite nature of the values revealed in his life.[14]

So far as we can see, there is no reason why a philosopher should not be allowed an assumption, but his conviction must be justified by its ability to explain the facts of experience most coherently and must not be allowed to blind him to experience in its fullness and variety. In contrast with Kant's view, Pringle-Pattison's position is that the place of the categories in experience will be illuminated by an ideal, not of pure reason, but of value. This analogy, however, suggests the problem: Does Pringle-Pattison, following the procedure of Kant with regard to the ideals of pure reason, consider his ultimate value (his ideal of pure conscience, as we shall see)

[12] Ibid., p. 232.
[13] Ibid., p. 341.
[14] Ibid., p. 236; cf. Two Lectures on Theism (1897), p. 63.

hypothetically, realizing that it is not *given* in the *whole* of experience; or does he, like Kant, finally hold that the (moral) ideal is an ultimate certainty? Pringle-Pattison affirms, as we can see, the latter conviction, a conviction which, he contends, is backed by a whole system, and which *we* shall treat as an hypothesis. His thought, therefore, is the justification of an ultimate conviction, and the student can only attempt to see the way in which it is held and evaluate the system by which it is supposed to be corroborated. It is pertinent to remark that, though more fully developed and justified, the approach is not essentially different from Martineau's. We are ready, however, to examine the system which is to corroborate this belief in the value of man's spiritual life.

C. MECHANICAL VERSUS TELEOLOGICAL, NATURALISM

The naturalistic theory of the universe suffers incurable defects in its resort to a mechanical explanation which describes the universe simply as a collocation of facts and events to be accounted for solely by their antecedents. But "mechanical explanation is a *progressus in infinitum,* which can ultimately explain nothing," [15] since it can assign causes but never give *reasons* and motives for change. Though such procedure is adequate in the limited realm of science, it is false as philosophical explanation, which must be teleological. Rejecting the mechanical teleology, such as Martineau's for example, which tried to explain particular phenomena by adaptation to external ends, philosophy must try to see the cosmic process as an organic unity bound by a purpose which permeates and transforms mere change into *evolution* toward an end. "In the last resort, *causae efficientes pendent a finalibus. . . ."* [16]

This general objection is repeated and made concrete in the *Idea of God.* The zeal of the naturalist for continuity which avoids appeal to an external Creator has either blinded him to the real differences between various steps of a continuous process, or driven him to protect continuity by re-

---

[15] *Man's Place,* p. 41, "The Present Position of the Philosophical Sciences."
[16] *Ibid.*

ducing all experience to the one level of the inorganic. But in the truly philosophical explanation of the evolutionary process every part must be read in the light of its end, or of the process as a whole. Indeed, to explain the higher by the lower is to commit the fallacy of hysteron proteron, for the antecedents are not to be considered first in abstraction from their consequences and then as the causes of them,[17] since for our actual knowledge antecedents "are mere *entia rationis*, abstract aspects of one concrete fact which we call the universe. . . . If we are in earnest with the doctrine that the universe is one, we have to read back the nature of the latest consequent into the remotest antecedent." [18] This part of Pringle-Pattison's argument is rendered complete by his claim that the time at which the new qualities appear is of no importance.

In so far as Pringle-Pattison demands that philosophy take into account the uniqueness and variety of experience, and insists that explanation is most complete if it renders purpose as well as cause intelligible, his rejection of naturalism is the logical outcome of the application of the coherence-criterion of truth. For that criterion requires both efficient and final causes to be considered. Again, in so far as he protests that the disjunction of reason, as valid in the scientific realm, and spiritual insight, as valid in the realm of value, leaves theology "in the air," [19] and that no lasting victory for religion can be won by the division of the mind into conflicting faculties and "needs" which have equal validity in their respective realms, Pringle-Pattison gives clear evidence of a realization that "the mere assertion of the principle [of value] is not enough." Rather must the principle "be articulated as far as possible in a coherent system of reality, and shown to represent the ultimate insight of a larger knowledge." [20] But into his argument a new element is creeping when he appeals to the doctrine of the universe as one in defense of his teleological explanation. To our knowledge, nowhere is the prin-

[17] Cf. *Idea of God*, p. 106.
[18] *Ibid.*, p. 107, quoting *Man's Place*, pp. 11–12.
[19] Cf. *Idea of God*, pp. 57 ff.   [20] *Ibid.*, p. 65.

ciple that the universe is *one* [21] defended or adequately
explained; for, so stated, with "one" undefined, the doctrine
is ambiguous. Indeed, only the *success* of a particular teleological explanation would prove that the universe is the
teleological unity Pringle-Pattison has in mind. But the particular explanation, which is to be sought, seems here to be
assumed by Pringle-Pattison. To be sure, in a criticism of
Bradley, Pringle-Pattison holds that "the mere consideration
. . . that the universe exists — that Being is — proves that
it is in some sense a harmony," [22] and he adds that unity
and harmony must mean more than this tautology, "if their
presence or absence is to be of any vital concern to men." [23]
Be this as it may, to argue in favor of a teleological explanation *because* the universe is one is to introduce ambiguously
or gratuitously a question-begging argument of the form: The
universe is teleological because it is (a teleological) *one*.

More light will be thrown on this subject as we proceed,
but the statement that the point in the temporal series at
which a new quality appears is unimportant for philosophy
is not easily acceptable, unless time is not real. For how can
the philosopher who is trying to judge the value of any quality
omit from his judgment considerations involving the oppor-
tuneness, for example, of its appearance? Is it unimportant
that man became a part of the cosmos later than animals, and
would judgments about the universe not be affected if the
reverse were true? It is true enough, as Pringle-Pattison says,
that epigenesis does not in itself involve contingency, especially from the point of view of an Absolute Experience,[24]
but would not a Ward be correct in answering that biological
epigenesis from the finite point of view to which we are restricted does mean contingency in the sense that a new quality
could not be predicted from our knowledge of the antecedents? In both of these instances Pringle-Pattison's statements
are true only if a certain theory of the universe, not yet

[21] As we shall see, he really means an organic whole, but the same criticism
applies.
[22] *Man's Place*, p. 127, and *Idea of God*, p. 230n.
[23] *Man's Place*, p. 128.   [24] Cf. *Idea of God*, p. 95n.

explicated and justified, is assumed. One who knows the conclusions has difficulty in avoiding the suspicion that Pringle-
Pattison is lapsing in his attention to empirical facts and
thinking in terms of a rounded theory. Even if these criticisms
are justified, however, Pringle-Pattison's essential argument,
that the mechanical explanation cannot do justice to the facts
of experience, is left unscathed. To this he adds another less
cogent point, which we shall do well to remember in connection with his theory of value, namely, that even if naturalism
were intellectually conceivable, it would so outrage "our
deepest convictions" about the objectivity of our value-judgments as to be incredible.

D.   MAN AS ORGANIC TO NATURE

A point of transition to the most important and yet ambiguous position Pringle-Pattison takes is afforded by passages
in "The Present Position of the Philosophical Sciences."
Here, having said that philosophy must indicate a purpose
in the universe, he states that "philosophy must be unflinch-
ingly *humanistic*, anthropocentric," as against the naturalistic
thought of his day which made man only a part of nature in
general, and overlooked the fact that "to man as rational, all
things are relative." [25] That is, it is not enough, in Pringle-
Pattison's view, to say that man is a unique part of nature
and that his mental and moral life cannot be explained in
terms of the clash of atoms. Man, in Martineau's terms, is
the crowning feature of the whole creation which he mirrors;
he is for Pringle-Pattison not only a unique appearance; he
stands in a unique relation to nature. As expressed in the
dominating theme of the *Idea of God*: "man is organic to the
world. . . . The intelligent being is, as it were, the organ
through which the universe beholds and enjoys itself." [26] In
the same context, we are told, as an equivalent statement,
that the world is not complete without man, and that "man's
rootedness in nature" shows his rational intelligence to be the
"culmination of a continuous process of immanent develop-

[25] *Man's Place*, p. 42; see also pp. 23, 242.
[26] *Idea of God*, p. 111.

ment." [27] There is no doubt that Pringle-Pattison is trying to stress man's continuity with the rest of nature; that he is trying to avoid the view which, he thinks, underlies defective epistemologies, namely, that an independent and finished world is known by a foreigner "equipped, from heaven knows where, with a peculiar apparatus of faculties"; [28] that he is attempting to replace the conception of man's relation as contingent and accidental by one which finds man essential and complementary to nature.

But despite a host of such statements, at no point in the discussion are the inherent ambiguities clarified. To be sure, we are told that man *as rational* is organic to nature, but the meaning of the statement depends upon the meaning of "nature" and "organic." If "nature" means the non-human and non-divine realm of being, and if "organic" is meant to denote a relation of interdependence, the statement is clearly false, for nature does not depend on man. If "organic" means complementary in the sense of additional, then the statement is a mere truism. If "organic" means complementary in the sense of fulfilling a purpose immanent in nature which is a means to man, the goal, then the statement is intelligible and meaningful but *not* proved. Here, as with the unity of the world, if the relation of man to the universe is organic in the sense that man is a member of a life and the end of a purpose which dominates the whole, then the very thesis to be proved is assumed, couched as it may be in the ambiguous words "organic" and "nature." *This* particular type of organicity and unity must be proved, for the data are a plurality of men, things, and the various forms of life, and though there may seem to be a general gradation or continuity from the inorganic through the organic to mind, a specific kind of unity may be suggested but its truth cannot be assumed.

This doctrine that man is organic to nature is particularly difficult in view of Pringle-Pattison's own argument that man's moral and intellectual characteristics cannot be explained in terms of the lower stages, which means all of nature. The

[27] *Ibid.* [28] *Ibid.*, p. 112.

long and short of it seems to be that Pringle-Pattison has assumed an idealistic metaphysics *within which* his empiricism operates. Surely, if nature meant for him the realm of being excluding the human and divine, the statement that the universe beholds and enjoys itself through its organ, the intelligible being, would be little more than poetry. For this particular statement of the connection between man and nature emphasizes a cognitive and appreciative relationship, but, unless an idealistic view of reality is granted, it does no more than poetically personalize nature. The gap between man and nature cannot be better expressed than as Pringle-Pattison himself expresses it in the essay last mentioned. "Nature is non-moral, indifferent and pitiless; but man is pitiful, and human nature flowers in love and self-denial, in purity and stainless honour." And, conscious of the chasm, he adds: "If these have no root [not in nature but] in the nature of things, then indeed

> The pillared firmament is rottenness,
> And earth's base built on stubble. . . ." [29]

Be this as it may, here is the problem, and it cannot be solved by a doctrine which in the ambiguous phrase, "man is organic to nature," assumes that man is organic to the "nature of things." What is even worse, however, is that this doctrine instead of being verified by *independent* considerations from the theory of knowledge is used to justify a particular theory of natural and moral knowledge. For instance, in reviewing the argument of the first course of lectures in *The Idea of God*, Pringle-Pattison says: ". . . I emphasized the essential relatedness of nature and mind as the guarantee of the naturalness of the knowledge-process and the truthfulness of the result." [30]

We may now turn our attention to Pringle-Pattison's theory of natural knowledge for the sake of the light it throws on our main concern, his view of moral knowledge. In order that we may be sure of doing justice to Pringle-Pattison's

[29] *Man's Place*, p. 43; cf. *Idea of God*, p. 213.
[30] *Idea of God*, pp. 211, 212.

position, we shall trace his theory of knowledge independently of any conclusions suggested hitherto, and then his theory of value as independently of it as possible.

E. The Theory of Natural Knowledge

In the second set of Balfour Lectures, *Hegelianism and Personality*, a fundamental charge brought against the Hegelian philosophy is its confusion of existence and knowledge. No number of thought-relations are equivalent to an existent thing.[31] The categories of thought may be valid for nature, but "we require to be on our guard against the idea that logical abstractions can *thicken*, as it were, into real existences." [32] But whatever the fault of the Hegelian system may be, "its insistence on self-consciousness as the ultimate principle of explanation, is also an imperishable gift." [33]

In *The Balfour Lectures on Realism* (the third set), Pringle-Pattison holds that: "Epistemology starts, and must start, from the individual human consciousness — the only consciousness known to us," [34] and considers the nature of the relation between the idea and what it refers to. On any theory of knowledge a dualism exists, and "no theory can deny the contrast between the present content of consciousness and that which it symbolizes or stands for." [35] We may, indeed, never be *logically* coerced to go beyond our own consciousness, but the problem of knowledge is: Are the subjective states which form our data valid for the trans-subjective reality?

Now the difficulty with Neo-Hegelians is that they forget that knowing involves a subjective process, and though justly freeing themselves from the unrelated metaphysical *ding-an-sich*, they go too far and identify thought and thing, thus denying the subject-object dualism which must be granted no matter how identical the independent world and the knower's ideas may be. The Scottish philosophers, on the other hand (whom Pringle-Pattison criticized in his first set of Balfour

[31] Cf. *Hegelianism and Personality* (1897), p. 126.
[32] *Ibid.*, p. 125.
[33] *Ibid.*, p. 230.
[34] Pp. 179, 180.
[35] *Ibid.*, p. 168.

Lectures), correctly insisted on an epistemological dualism but then erred in hypostatizing it as a metaphysical dualism. "Dualism in knowledge," Pringle-Pattison correctly holds, "is no more a proof of metaphysical heterogeneity than identity of metaphysical essence in Hegel's sense can be taken as eliminating the epistemological problem" [36] of the relation of the conscious object to the extra-conscious or trans-subjective object, which all knowledge implies.

Knowing, then, is a subjective process which nevertheless "bears in its heart, in its very notion, this reference to a reality distinct from itself," [37] which knowledge represents or symbolizes. Now for "the plain man," the "appearance *is* the reality," [38] and such Realism has an instinctive priority to other theories. Idealism is simply a criticism of *crude* Realism, but it lives "and derives any plausibility it possesses from the surreptitious or unobserved importation into its statements of our ineradicable realistic assumptions." [39] Furthermore, in attempting to obliterate the distinction between being and knowing, it never can explain how the distinction ever arose. Yet, Idealism is correct in so far as it insists, against the crude Realism which uncritically holds that we know the object immediately, that knowledge is mediate and the result of a process. "A critical Realism" must acknowledge this fact and, realizing that "the transcendence of the real does give scepticism its opportunity," [40] must face fairly the sceptical insinuation that the appearance may not be the reality.

The conclusion of these lectures is that, though there is always room for doubt that our mental categories are only subjective and do not disclose the actual connection with a trans-subjective world, this contention is ultimately untenable. To be sure, the fact that we cannot compare our ideas with reality makes proof or disproof of either thesis impossible, so that in the end "we are thrown back upon a species of trust . . . that knowledge in its fundamental characteristics

[36] *Balfour Lectures*, p. 182.
[37] *Ibid.*, p. 183.
[38] *Ibid.*, p. 185.
[39] *Ibid.*, p. 191.
[40] *Ibid.*, p. 197.

renders correctly the world of existence." We must therefore balance the probabilities in the situation, but since "to suppose that the mechanism of knowledge has been expressly devised to defeat its own purpose," as scepticism would hold, is to "take the universe for a bad joke" and is "incompatible with any belief in the rationality of existence," the probability that there is an absence of correspondence "between the forms of knowledge and the forms of existence" [41] is negligible. The trouble is that "the knower is practically extruded from the real universe" and "treated as if he did not belong to it, as if he came to inspect it like a stranger from afar. His forms of thought come thus to be regarded as an alien product with no inherent fitness to express the nature of things," [42] and which consequently distort the things conceived in independence of them. But to conceive matters thus, Pringle-Pattison continues, is to hypostatize the epistemological realism or dualism into an unwarranted metaphysical dualism.

The knower is in the world which he comes to know; and the forms of his thought, so far from being an alien growth or an imported product, are themselves a function of the whole. As M. Fouillée puts it: "Consciousness, so far from being outside reality, is the immediate presence of reality to itself and the inward unrolling of its riches." [43]

If the universe is dichotomized into two substances foreign to each other, it is no wonder that thought should not apply to it. "The possibility of knowledge becomes, on the other hand, the surest guarantee of metaphysical monism — of a unity which underlies all differences." [44] Hence, Pringle-Pattison says that he knows no more than Berkeley did about the

[41] *Ibid.*, p. 254.

[42] *Ibid.*, p. 255.

[43] *Ibid.* In these quotations note how, despite the emphasis on organicity, man's cognitive faculties are (rationalistically) regarded as ready-made for the world to be known; the contrast with Tennant's view (cf. Chapter VI, Section D) is interesting and instructive, for the latter, by employing the genetic-analytic psychological approach, avoids the error of supposing that man's intellectual organs and categories are specifically made for the environment (as Martineau's natural teleology illustrated), rather than developed by interaction with it.

[44] *Ibid.*, p. 256.

existence of a brute, created matter placed outside the divine consciousness and will.[45] Unless epistemology is to issue in "sceptical idealism," it must "tacitly presuppose this metaphysical unity of the subjective and objective, or, to put it more strictly, the harmony of the subjective function with the universe from which it springs." [46]

One might quote confirmatory passages from the *Two Lectures on Theism* [47] delivered at Princeton University, in which Pringle-Pattison finds Hegel's criticism of the Kantian theory "absolutely conclusive," and asserts the Hegelian dictum that "Thoughts . . . do not stand between us and things, shutting us off from the things, they rather shut us together with them." The argument in the Gifford Lectures restates this and emphasizes certain other conclusions, as we shall learn, but we need no more than the purposely numerous quotations and detailed exposition given to see that the argument is different from Martineau's only in that it rejects his externalism and replaces it with an assumed immanence which indeed lurked in Martineau's thought. That is, the fundamental common-sense conviction, what might be called "the obsession for objectivity," that the knowledge process, whatever it be, does not distort but accurately represents a world independent of and antecedent to it dominates both views.[48] Despite the fuss that is made about the mind's creative activity, and no matter how strongly he insists with Lotze that the function of intelligence is not a mirroring of a finished reality, not a "barren rehearsal" or "a passionless duplication of existence," ultimately it is hard to see how Pringle-Pattison's theory of knowledge avoids this. On his view, it is impossible to see in what way mind is creative, for appearance *is* reality and both secondary and tertiary qualities are as independent and uncreated as the primary.[49] Indeed, mind's function is simply to "show off" the nature of things antecedent to and independent of it; and though Pringle-Pattison asserts that nature could not be what it is without the mind which knows

[45] Cf. *Balfour Lectures*, p. 257.
[46] *Ibid.*, p. 258.
[47] P. 20.
[48] Cf. *Idea of God*, p. 118.
[49] Cf. *ibid.*, pp. 120–123, 128–130.

it (any more, we must say, than the mirror object could be what it is without the mirror), this is a mere truism, confused, if anything, by Pringle-Pattison's assertion that the mind is creative. On the one hand he asserts that the soul is the only significant being in the universe, since it alone can feel nature's beauty and grandeur, and on the other he holds that mind is simply the end toward which (personalized) nature has worked in order that she "may become conscious of herself and enter into the joy of her own being." [50] However he may protest against the eye-metaphor of "speculative idealism," Pringle-Pattison, as we shall now show to be so even in regard to moral values, never escapes from it. In order to be as fair as possible and not to allow our conclusions about one aspect of Pringle-Pattison's thought to prejudice our conclusions on another, we shall burden the reader with an independent discussion of the theory of moral knowledge.

F. The Theory of Moral Knowledge

A contrast of Martineau's and Pringle-Pattison's views on the moral consciousness is supplied by the latter in an earlier essay, in 1903, on "Martineau's Philosophy." [51] Here, though paying tribute to Martineau's "splendid insistence on the moral life and its implications, as furnishing the key to human existence and man's relation to the divine . . . ," [52] Pringle-Pattison rejects, however, "his specific theory of Conscience as in every case intuitively deciding between two conflicting motives" as psychologically and philosophically unsound.[53] The dictates of conscience must be tested in every instance by reference to the results of the actions they prescribe. Having gone thus far, Pringle-Pattison also realizes that "this conclusion . . . also disposes of the notion of a special faculty issuing immediate decision on the moral question at issue." [54]

Indeed, the difficulty pervading the whole of Martineau's thought is its deism and individualism. Conscience, for Pringle-Pattison, means little more than "the response of the

[50] *Ibid.*, p. 114; cf. also pp. 127, 211.
[51] *Philosophical Radicals*, pp. 78–108.   [53] *Philosophical Radicals*, p. 91.
[52] *Ibid.*, p. 82.   [54] *Ibid.*, p. 92.

trained moral nature in view of any ethical alternative," [55] which may furnish swift and in most cases infallible decisions that in turn are not abstract judgments made independently of the effects of action. Martineau's revolt against the Utilitarians resulted in an excessive individualism which overlooked the molding effects of society's institutions and customs. "But it is not really open to doubt that we are men and moral beings at all only as we share in the corporated and inherited life of humanity . . . the subjective conscience is in its main contents, the organ of the objective ethos. . . ." [56]

Pringle-Pattison does approve, however, Martineau's insistence on the ultimate authority and irreducibility of moral obligation. Yet even here, he thinks, Martineau suffers from his deism, for he finds that the moral law has authority because it is imposed by God, as *an authority foreign to our personality.*" [57] In denying that the moral law can be self-imposed, Martineau is destroying the autonomy of the self which is Kant's "most valuable contribution to modern thought." Pringle-Pattison contends: "So long as the law comes to me from without, I can demand its warrant and evade its claims; but I cannot escape from my own law. . . ." [58] Here, as in the rest of his criticism of Martineau, one feels that Pringle-Pattison does not do sufficient justice to the other aspect of Martineau's thinking which emphasizes the immanence of God in nature and in the conscience which may "act as human before it is discovered to be divine." [59]

But these criticisms are interesting for the light they shed on Pringle-Pattison's view, which, we are beginning to see, is of the same fundamental nature and presents the same difficulties as did his theory of natural knowledge. For his objection is not to the essence of Martineau's theory, that God is really the source of the moral law, but to the externalism of the relationship as Martineau conceived it in his less religious

[55] *Philosophical Radicals*, p. 93.
[56] *Ibid.*, p. 94.
[57] *Ibid.*, p. 95, quoting Martineau, *Study of Religion*, II, 7 (but it should be p. 6, second edition).
[58] *Philosophical Radicals*, p. 96.
[59] Martineau, *Study of Religion*, I, 20.

moments. Pringle-Pattison rejoices when Martineau speaks of God not as "another and higher person" who is the result of inference from resistance in will and restraint in conscience, but as "the soul of souls" immanent and expressed in their ideals. For Pringle-Pattison:

> Consciousness of imperfection, the capacity for progress, and the pursuit of perfection are alike possible to man only through the universal life of thought and goodness in which he shares, and which, at once an indwelling presence and an unattainable ideal, draws him "on and always on." [60]

Yet, as Upton says, the reason why Martineau avoided such conceptions was his fear of pantheism, whereas Pringle-Pattison seems to have no such fear, though all of his argument so far leads directly to pantheism. What else, indeed, has he done but invert Martineau's position, so that what was once external is now internal?

This is evident from developments expressed in the Princeton Lectures and in the *Idea of God*. In the latter, after quoting the passage just cited, he adds: "The authority claimed by what is commonly called the higher self is thus only intelligible, if the ideals of that self are recognized as the immediate presence within us of a Spirit leading us into all truth and goodness." [61] In the Princeton Lectures Pringle-Pattison repeats the objection that Kant's ethical theism suffers from the externalism which led him to regard the moral law as first imposed by the self and then reimposed by a deistic God who coördinated it with the achievement of happiness. Kant does not see that if the law is imposed by the isolated individual he is thrown back into subjectivity and cannot account for the absolute obligation which it has for all rational beings. Such authority is only intelligible if the ideals "are recognized as the immediate presence within us of a spirit leading us into all truth and goodness." [62] Again, "God is the source and author of the law, but only in the sense that he is the

[60] *Philosophical Radicals*, p. 98.
[61] *Idea of God*, p. 37.
[62] *Lectures on Theism*, p. 27. We have already noted the similarity of A. E. Taylor's thought with Martineau's at this point. Cf. Chapter II, pp. 35 f.

higher self within the self which inwardly illuminates our lives." [63] Hegel saw the truth Kant never realized, that the individual is in organic connection with the whole course of human intellectual and moral evolution, which in turn is "directly" connected with the life of God as the unfolding of an ideal of goodness "which in itself is the most real of realities." [64] We thus see that though Pringle-Pattison rejects the conscience as an intuitive faculty, he nevertheless holds an equivalent position in his insistence that moral knowledge is the revelation of an antecedent reality, the result of the immanence of God in individuals. The judgment of value is impartial and unhesitating, and though it makes mistakes in detail, "in its pronouncements as to what possesses value and what does not — in its recognition of the main forms of value, and in its general scale of higher and lower," [65] it is essentially true. Mind does not create moral truth or value; it simply recognizes what is already independently there. The truth of any cognition depends upon its degree of revelation.

We may, then, fittingly complete the exposition of both the natural and moral epistemology by considering the doctrine of the degrees of truth or revelation. It may be said that moral knowledge, to take the type most pertinent here, is knowledge of moral reality in its appearance. But the moral ideal is not "communicated" in the same form and in the same degree to all,[66] "for all revelation must be *ad modum recipientis*," [67] in the same way as knowledge of the physical world is relative to the structure of the sense organs and nervous system.[68] Each creature lives in his own world, "but what it apprehends, up to the limit of its capacities, is a true account of the environment, so far as it goes." [69] Indeed, the evolution of the sense organs is inexplicable unless we assume the reality of the new qualities they reveal to us. What is seen was always there waiting for the eye which could see it, and the same is true with regard to moral qualities. The only

[63] *Lectures on Theism*, p. 28.
[64] *Ibid.*, p. 31.
[65] *Idea of God*, p. 41.
[66] *Ibid.*, p. 32.
[67] *Ibid.*, p. 175.
[68] Cf. *ibid.*, p. 126.
[69] *Ibid.*, p. 127.

distinction between appearance and reality "is, in short, between the thing as it first appears, and the thing as it eventually appears in the light of a fuller experience." [70] It is only
a "misguided philosophy" which takes this distinction "within
experience" to mean that therefore our experience is to be
set over against an unaccessible reality.

Thus we see that the validity of moral and natural knowledge, based on the argument that appearances do not distort
reality, is defended by the doctrine of immanence or organicity. Then the disturbing fact which endangers the validity
of a realistic theory of knowledge, namely, that there are differences between appearances of reality, is nullified by the
contention that the differences are not in quality but only in
the degree of revelation. Consequently, on this theory the
word "partial" would replace the word "distorted" when we
realize that what *appeared* to be the reality is no longer so.

But to redefine error is not to explain it. If the explanation of error is, as Bradley says, that we are forced to see reality only partially, through a keyhole, then the sole criterion
of truth is the rationalistic coherence to which Bradley was
confined and which Pringle-Pattison rejected. And where
now is the cognitive security which Pringle-Pattison tried to
guarantee by forfeiting the creative contribution of the mind
to known reality? If it is security we want, we do not gain it
through veridical faculties, which do not distort, but which
nevertheless give only partial knowledge. The same uncertainty which Pringle-Pattison avoided by reducing the mind
to a mirror, after he had rightly granted epistemological
dualism, returns when the mirror reflects only the part and
not the whole of reality. And once having admitted that appearance is only partially true of reality, we are then forced
for want of any other alternative, to forsake the gleam of
experience as we *seek* the coherent, and to judge experience
by an abstract and formal coherence, which, as Bradley illustrated, would lead to the denial of the ultimate reality of
important characteristics of known experience. Instead of
judging the conceptual by the given we should have to forsake

[70] *Ibid.*, p. 217.

empiricism and judge the given by the conceptual, on the *assumption* that reality is coherent in a special sense, that is, noncontradictory. Pringle-Pattison and Martineau were led astray by the vain hope that knowledge could be photographic, and this led them to deny the creative activity of the mind and to overlook the fact that all we need (and can hope for) is knowledge *relevant to* and not identical with reality.

G. The Argument for God

So far we have been trying to disentangle fundamental lines of thought which intermingle with almost baffling confusion in the process of Pringle-Pattison's criticism of other views and the development of his own. Our point has been that, though Pringle-Pattison begins empirically, his conclusions are based on the prior conviction of an existent unity which, immanent in the experience of the members organic to it, therefore guarantees the truth of their ideas. In order, however, that the argument for God may be seen as a whole and this conflict between the a priori and the empirical be presented from another point of view, the argument will be traced in its natural setting as found in the *Idea of God*.

Pringle-Pattison's argument for God may be seen as a series of answers to the challenges he accepts from Hume. He agrees with Hume in rejecting the ontological argument, for it is illegitimate to pass from essence to existence. He further maintains that the only meaning the statement "God necessarily exists" can have, is that "Given certain facts of experience God is the necessary hypothesis to explain them." These contentions indicate Pringle-Pattison's desire to follow experience wherever it leads. His empiricism is even more admirable when he agrees with Hume's answer to Demea's claim that the evil of the present world may be rectified in a future period or seen to be good from a broader perspective. Pringle-Pattison writes: " 'No!' replies Cleanthes, with a vehement disclaimer of this crooked logic, 'these arbitrary suppositions can never be admitted contrary to matter of fact, visible and uncontroverted. Whence can any cause be known but from its known effects? Whence can any hypothesis be proved but from the apparent phenomena?' " [71] In principle, undoubtedly, Pringle-Pattison accepts Hume's position, which seems to us to be the essence of empirical procedure, namely, to rest hypotheses on known facts only. And quite correctly Pringle-Pattison criticizes Hume for the halting empiricism which disregarded man's moral experience in the explanation of the cosmos.

But the tide begins to turn when Pringle-Pattison says that the existence of a mere superhuman Intellect who is indifferent "not only to human weal and woe, but also to . . . the highest and best we know" is "hardly a matter of human concern." [72] For, empirical as it may be to say that the whole of human experience must be considered, it is an unworthy and unwise empiricism which seeks only that which *seems* to be of present concern. Pringle-Pattison and many other theists jump too hastily to the conclusion cited. Supposing one did arrive at the conclusion that only a cosmic Intellect existed, could this Intellect be meaningfully conceived as nonmoral? If any evil nature were ascribed to Him, then it would be of human concern to resist it, and Huxley's defiance of nature would be the minimum a reasonable ethics could sanction. But, though it sound fantastic, if the facts indicated a conflict between good and evil in the experience of that Intellect, would it not be of moral concern to decide as far as possible the attitude we should take to that experience? Or is morality the spoiled child that will play only when it is sure of its advantage? If the empirical spirit means anything in the philosophy of religion, it means the persistent attempt to discover the place of man's values in the universe, the only assumption being that the *truth* is of human concern. Any other conviction, of "the profound significance of human life," [73] for example, must be held as an hypothesis to be proved by the remaining facts of experience, and not as one which must be justified at all cost, as one without which "argument about God or the universe would seem to be mere waste of time." [74] In other words, though Pringle-Pattison

[71] *Idea of God*, p. 18; cf. p. 176.
[72] *Ibid.*, p. 24.
[73] *Ibid.*, p. 236.
[74] *Ibid.*

seems to espouse the empirical method, the empirical spirit is lacking, for he begins with an absolute conviction about a particular truth. To be sure, to give Caesar his due, he does hold that Kant and Comte paid too little attention to the dependence of the moral on the natural life, and he does say that "man is a child of nature, and it is on the basis of natural impulses and in commerce with the system of external things, that his ethical being is built up." [75] Nevertheless, in the final analysis, he himself isolates the moral life and finds its roots *beyond* nature.

At this point several comments on Hume and Kant may help to show our meaning. Hume thought that what Kant might call "the niggardly provision of a step-motherly nature" could give only an attenuated theism, as Pringle-Pattison puts it. But Kant, whose finding of God through the moral consciousness Pringle-Pattison approves as an important step toward a more inclusive empiricism, says of the good will, "*even if* it should happen that, owing to the special disfavour of fortune or the niggardly provision of a step-motherly nature, this will should wholly lack power to accomplish its purpose, . . . it would still shine like a jewel by its own light as something which has its whole value in itself." [76]

Now Pringle-Pattison criticizes Kant for the isolation of the moral life and for his refusal to judge goodness by consequences, but his own position is not essentially different, for by replacing several words in the above quotation we find Pringle-Pattison's view. The *moral ideals* of which we are conscious, "even if it should happen that, owing . . . to the niggardly provision of a step-motherly nature they should wholly lack power to accomplish their purpose, . . . would still be real." In other words, Pringle-Pattison does not rest the ultimate truth of the moral ideals on their application to man in his interrelation with other men and nonmoral nature, but on the veracity of our moral faculties, which in turn is guaranteed by the immanence of God in man or

---

[75] *Idea of God*, p. 156.
[76] Kant, *Grundlegung zur Metaphysik der Sitten* (Abbot's translation), quoted in *Idea of God*, p. 28 (italics mine).

man's organic relation (not to nonmoral nature but) to God. The following outline of his argument is given in verification of this.

Objecting, as we have seen, to the narrowness of Hume's empiricism, Pringle-Pattison pleads that man's moral consciousness has as much claim to objectivity as his cognitive nature, and that in any case it cannot be explained by "nature conceived as an independent system of causes." [77] Yet, at this very point he insists that we remember the principle of the unity of the world and not cut the world in two with a hatchet,[78] coming finally to the realization that man is not "incongruously superinduced" on a nonspiritual world. Furthermore, since ultimate explanation is impossible apart from some intrinsically worthy end which we can find only in man, "we must take our courage in both hands and carry our convictions to their legitimate conclusion." [79] We must contend, therefore, that man's moral life is "the open secret of the universe." [80] It is only because we consider man a stranger in the universe that the separation of him and his faculties from the world he knows results in the view that man creates values which he then imposes on a universe indifferent to him. We have studied separately the details of this argument and need not repeat them. The point is that we can only know the nature of reality through its highest manifestations as found in the moral consciousness of man, which, being inexplicable by any of the prehuman stages, must be referred to a source worthy of them. For moral ideals cannot be explained with reference to man alone, since man does not create them but knows them. Consequently, Pringle-Pattison concludes, God expresses himself in the universe as complete in man. "God as immanent — the divine as revealed in the structure and system of finite experience — this may be said to have been the text of last year's discourse and the outcome of my argument." [81] If we keep the whole range of experience in sight and follow "the evolutionary scheme to its obvious culmina-

[77] *Man's Place*, p. 21.
[78] *Idea of God*, p. 154.
[79] *Man's Place*, p. 22.

[80] *Ibid.*
[81] *Idea of God*, p. 215.

tion in . . . mind that knows and appreciates, and thus rounds and completes what were otherwise a broken arch," [82] then we have adequate ground for belief in God and the objectivity of our values.

But Hume would justly answer that if God's predicates are the world's,[83] including man, then since neither the world nor man exhibits perfection, God cannot be perfect. To this, Pringle-Pattison gives his final answer in the chapter, hitherto unconsidered, on "The Ideal and the Actual." Hume is insufficiently empirical not only in neglecting man's moral life, but also in his failure to realize that "man's experience is not limited, in the moral life . . . to the 'is' of his actual achievement. . . ." [84] Hume judges human phenomena as an external spectator limited only to results, and therefore overlooks the fact that "man's 'reach' as well as his 'grasp' must be taken into account; for the presence of the ideal in human experience is as much a fact as any other. It is, indeed, much more; it is the fundamental characteristic of that experience." [85] The point is that man's moral experience, "finite and even paltry as the outcome in word and deed may appear," [86] is inexplicable apart from an "infinite factor," namely, the ideals in accordance with which he shapes his life. "Whence, then, are these ideals derived and what is the meaning of their presence in the human soul? . . . Man did not weave them out of nothing any more than he brought himself into being. . . . The presence of the Ideal is the reality of God within us." [87]

Thus we are brought back to Descartes' causal argument, except that, unlike Descartes, we must realize that the finite self with which this Ideal is indissolubly connected does not exist in isolation but "knows itself only as a member of a larger life."

Man is by contrast [with an isolated self] a finite-infinite being, conscious of finitude only through the presence of an infinite nature within him. The possibility of aspiration, infinite dissatisfaction and its obverse, the capacity for infinite progress — these fundamental characteristics

[82] *Idea of God*, p. 215.   [84] *Ibid.*, p. 243.   [86] *Ibid.*, p. 245.
[83] *Ibid.*   [85] *Ibid.*, p. 244.   [87] *Ibid.*, p. 246.

of the human and rational life are based by Descartes [and Pringle-Pattison] on the existence of a Perfect Being revealing himself in our minds.[88]

Pringle-Pattison admits that we do not use the "full-orbed conception" of perfection as our criterion of value, but this does not bother him, for our idea of God is one which grows endlessly with fresh advance in knowledge and goodness. "The movement and direction imply the goal; they define it sufficiently for our purpose; and in direct experience we are never at a loss to know what is higher and what is lower. . . ." [89]

The difficulty with Hume, in other words, is that he accepts the empirical finite facts which are the starting point, and, in concluding that from finite premises the infinite and perfect cannot be reached, "misreads entirely the logic [now] of religion and indeed the procedure of living thought in any sphere, which perpetually carries us in the conclusion *beyond* our premisses." [90] Because we cannot advance without the presence of the ideal, "the ideal is precisely the most real thing in the world; and those ranges of our experience, such as religion, which are specifically concerned with the ideal . . . may reasonably be accepted as the best interpreters we have of the true nature of reality." [91] The moral and religious consciousness strongly claim objectivity, "and it is to the moral and religious man himself that we must go, not to the philosopher weaving theories about him, if we are to understand his experience aright." [92]

That this argument at its most critical point depends on the deliverances of the moral and religious faculties as such shows the truth in our contention that ultimately Pringle-Pattison, like Kant and Martineau, rests his case on the objective claim of certain intuitions whose truth does not need to be tested even by consequences. His claim is that unless the ideal were present as a cognitive standard within us, we should never know moral guilt or error; yet his very admission that we never have a clear idea of perfection suggests that

[88] *Ibid.*, p. 247.   [90] *Ibid.*, p. 250.
[89] *Ibid.*, p. 249.   [91] *Ibid.*, p. 252.   [92] *Ibid.*

morality does not rest in the complete assurance of the *Perfect*. For even if the Perfect exists, the admitted fact that we always know only one step ahead ought to paralyze a morality which depended on the knowledge that the (unknown) Perfect was realized. As a matter of fact, the reason, we suggest, why morality lives is that we find that certain moral principles, which we *do* see clearly, satisfy the needs we have critically approved.

But, further, the goodness of a person is not something like a sense impression which we merely "see." It is something we can *infer* only from the activities of one person toward other persons. Consequently, even if we could have intuitions, or immediate certainty (as in sense perception) of the realized goodness of God, we should have to doubt them if nature *were* so niggardly that these supposedly realized ideals "wholly" lacked power to realize themselves *in their relation to us*. Faith in God when not founded on his works is as dead as human faith without works. But what would the realized goodness of God mean *for us* unless the world and the human nature he had made possible were at least predominantly good? There might be much aesthetic satisfaction in the vision of the goodness of God (if vision, not inferential knowledge of such a quality were possible), but no moral encouragement.

Aside from this, the presence in us of a perfection we *imperfectly* know is a dubious blessing, and, as we shall argue later, the idea of the Good is one which can be derived from experience. As a matter of fact, even for Pringle-Pattison, the knowledge of the supreme Good which is realized in God must be gained through moral and intellectual struggle, so that the Good *we* know and achieve is our own creation, or at most phenomenal (rather than of the Good in itself, which is the source of our knowledge on Pringle-Pattison's view). And this brings us to a central difficulty in the whole conception.

Pringle-Pattison's theory of value is ultimately realistic, as is his theory of knowledge; for, much as he insists that there is no value without consciousness and feeling, these for him are merely the indispensable psychological conditions for a *cognition* of value they do not themselves produce. But, even though the realistic argument might sound intelligible for primary and secondary qualities, when we deal with moral values, we are plainly not dealing with simple characteristics like *red* or *long*. Rather are we observing a dynamic *relational quality*,[93] value, which cannot exist until desired by a conscious person. Furthermore, an action has no *moral* value unless it is desired and willed by a conscious person. Even supposing a cosmic Mind for whom the ocean, or fair dealing, for example, have value, we maintain that another value and perhaps a different kind or degree of value is *created* as soon as a second mind desires them. The existence of persons, then, makes possible an indefinite number of values which could not be said to exist or be realized previous to their conations. Values are created and saturated by the general needs of determinate finite beings, and by their specific needs in specific situations. If the same is true of the Good, meaning that value or complex of values prized as a *human* state superior to all others, in what sense can this Good be said to be objectively realized in any nonhuman realm, and therefore be something we do not create but simply recognize?

The underlying difficulty is that the eye-analogy, suitable as it *may* be for physical qualities, breaks down completely when values are involved. Both Martineau and Pringle-Pattison are deceived by analogies drawn from their theories of natural knowledge and applied uncritically to our knowledge of moral values. Epistemological realism in the one realm seduces and betrays them in the other. The additional reason for their error lies in their belief that morality can have authority only when its object is not created but already realized. Their position is based on the assumption that morality can function only when men are sure they see a metaphysically real, moral object. Just as a man will not sit down unless he can be sure that his eyes see a real chair, it is

---

[93] That is, the relation is not logical or spatial but volitional or causal, for goodness results from desire, thought, *and deed.*

assumed that man will not be moral if his object is not already real. But if man is creative anywhere, it is in the realm of values, and here, as we shall see, his ideals are built upon the basis of his knowledge of himself and nature. The real question to which, we believe, a more accurate theistic conclusion may be given, is: In what way can we fairly conceive an ultimate Being that makes possible a nature in which and through which human nature can achieve values?

The problem, we would finally add, is not correctly put by Pringle-Pattison when he asks: "Is the spirit of the universe or the ultimate nature of things *akin* to what we recognize as greatest and best, or are such standards and distinctions but human parochialisms, *sheerly irrelevant* in a wider reference?" [94] To canalize the alternatives thus into either perfect harmony *or* chaos and irrelevance, into either reality or dream, shows the influence of preconceptions. There is at least another relation besides these of perfect disjunction and conjunction, and that is partial conjunction and disjunction. Do the alternatives have to be that goodness and beauty are either "born of the clash of atoms" or "effluences of something more perfect and more divine"? [95]

H.   THE NATURE OF THE SELF

The dominant theme of Pringle-Pattison's philosophy thus far, we have seen, is the immanence of a God who is interpreted in terms of the most characteristic features of human experience. So great has been the emphasis on immanence that individuals seem to be like "telephone wires along which that Absolute acts or thinks." [96] But this simile states the very view that Pringle-Pattison energetically opposes in the second set of lectures which deal with God's relation to man. Here, if anywhere, is the conflict between the empirical and nonempirical elements in Pringle-Pattison's thought. Confusion may be avoided if we can bring together, and see as a whole,

---

[94] *Idea of God*, p. 40 (italics mine).
[95] *Ibid.*, p. 42. This same setting of the problem and realistic view of value may be found in A. E. Taylor's *The Faith of a Moralist*, I, 58–65, especially.
[96] *Idea of God*, p. 291.

scattered remarks about the nature of the self, before we consider its relation to God and the light it throws on his nature.

We may first note the problem as his own works indicate it. In *Hegelianism and Personality* (1887), Pringle-Pattison, seeking to expose the "radical error both of Hegelianism and of the allied English doctrine," which consisted in the "identification of the human and divine self-consciousness," [97] goes so far in denying "one universal self in all so-called thinkers" as to say ". . . that each Self is a unique existence, which is perfectly *impervious*, if I may so speak, to other selves — impervious in a fashion of which the impenetrability of matter is a faint analogue." [98] But his stress on the fact that the self "resists invasion" and "refuses to admit another self within itself," [99] on its being "the very apex of separation and differentiation," and "in existence or metaphysically, [being] a principle of isolation," [100] was misinterpreted. Consequently, regretting the use of the word "impervious," Pringle-Pattison grants in the *Idea of God* that: "The exclusiveness of the self, *especially in its relation to the divine*, was . . . too strongly emphasized in my argument." [101] Pringle-Pattison's problem, as he reacted from Hegelianism, was that of the relation of the self to God, but, as we shall soon see, he never succeeds in achieving the compromise between the "coincidence or literal identification of several selves," [102] human and divine, and their exclusiveness.

All knowledge about our whole self or the world is based upon the experience and development of the specious present. So far Pringle-Pattison, Bradley, Bosanquet, and James are on common ground. This specious present is a complex of cognitive, conative, and emotional elements which, as James said, is not a "knife-edge, but a saddle-back with a certain breadth of its own on which we sit perched, and from which we look in two directions into time." [103] But the very

---

[97] *Hegelianism and Personality*, p. 215.
[98] *Ibid.*, p. 216.
[99] *Ibid.*
[100] *Ibid.*, p. 217.
[101] *Idea of God*, p. 389n. (italics mine).
[102] *Ibid.*
[103] *Ibid.*, p. 352.

fact that this is an *experience* of flux, an experience of succession and not a succession of appearances, shows that there
is self-conscious unity. The self is not, as Bradley and Bosanquet seem to hold, a "flocking together" of universals. It is
concrete individuality. "To exist means to be the subject of
qualities, to have or possess a nature." [104] And yet the "that"
of a self is "not to be thought of as a solid core of being, . . .
to which as a support, the qualities are attached" [105] (as
Martineau thought). "The unity of the subject, we may
agree, simply expresses the peculiar organization or systematization of the content," [106] and, Pringle-Pattison adds, this
unity is a self-conscious unity which is the meaning of the
word "self."

Because selves are reflexive unities, "they necessarily im-
port into the universe an element of *relative* independence
and separateness which is not involved in the notion of externality as such. . . ." [107] This unity for self, distinguishing
the self from other objects, is what demands for its explanation the term *creation,* which represents the mysterious process by which the independent finite center "separates itself
from the common foundation of all things." [108] Every self
acts from itself and sees the world from its own center and
"dichotomizes the universe in a different place." [109]

This view obviously issues into the conception of the self
as free, for, according to Pringle-Pattison, determinism "is
simply the denial of self-hood altogether." [110] Selves are not
mere channels or pipes through which the Absolute flows,
nor are they "radiating centres of a single force," [111] for any
self which is merely the "mouthpiece" of another self is no
self at all. Unless selves have some independence, worship
is meaningless. Concrete personality is "a formed will, originating its own actions and accepting ultimate responsibility
for them." God will not force obedience, for the freedom
which "belongs to a self-conscious being as such" is "the
fundamental condition of the ethical life." [112] This freedom

[104] *Idea of God,* p. 282.   [107] *Ibid.* (italics mine).   [110] *Ibid.*
[105] *Ibid.,* p. 283.   [108] *Ibid.,* p. 287.   [111] *Ibid.*
[106] *Ibid.,* p. 285.   [109] *Ibid.,* p. 288.   [112] *Ibid.,* p. 292.

is a certainty based on direct experience, and no amount of speculation can deny it.[113]

The fundamental truth expressed in this theory of the self is that the self is a distinct reality with a definite nature of its own, that one of the characteristics of that nature, as much a part of it as its emotional nature, is the power to *initiate* activity. It might well be said that the principle of individuation among selves is free will. There can now be no doubt that Pringle-Pattison means to recognize this fact and to resist all attempts to reduce selves to adjectives or modes of an Absolute experience. Selves are distinct from each other, and one self cannot experience the other's experience directly. But there is another tendency in his thought which seems to run contrary to these observations. It was present in the first set of Gifford Lectures, and it is nowhere to our knowledge expressly denied, namely, the concept of the relation between the Absolute and the finite self as that of whole and part.

Pringle-Pattison struggles against an all-absorbing Absolute, and yet his campaign against deism and the isolation of selves brings him to regard the selves not only as parts of a substantial objective humanity [114] but also as parts of the life of the Absolute, and to insist in words reminiscent of Bradley that *somehow* the Absolute incorporates them in its experience. Passages which hold that the self is a "focus" or "depositary" or "organ" or "expression " [115] of the divine life seem to result in the conclusion that each self is a "separate and exclusive focalization of a common universe," [116] "that every individual is a unique nature, a little world of content which . . . constitutes an expression or focalization of the universe which is nowhere exactly repeated." [117] The universe is a vale of soul-making, and the Absolute realizes himself in and through these selves, which make (in some mysterious sense on this view) their "unique contribution to the life of the

---

[113] In this volume the problem of freedom will not be discussed, though, for reasons similar to those given by Martineau, Ward, and Tennant, determinism is rejected. Unless there is the possibility of freedom, bias cannot be escaped, and truth is impossible.

[114] Cf. *Idea of God*, pp. 141, 143.
[115] Cf. *ibid.*, p. 258.
[116] *Ibid.*, p. 264.
[117] *Ibid.*, p. 267; cf. also p. 269.

whole." [118] God is the "Soul of souls" of which Martineau speaks.

This doctrine seems to agree with Leibniz's view that every soul mirrors the universe from a different point of view, but at the same time it rejects the ontological self-subsistence the pluralist gives to souls. Bradley and Bosanquet held that the alternative to their view was such pluralism, and though Pringle-Pattison is bravely trying to strike a mean between the two extremes, he ultimately leaves us in mystery. For, consistent with the statements just cited, he concludes that "the infinite reality reflects itself in the finite nature," and that finite souls repeat (not contribute) "in the process of their own experience the flux and reflux of the cosmic life." [119] The divine life is one of self-communication.[120] Yet, though the distinctness and independence of finite selves from each other is emphasized, their independence of God is the main miracle of the universe. And Pringle-Pattison holds that the inability to understand the relation between God and man must not lead us to attribute to it limitations similar to those we find in our finite relationships. In the latter the knower cannot have immediate experience of another center, "but there can be no such barrier, we may suppose, between the finite consciousness and the Being in which its existence is rooted. It must remain open and accessible — it must enter into the divine experience in a way for which our mode of knowing hardly furnishes us with an analogy." [121] Our attempt to schematize the relation must, at any cost, not lead us to regard selves as pipes, or to "lose hold of the creative unity altogether by treating the individuals as independent, self-subsistent units," [122] for freedom is a fact of experience which must be recognized.

Thus we see Pringle-Pattison struggle to avoid pluralism, on the one hand, and the Absolute on the other; but the reason why the relationship between man and God should completely transcend mutual intercourse as we know it is not given! Once more Pringle-Pattison is interpreting experience

[118] *Idea of God*, p. 269.   [120] *Ibid.*
[119] *Ibid.*, p. 295.   [121] *Ibid.*, p. 293.   [122] *Ibid.*

in terms of a preconceived view of God's nature. Merely to say: Because God is God, is not enough as an explanation for the removal of the limitations, so long as the empirical method is followed, for if we use this method we cannot know *what* God is apart from facts of experience which demand that our hypothesis be further modified or enlarged to explain them. But Pringle-Pattison has not exhibited the data explained by his mysterious relationship which transcends any we know, and, furthermore, his position leads him to deny in fact the relative independence he verbally ascribes to selves. If selves cannot know each other directly, it is, we should suppose, because they are ontologically distinct, in the sense that they cannot overlap or flow into each other. For Pringle-Pattison to say that finite limitations are overcome in the *knowledge* God has of man is to imply that God and the self are not ontologically distinct, for how else could God have "the immediate experience of another centre" which is denied human beings? [123] Further, how human freedom is compatible with the ontological connection implied in this relation between part and whole is difficult to see. In any case, so long as we hold, in accordance with the empirical method, that we must argue from what we know, we have no right to appeal to mysteries until all other explanations have been found to involve greater mystery.

The difficulties in which Pringle-Pattison finds himself arise, perhaps, from his failure to realize that ontological distinctness need not mean self-subsistence and isolation. This may be made clear first in the relation of different individuals to each other. If a distinction is made between the *cultured* and the ontological or structural self which *becomes* cultured, the relation between the self and society may be expressed by saying that the existence of the cultured self is impossible if isolated from society. But to say that the ontological self, that the entity capable of reasoning, feeling, and willing (powers which indeed develop in society) could not exist apart from society is to hold unreasonably that no single

[123] Pringle-Pattison says later (*Idea of God*, p. 363) that God's idea of a mind and life "would be the very life itself."

self could ever have existed solely in relation to nature. In the same way, it is at least possible to conceive that selves were created as beings ontologically separate from God, but with powers of interacting with nature, other human beings, and God — the extent of their interaction being determined by the strength of their original capabilities and their desire to live a physical, social, ethical, and religious existence. Such a possibility involves an act of creation and brings up the problem of interaction, but, dismissing the latter for the present,[124] we may now consider Pringle-Pattison's objection to the idea of creation as applied to God.

I.   GOD AND CREATION

Pringle-Pattison rejects the idea of creation because it implies that God is "one more phenomenon added to the series," or that creation is a temporal act which "represents the universe as in no way organic to the divine life," and, consequently, is an "after-thought" [125] of a pre-existent God who becomes a mere spectator of his product. For Pringle-Pattison creation is not an incidental act of God's will but "an eternal act, an act grounded in the divine nature and, therefore, . . . coeval with the divine existence," [126] and he quotes Ulrici [127] approvingly thus: ". . . God is not *first* God and *then* creator of the world, but *as* God he is creator of the world, and only *as* creator of the world is he God." God must not be abstracted from the world, which is actually coeternal with him as his eternal creation and not as a datum.

So far the discussion has been limited to God's connection with the world; but in the midst of what seems to be a purely historical outline of the idea of creation, Pringle-Pattison appears to distinguish God's relation to the world from his relation to man. His conclusion seems to be that God, the world, and selves are stages or moments of one tremendous process, each of which is meaningless and cannot exist apart from the other. But nature is "the intermediary or connect-

---

[124] Cf. the next chapter.
[125] *Idea of God*, p. 302.   [126] *Ibid.*, p. 304.
[127] *Gott und Welt*, pp. 531–532, quoted in *Idea of God*, p. 305.

ing term" [128] between God and man. Through it God reveals himself to man, while man, the ultimate end of nature and God, terminates the process of creation and the self-expression of God, since in man's experience the ultimate meaning of nature and God is seen.[129]

Now, as long as no independent power is given the world, there is no inherent difficulty in denying to it an efficient, metaphysical causation. The difficulty comes when finite spirits are included as similar though different parts of the world. The statement: "God, then, becomes an abstraction if separated from the universe of his manifestation . . . ," is not inconceivable, but the continuation, "just as the finite subjects have no independent subsistence outside of the universal Life which mediates itself to them in a world of objects," [130] treats the selves as any part of nature would be treated and therefore denies their uniqueness. The following statements approximate the rejected view of Bradley:

> We may conceive God as an experience in which the universe is felt and apprehended as an ultimately harmonious whole. . . . We have no right to suppose the possibility of such an infinite experience as a solitary monad — an absolute . . . self-sufficient and entirely independent of the finite intelligences to whom, in the actual world which we know, it freely communicates itself.[131]

Spirits are not to be "regarded as things made, detached like products from their maker; they are more aptly described . . . as 'partakers of the divine nature' and admitted to the fellowship of a common life." [132] God is not a pre-existent deity, for as such there would be a time in his experience when he was "not yet crowned with the highest attribute of Goodness or self-revealing Love." [133]

These last few words, we believe, express the underlying (Spinozistic?) motive of the rejection of creation as in any sense efficient causation. Pringle-Pattison is really arguing for the eternity of Goodness and Love; he is laboring to give them a place at the very heart of reality. If the creation of spirits involved a temporal action, Love would not be the

---

[128] *Idea of God*, p. 309.   [130] *Ibid.*, p. 314.   [132] *Ibid.*, p. 315.
[129] Cf. *ibid.*, pp. 309, 310.   [131] *Ibid.*   [133] *Ibid.*

"eternal fashion of the cosmic Life," but a new development, a conclusion which the mutual implication of the infinite and the finite [134] avoids. This same motive dominates, as we shall see, Pringle-Pattison's discussion of cosmic purpose, time, and growth.

On the other hand, love, worship, and moral obligation involve, as Pringle-Pattison himself says, "relative independence." Yet it is impossible to see how free will and the independence ascribed to selves can be compatible with the ontological identity here described. To be sure, we are told in the thirteenth lecture that "the transcendence which must be retained, and which is intelligible, refers to a distinction of value or of quality, not to the ontological separateness of one being from another." [135] But the very question is: Is qualitative transcendence intelligible unless there is ontological separateness between God and selves? If "the filaments which unite the finite spirit to its creative source are never severed," and if "the Productive Reason remains at once the sustaining element of the dependent life, and the living content, continually offering itself to the soul which it has awakened [implying separate existence] to the knowledge and quest of itself," how account for qualitative differences? [136]

Once more the difficulty lies in Pringle-Pattison's inability to see that ontological distinctness may be consistent with mutual dependence. Hence he conceives of the relationship analogously to that between part and whole. But, why does the creation of a soul *have* to mean "the manufacture of an article, which remains throughout something separate from its maker . . ."? May not the cosmic Womb give birth, cutting all filaments, to children whom, through long ages of labor and travail, it has so endowed that they of their own free will find their joy and peace in the production of a symphony of love, a symphony in which unity of conscious purpose rather than metaphysical unity of the human and divine purposers is enjoyed? Must the relation be that of part to whole, or may it be the harmonizing of many ontologically separate musicians so blessed that they may read

[134] *Idea of God*, p. 315.   [135] *Ibid.*, p. 255.   [136] *Ibid.*

and play a common music under the guidance of the great Conductor? This may mean that Love is not eternal, but it at least becomes intelligible, and it is difficult to see what theoretical as well as practical gain is made possible by the alternative.[137]

J. Cosmic Teleology

The realization of purpose involves the voluntary fulfillment of a preconceived plan by the selection of proper means through a period of time. Since the method of argument is "from the structure of experience," Pringle-Pattison sets out to see whether, "when purged of demonstrably finite accomplishments," [138] the idea of purpose can be applied to the infinite experience.

Martineau's reluctance to reject the notion of the use of means by God is certainly not evident in Pringle-Pattison's thought. To be sure, if Martineau had conceived of such means as a limitation of God's power, he would have rejected the idea immediately, but Pringle-Pattison, drawing the implications of his metaphysical position, that reality is a process in which all the parts are continuous and contribute to the whole, immediately discards the notion that God makes better adjustments in a foreign existence by superinducing other ends on it.

Nor can operations in accordance with a preconceived plan be attributed to God. Pringle-Pattison's reasoning here is that it is only from the standpoint of the part that the plan of the whole process seems preconceived. To the nondiscursive understanding of God (to whom "the whole would appear as the necessary unity of its members, and the members as the necessary differentiation of the whole") [139] a teleological view would mean simply "that reality is a significant whole," [140] and not the realization of a preconceived plan. The only meaning, therefore, which teleology can have when applied to the cosmic process is that "rationality is not a lucky accident," that "reason is present at every stage as the shaping spirit of

[137] This theme will be developed in the next chapter.
[138] *Idea of God*, p. 324.   [139] *Ibid.*, p. 330.   [140] *Ibid.*

the whole." [141] Thus Pringle-Pattison dispenses with a second attribute of human purpose.

By this time the reader begins to wonder why the word "purpose" is used at all if two-thirds of its empirical meaning is found inapplicable — except perhaps to predispose him to such an "unhuman" view by appealing to connotations which the word "purpose" no longer possesses. In any case, if this is the way to show that the preconception of a plan is a "demonstrably finite" accompaniment of purpose, it is not the *empirical* way! On the contrary, it emphatically denies that the known structure of experience (purpose) applies to the cosmic Person, and yet persists in applying that word "Person" to him. We have simply been carried to the point of view of the Absolute, to which *our* experience was to be an index. Nowhere are we told why this infinite Experience should be a rational whole of the type described. Pringle-Pattison is still using the conception he never proves, that the world is what it is because God *is* what he is. He also seems to assume that God's rationality cannot be ultimate if time were as real for him as it is for us. The difficulty is that, despite all the empirical ornamentation, the unconsciously dominating motive is the defense of a rationalistic conception of reality which comes very near to Spinozistic Substance. For, does Pringle-Pattison not condemn the notion that anything can exist which was not in the Whole from the beginning?

This comes out in Pringle-Pattison's discussion of volition, the third aspect of purpose as we know it. In spite of his rejection of the other two, he introduces this discussion with the statement that any whole is philosophically meaningless "unless we read into . . . [it] a specific content from our own experience. . . ." [142] The importance, therefore, of the idea of purpose and its correlate, satisfaction, is that they bring us back to feeling and will, "which are incontestable marks of any experience known to us, and apart from which value is an unmeaning phrase." [143] Without conation, purpose, and

[141] *Idea of God*, p. 331.   [142] *Ibid.*, p. 334.   [143] *Ibid.*, p. 335.

realization, "value . . . becomes an abstraction." [144] Obviously the question now is: Can the defect which conation and purpose imply in human experience be attributed to God?

There can be no doubt that Pringle-Pattison strains to make conation play a part in the experience of the Absolute. But the way in which he removes defect is typical of his method of argument at critical points.

Since in our judgments of value we should never experience satisfaction "if we did not believe that we were judging *sub specie universi* or from the standpoint of the whole," these very judgments "seem to postulate a satisfaction of the Absolute itself" which we share.[145] In other words, we have a recurrence of the theme that unless God lived in complete realization of value, our judgments of value, not having their source in a universe in which these values were realized, would fail to give us the satisfaction resulting in the confidence "to stake our all on them." [146] And the only way in which Pringle-Pattison settles the problem of defect involved in the fulfillment of desire is by agreeing with Bosanquet, that in God *"the contradiction of a conation co-existing with fruition must be realized,"* [147] and by holding that this may be one of the paradoxes of religion. He sides with Spinoza "against transferring the idea of choice to a sphere where it is inapplicable, and thus founding the universe and its constitution upon a groundless act," but he insists that "will, not as a meaningless freedom of choice but in the sense of continuously affirming and possessing one's experience" [148] may be attributed to God. This, however, is an evasion of the question, especially since Pringle-Pattison admits that such continuous self-affirmation is only "the ideal" of the *finite* individuals which are supposed to furnish the *clue* to the infinite experience. The unconscious and unwarranted transition from conation to will completes the deception that enables him to continue thinking of God's life not as one of want but as one of self-affirmation in the

[144] *Ibid.* Of this idea he does not see the full significance in his realistic epistemology of value.
[145] *Ibid.,* p. 337.
[146] *Ibid.*
[147] *Ibid.,* p. 338.
[148] *Ibid.,* p. 339.

finite, which is "the divine necessity" or "the fundamental character of the divine life." [149] This divine necessity he speaks of as "the eternal purpose" of God, deprecating the association of time which even this phrase retains. Finally, as if afraid that the discussion has reduced the life of God to mere dreaming, he suggests that effort is involved in God's activity, "nay . . . *difficulty*."

What, however, does either effort or difficulty mean apart from the very *want* (even to keep on affirming oneself) which by intellectual somersaults has been both attributed and denied to God in the attempt to make a place for values in the very nature of things? A want-less God, Pringle-Pattison fears, would become a cold Intellect, and yet his conception of an ultimate *rerum natura* completely satisfied, safe against the inroads of time, as we shall see, freezes God into a fixed and immutable rigidity comparable to that of Plato's Ideas.

K. God and Time

If God's experience is a realized and rational whole, then time, at least in its aspect of not-yetness, would have to be denied it. For a view such as this, in which the being of a Personal [150] God is *constituted* by "Truth, Beauty, Goodness, Love" (and by self-conscious existence in partial possession of these and striving for more),[151] the meaning of time as we struggling creatures know it cannot be ascribed to God, who is better described as eternal. And this is Pringle-Pattison's solution. Yet his discussion begins as usual with the insistence that since appearance is not illusion but reality, and since our own experience is still to be the clue to God's, time cannot be a cosmic illusion, since time is concretely real in the continuous *"melting"* of one moment of our experience in another. Once more, then, the empirical spirit is in evidence. Eternity cannot be ascribed to God unless we find it in some sense in experience.

Eternity, however, does not mean *timelessness* either in the

[149] *Idea of God*, p. 340.
[150] Cf. *ibid.*, p. 390, and pp. 430–435.
[151] Cf. *ibid.*, p. 434.

sense that valid truths are timeless or in the sense of endlessness or nontemporality. All mathematical views of time are abstractions from the immediate experience of time, while eternity must be the correlative of time rather than its logical contradictory. Time cannot exist without eternity, and vice versa. An illustration of this is our own immediate experience of the moments of time as a whole. "In the compresence which is thus an essential feature of our consciousness of time we therefore already realize, though doubtless on an infinitesimal scale, the nature of an eternal consciousness," [152] for the divine consciousness may be considered a *"totum simul"* or an immediate intuition of a tremendous specious present within which "human distinctions of past and future disappear." [153]

Two comments may be made on the argument thus far. In the first place, no matter how much God's specious present is elongated, within our *known* specious present, as defined by Pringle-Pattison, it is the experience of the present dying away into the past and surging forward into the future that is stressed. If Pringle-Pattison is to be faithful to his method, must he not show why these elements should not be present in an expanded specious present? Instead, he really assumes eternity for God and then finds an analogy in human experience.

But, secondly, eternity now means simply the fact that self-consciousness is a unity through the presence of memory. It is only *a certain kind* of temporal experience, indeed the only kind we know, for time as broken up into distinct moments is an abstraction, being the way in which we conceive time after we have experienced it. If eternity be defined as the unity of consciousness, then it is not the correlate of time but simply time as any conscious being knows it if he is conscious at all. Thus, only if time is abstractly *conceived* as moments separate from each other, is eternity, as the consciousness of all these separate moments at a glance, to be distinguished from time. But since time is the very characteristic of that *unity* of experience which is our immediate consciousness, within which we can distinguish moments, there is no need for the word *eter-*

[152] *Ibid.*, p. 354.   [153] *Ibid.*

nity as a correlate of time, since time *rightly conceived* needs none.[154] Therefore, not only is time the characteristic of the divine specious present, in that, within it, past, present, and future may be conceptually distinguished, but these three distinctions are elements within *one* experience of duration experienced as a whole. Neither God nor human beings *make* a whole out of past, present, and future — these are rather elements in a whole experience with which they begin.

But eternity means more than this unity of the specious present for Pringle-Pattison. It really is the attribution to God of a unity of consciousness whose span is so great that the whole temporal process of the universe is both included within it, and *known*, not little by little (which is the defect of temporal knowledge), but as an organic whole.[155] Now, however, the problem has insensibly shifted and is no longer the question of the sense in which time as we know it may be attributed to God, but of the way in which He knows the world-process. Since to know means to know the purpose of, "the eternal view of the time-process is not the view of all its stages simultaneously, but the view of them as elements or members of a completed purpose." [156] And the meaning of time also has been changed. "Time is not an element in which consciousness passes, or a procession which passes before consciousness," [157] but it is "the abstraction of unachieved purpose or purpose on the way to achievement." [158] The ground for *this* meaning of time is that mental experience is not a mere process but a conative process toward some end,[159] in the light of which the future and the past are distinguished. Since time in this sense means incomplete achievement of purpose, and since we saw that the defectiveness involved in the notion of purpose could not be applied to God, time can be attributed only to finite human beings, and not to God. He, therefore, is eternal, because he sees all the stages of the time-process as members of his own completed purpose. Hence, eternity as

[154] This discussion of time and eternity will be continued in Chapter VI, where Tennant's more empirical view is considered.

[155] Cf. *Idea of God*, p. 355.

[156] *Ibid.*, p. 358.

[157] *Ibid.*, p. 356.

[158] *Ibid.*, p. 358.

[159] Cf. *ibid.*, p. 357.

applied to God is simply another way of saying that the whole world-process is known by God as we know our specious present. He knows the world-process not, as we do, incompletely in matters of detail, but completely as immutable purpose. The stages of the cosmic process which we view as contingent, "side by side," are felt by God as necessary parts in a whole, the end or whole being felt in every part.[160] Pringle-Pattison goes so far as to say that whatever independence selves might have, *all* is open to God. "The divine idea of 'a mind and life' would therefore be the very life itself, experienced as significant because experienced as a whole, and, what is more, as part of the meaning of the all-inclusive whole." [161]

All that Pringle-Pattison has done, we now see, is to redefine his position in terms of words which have temporal connotations but which have in reality lost every feature of time as we know it. Even if time is the abstraction of purpose,[162] then the "not-yetness" and "no-moreness" with which our experience is saturated and to which our experience of time is supposed to be due, is lost in the divine Experience of completed Purpose (which does not mean purpose as we know it). We have been told in words *how* an eternal experience might be conceived but not *why* it should be so conceived. When Pringle-Pattison answers McGilvary's objections: (a) that God is in "untimed time," since for him the order of events can bring neither novelty nor anxiety, and (b) that God therefore can never have an "inkling" of expectation or suspense, he simply says to (a) that "it is an unreasoning procedure to seek to transfer this attitude to a universal Spirit," [163] and that time is "somehow transcended in the ultimate Experience on which we depend." [164] His answer to (b) is that God can have an

---

[160] Cf. *ibid.*, pp. 361, 362. A similar conception of time and eternity, defined in terms of the life of desire and its fulfillment, and similarly confused with metaphysical time, or *durée réelle*, pervades A. E. Taylor's *Faith of a Moralist*. See especially, pp. 74 ff.

[161] *Idea of God*, p. 363.

[162] Yet time is not the abstraction of purpose, but the characteristic form of the unity of self-consciousness which is the *sine qua non* of any purpose. Desires may be unified by purpose, but the unity of the metaphysical self is original. Cf. Chapter VI, pp. 240 ff.

[163] *Idea of God*, p. 364.   [164] *Ibid.*, p. 365.

inkling into the suffering of creatures in time, since "it is everywhere the mark of the higher and wider experience to comprehend the lower and narrower." [165]

But this clearly misses the point. For the analogy he suggests, that God is to the parent as the parent is to the child with whom he can share joy and sorrow, is false, since the only reason why the parent can understand his child is that he once experienced similar joys and sorrows, while God, unlike the parent, never, on Pringle-Pattison's view, could experience a "not-yet." The difference between man's experience of time and God's is not one of degree but of quality. As long as eternity meant the unity of God's greater time-span there was no need of transcendence of the time-process rightly understood. But as soon as God's eternity was interpreted as experience of the whole temporal process, including our own, as a realized purpose, then man's experience no longer could be said to serve as an index to that eternity.

This whole discussion, furthermore, confirms the contention that the independence of selves is really lost! For how, so long as man has free will, can God know a future series of consequences which *we* must decide to realize? Martineau, realizing this difficulty, rightly denied God's foreknowledge of human actions. It is only as selves are simply parts of the divine experiences that foreknowledge is possible, unless we are going to say that freedom and foreknowledge are *somehow* compatible in God, and then once more break the promise to be empirical.

The summary of this chapter on Time shows that what has happened is not the promised development of what is found in appearance, but its development to a stage which has lost all contact with human experience. "Time, then, seems one with the existence of the finite; and although the experience and the relations of time must be represented in the infinite Experience, this must be in a way which transcends our human perspective." [166] The logical conclusion of this position is expressed in the next sentence but one.

[165] *Idea of God.*
[166] *Ibid.*, p. 367.

It was a silent presupposition of the argument that time cannot be taken . . . as ultimately real; that is to say, time, with all its implications of development and progress, is an aspect of facts *within* the universe, . . . not . . . a containing element in which the Absolute . . . exists, and through which it advances, garnering new being and perfections as it proceeds.[167]

Such a growing universe is set aside as "intrinsically incredible," and the rejection of this notion at critical points is owing to the instinctive feeling [168] and the ultimate conviction, supposedly corroborated by religious experience, that values are completely realized at the very core of the universe and are not created. Man, as part of the universe, may grow, but his ideals reflect immutable realities. "The reality of the ideal and its infinite transcendence of finite attainment is the very note of moral and religious experience." [169] *The Idea of God* is an extended rejection of any attempt to introduce the least bit of contingency into the Ideals of the universe. And it represents the thinking of a mind empirical enough to struggle against Absolutism but ultimately imprisoned by earlier loyalties.

L. ESTIMATE AND SUMMARY

In the foregoing it may have been noticed that only Pringle-Pattison's positive argument has been held to be inconclusive and inadequate. His rejection of the rationalism of naturalism on the one hand, and that of Absolutism on the other, his insistence, in other words, that the uniqueness of human experience be recognized is heartily endorsed. The weakness of the positive argument for God has been indicated. Unfortunately, Nédoncelle is correct when he says:

Son [Pringle-Pattison's] souci de sauver toutes les tendances philosophiques les plus diverses laisse à sa pensée une imprécision peut-être incurable et qui fait une contraste pénible avec l'exactitude [?] constante de son langage. Finalement il se réfugie dans un aveu d'impuissance. . . . Dans tous les ouvrages de Pringle-Pattison, on peut glaner des phrases . . . où il demande que les difficultés théoriques n'entament pas le bloc de nos certitudes primordiales.[170]

[167] *Ibid.*   [168] Cf. *ibid.*, pp. 372, 376.
[169] *Ibid.*, p. 382; cf. pp. 383, 395.
[170] M. Nédoncelle, *La Philosophie Religieuse en Grande-Bretagne de 1850 à nos jours* (1934), p. 92.

Pringle-Pattison himself accepts Mr. Yeats's statement that "whatever of philosophy has been made poetry is alone permanent." [171]

The following propositions may help to bring together the more important points in this extended discussion.

1. The use of the empirical method and the coherence-criterion of truth in the interpretation of experience implies that teleological explanation alone is philosophical. But empiricism demands that any particular end be held tentatively until verified.

2. Mechanical explanation is tautologous and does not adequately explain the appearance of unique differences in the process of evolution; but teleology must prove and not presuppose any specific kind of unity, at the same time taking account of temporal factors in the development of value.

3. The organic relation of mental activity to the nature of things guarantees the validity of the realistic theory of knowledge and the assertion, specifically, that secondary and tertiary qualities are real. But the professed creativity of mind is thus denied, and both the doctrine of organicity and the theory of knowledge presuppose an idealistic metaphysics.

4. Appearances are always true of reality in different degrees. But this leads to the rejected formal coherence.

5. Since man's moral consciousness testifies to the reality of ideals, without whose presence within him man's moral progress would be inexplicable, God is said to exist. But our admittedly imperfect knowledge of the ideal implies that we do not need the presence of *perfection* for progress, and the eye-metaphor involved in the underlying theory of moral knowledge overlooks the fact that goodness is a dynamic *relational* quality *created* by man in interaction with nature.

6. The self is a unique conscious unity possessing freedom of will and relative independence from other selves and God, though the limitations in finite relationships are

[171] *Idea of God*, p. vii.

somehow transcended by God. But no empirical reason is given for this transcendence, and the confusion of ontological with cultural independence, the emphasis on the part-whole relationship, and the denial of creation leave no place for the alleged independence of selves.

7. Purpose as applied to God ultimately means that conation and fruition without want somehow exist in the nature of God, who continually reaffirms his experience. But in this discussion every aspect of purpose as experienced is denied, the promise of empirical procedure is violated, and the argument ultimately rests on the supposed sanction of religious experience for contradiction.

8. The eternity of God means that the whole time-process exists in God's experience as the specious present does for human beings, and since time is only the abstract form of unachieved purpose, it can be attributed only to the finite part and not to God. But once more professed empirical procedure is violated, terms are used ambiguously, while religious experience and subjective convictions are substituted for argument at critical points.

CHAPTER IV

THE HALTING EMPIRICISM IN JAMES WARD'S
THEISTIC MONADISM

A. Ward's Intellectual Development

James Ward (1843–1925) at nineteen was "writing to warn his sisters that not the most virtuous life is of the slightest use for salvation without the direct intervention of Christ." [1] With such narrow, evangelical, religious ideas and a love of nature did Ward, in his twentieth year, begin serious study for the Congregational ministry at Spring Hill College (afterwards incorporated in Mansfield College, Oxford), where, nevertheless, he was soon to be commended for his "scientific mode of thought."

His later studies at Berlin under Dorner and Trendelenburg soon produced a decided change in his mode of thinking, and the problem of immortality and the relation between mind and matter began to trouble him. "Enamoured of philosophy," he determined to attend Lotze's lectures at Göttingen, and thus, through Ward's work, the latter's influence was once more felt in England. The fundamental characteristics of Lotze's thought are evident throughout Ward's works, and Lotze's emphasis on personality and the application of empirical methods turned Ward away from the pantheism which had been attracting him. (On Ward's psychology Herbart and his followers, in addition to Lotze, had no little influence.) It is not surprising that in 1872 Ward, his acquired liberalism having caused him and others much trouble, left the ministry and became a noncollegiate student in the University of Cambridge.

There Henry Sidgwick [2] was his greatest benefactor. "His

---

[1] W. R. Sorley and G. F. Stout, eds., *Essays in Philosophy* (1927), p. 10. Unless otherwise stated, all other references in this chapter will be to Ward's works.

[2] Cf. *Essays*, p. 92, where Ward has said: "If I am anything at all, I owe it to two men, Hermann Lotze and Henry Sidgwick."

thwarted Evangelicism, based on that deeper craving of his nature to teach and serve humanity, found new life and hope in Sidgwick and the work and ideals he held out." [3] After a year of work in physiology at Leipzig, in 1876, Ward returned to Cambridge and lectured on psychology, modern philosophy, and education, and in 1881, through Sidgwick's help, he was elected to a College lectureship in moral science. As a result of lectures and papers read before the Moral Science Club, the famous article on psychology in the ninth edition of the *Encyclopaedia Britannica* was written, only to be revised for the eleventh edition, published in 1911. His lifelong dream was realized in 1918, when his *Psychological Principles*, which turned over anew the psychological soil in England for the sake of a better sowing, was printed.

In the meantime, in 1894, Edinburgh had rewarded him with an honorary degree.[4] And in the same year he had been offered and had accepted the Gifford Lectureship, which resulted in the publication in 1889 of *Naturalism and Agnosticism*. This work was complemented by the Gifford Lectures, delivered at St. Andrews in 1907–10 and published in 1911 as the *Realm of Ends*. We may conclude this sketch by quoting an appreciation (which would not be lamented by other contemporaries) given by A. E. Taylor in his review of this last work.

It is superfluous to summarise the argument of a book which all who care seriously for philosophy in Great Britain may be expected to study closely, sentence by sentence, for themselves, and elaborate criticism is hardly possible to a reviewer who agrees so thoroughly with all the main positions contended for that his natural impulse is simply to thank God that we have such a philosopher as Dr. Ward among us.[5]

B. WARD'S PHILOSOPHICAL EMPIRICISM

"The dream of a system of knowledge without assumptions only results in assumption[s] which are disconnected and in all probability opposed. Here we are *in mediis rebus*, and here

[3] *Essays*, p. 64.

[4] He was also a member of the *Institut de France*, and a charter member of the British Academy.

[5] Quoted in *Essays*, p. 88, from *Mind*, XXI (1912), 427.

we must begin whether we will or no; but without assumptions at the outset we cannot begin at all." [6] For Ward, evidently, there is no way to truth about this world apart from the avenue of empiricism. The sciences of course all make assumptions, and it is the task of philosophy to "find the final and all-conditioning assumption. . . ." [7] Philosophy, however, must not only criticize the fundamental concepts of the sciences, but it must complement them by discovering the relation of the true, the beautiful, and the good to the soul, the world, and God.[8] It must, as Goethe said, approach problems "nach allen Seiten," and in every instance, Ward continues, procedure must be from the more known *in mediis rebus* to the less known.[9] Induction in any universe of discourse must be followed by deduction, but never to a point where the particulars on which the induction is based lose their uniqueness. Hence, philosophy for Ward represents reason, "the subjective factor which by its theoretical and practical demands helps us to determine our ποῦ στῶ and to find our bearings"; [10] while science, on the other hand, represents the analytic understanding.

But philosophy, as indicated in the first quotation, also has its postulate, "that of the unity and rationality of all experience, theoretical and practical alike." [11] Yet Ward's conception of this unity and rationality is not pervaded by the subtle rationalism found underlying Pringle-Pattison's thought. Ward holds that "the first requisite of philosophy is organic coherence," since "it cannot . . . have two independent growing points." [12] But rationality itself is only an ideal of pure reason, and we cannot *begin* with the certainty of its attainment. Indeed, the only certainties are the immediate qualities of sensation and the realms of pure reason, but

---

[6] "A General Analysis of Mind," p. 4, in *Psychological Papers* (1880).
[7] *Ibid.*
[8] *Essays*, p. 186.
[9] *Ibid.*, p. 279.
[10] *Ibid.*, p. 184. One is reminded of William James's essay, "The Sentiment of Rationality," which strikes the same note that Borden Parker Bowne was playing at the same time.
[11] *Essays*, p. 111.   [12] *The Realm of Ends* (3rd ed., 1920), p. 22.

neither of these constitutes knowledge. Thus, the philosopher must begin where he is with the trust that the real is the rational and, "letting knowledge grow from more to more," hope that the original confidence will be justified.[13] At the beginning, the philosopher must strive to be systematic, with the realization that philosophy can never be complete.[14] "To advance continuously and to be coherent — that, it seems to me, should be our golden rule," even though the whole procedure will be tentative.[15] The rational ideal is flawless, but its function is regulative and not constitutive.

This very fact, however, makes it imperative that (as William James would say) practical interests be considered in the search for truth, since "practice may enlarge our theoretical horizon; and this in a twofold way; it may lead into new worlds, and secure new powers. Knowledge we could never attain, remaining what we are, may be attainable in consequence of higher powers and a higher life, which we may morally achieve." [16] Philosophy can never attain speculative certitude, but its hypotheses must be fertile not only theoretically but practically; indeed, the two cannot be separated in the long run. Here, we must carefully note, an hypothesis which works is the guide to further truth than that already gained, but the fact that it works is not in itself the test of truth.

Thus there is good reason why G. Dawes Hicks should say of Ward: ". . . it was well-nigh inevitable that a mind imbued as his was with a sense of the importance of testing philosophical generalizations by their compatibility or incompatibility with empirical details should look upon Hegel's idealism as having been too cheaply and easily won." [17] Ward is so earnest in his empiricism that he is the first to tell the

[13] *Ibid.*, p. 23.

[14] *Ibid.*, p. 22, and *Essays*, p. 30. This is one of the lessons which Ward taught A. E. Taylor, who emphasizes, as a result of Ward's influence, "the impossibility of eliminating contingency from Nature" (J. H. Muirhead, ed., *Contemporary British Philosophy*, 1924–25, II, 271).

[15] *Essays*, p. 301.

[16] *Ibid.*, p. 140.

[17] "The Philosophy of James Ward," *Mind*, XXXIV (1925), 288.

reader where empirical evidence fails him and where his empiricism can be called such only because it carries him beyond the concrete experiential horizon without *contradicting* experience. In Pringle-Pattison rationalism sought empirical foundations; in Ward empiricism becomes supplemented at critical points by rationalism, as we shall see.

C. WARD'S CONCEPTION OF EXPERIENCE

If philosophy is to begin *in mediis rebus*, what better starting point is there than the psychology of experience? Accordingly, Ward's philosophy has its base in psychology, whence his epistemological, metaphysical, and theological investigations proceed. The order of his works illustrates this, for the famous article in the *Encyclopaedia Britannica*, which his *Psychological Principles* developed, preceded Ward's rejection of naturalistic, dualistic, and absolutistic metaphysics in the two volumes on *Naturalism and Agnosticism*, which, in turn, paved the way for the completion of his philosophy in the *Realm of Ends*. Since our concern is mainly with problems relating to Ward's theism, we shall deal very summarily with Ward's psychology and epistemology. More attention will be given to them in the consideration of Ward's disciple in psychology and epistemology, F. R. Tennant.

For Ward, *"Experience is the process of becoming expert by experiment."* [18] Experience, as the etymology of the word implies, is basically conative, and it develops in the pursuit of those adjustments to the whole environment (meaning, perhaps, more than the physical and the social) which will be most conducive to self-preservation (again ultimately meaning more than the physical and the social self, though at the beginning it is only these). "Now we have from the first regarded experience not as simply passively moulded by circumstances but as also actively shaped by our own endeavour towards self-conservation and betterment." [19] All thought and knowledge,

---

[18] "Psychology," *Encyclopaedia Britannica* (11th ed.), XXII, 548. Here experience indicates a whole mental life.

[19] *Psychological Principles* (1918), p. 358.

then, is initially inspired by, but not subservient to, the fundamental desire for self-preservation.

All knowledge, in turn, involves an experiencer and the
experienced, a subject and an object. The object is not a state
of the subject but a presentation to it. In addition, any one
object is only a selected part of a "presentational continuum." [20] The subject, on the other hand, is a complex
unity of feeling, thought, and conation, a unity in variety.

Experience can *not* without mutilation be resolved into three depart-
ments, one cognitive or theoretical, one emotional, and one practical.
. . . It is true that what we take and what we find we must take and find
as it is given. But, on the other hand, it is also true that we do not take —
at least do not take up — what is uninteresting; . . . [On the next page
he continues:] Regarding experience in this wise as life, self-conservation, self-realization, and taking conation not cognition as its central
feature, we must conclude that it is not that 'content' of objects, which
the subject cannot alter, that gives them their place in its experience,
but their worth positive or negative, their goodness or badness as ends or
means to life.[21]

Furthermore, every individual experience is not only a
unity in duality of subject and object, but its self-consciousness
is the result of interaction with the not-self.[22] Some of the
objects in the objective continuum are other people's bodies [23]
into which we read an experience analogous to our own, and
it is through intercourse with other selves that we better understand ourselves and build up a common world out of the
private objects.[24] For example, the sun of common discourse
(as distinct from the psychological object of private experience) is a construct resulting from the interpretation of private
experience influenced by social discourse. In this way, knowledge about the self, the world, and other selves grows from
more to more. Ward is fond of quoting Comte's sentence:
"Entre l'homme et le monde il faut l'humanité." [25]

[20] *Essays*, pp. 333, 334; see also *Naturalism and Agnosticism* (1899), II, 264,
265.
[21] *Naturalism and Agnosticism*, II, 134, 135.
[22] See *Essays*, p. 238.
[23] *Ibid.*, p. 104.
[24] See *Naturalism and Agnosticism*, II, 168.
[25] See *Essays*, p. 354.

The interaction between subjects is the basis of mutual sympathy, understanding, or sympathetic *rapport*,[26] and the commerce which human selves have with each other and their environment results in the establishment of custom and law. Such social necessities indicate the development of part, at least, of persons' natures, to the extent that predictions can often be made about their activities. That is, conative human beings find a certain adaptation to their environment profitable, and they "settle down" and develop certain habitual modes of activity which become relatively passive and conveniently organized. Hence, attitudes gained through experiment with the human and natural environment are now taken for granted. Human nature, accordingly, might be considered as partly *naturata*, ordered and automatic, and partly *naturans*. The former was originally the fresh, spontaneous striving of the latter, but the latter, rooting and preserving itself *via* the regularity of the former, from time to time brings disturbance and change into its routine existence by attempting a new adaptation to environment. The impulsive aspect of human nature is, of course, little predictable; but even the laws of the interaction of individuals are at most only statistical. Hence, it is to our experience of such human interaction and subjective intercourse that we must turn to explain the conception of the regularity of nature and its laws.[27]

Such, then, is the historical world, the world in which no two individuals are alike, though they are not completely different. Consequently, it is in this human world of concrete, struggling individuals that we can find the best clues to the riddles of time. Therefore, "To reduce these finite centres to appearances means, I think, the 'Disappearance of Reality' for us." [28] The problem for Ward now remains: Can the rest of reality be similarly conceived as composed of struggling, finite spirits? In the following, we shall outline the more pertinent elements of Ward's metaphysics, after pausing to note the more important steps Ward takes in preparation for his own positive construction.

[26] See *Naturalism and Agnosticism*, II, 250.
[27] *Ibid.*   [28] *Essays*, p. 298.

D. Naturalism and Life

The world as it appears to us is a "tangible, visible, sonorous world," but these aspects are completely lost in the deductive and mathematical treatment of abstract or analytical mechanics, especially as expressed in kinematics. The laws of the latter may indeed be found to hold for molar bodies, but the difficulties a rigid, mechanical scheme encounters in the microscopic realm alone forbid the universal application of it. As Ward humorously remarks, once the logic of kinematics has taken it to the mere movement "of a something that is neither solid nor liquid nor gas," [29] we find ourselves in Alice's predicament when the Cheshire cat disappeared and left her grin. The mechanical theory, if not before, received its death blow when physics advanced beyond Newton's solid and impenetrable bits of extended matter. But Ward's main point is that the strictly mechanical account of the universe "was after all but an abstract and ideal scheme" which could be applied to the concrete world only with the help of the calculus of probability, and that from this scheme there was no way back to the world as we know it. Such scientific Absolutism is no more desirable than philosophical Absolutism. Furthermore, if, as a development of strict mechanism maintained, mind is a mere epiphenomenon of matter, then the mechanist, in holding this conceptual (epiphenomenal) scheme to be true, is really presupposing in practice what he denies in theory, a connection between matter and mind.

But naturalism (or mechanism) confronts insuperable difficulties when confronted with the data of biology. Biological evolution is much more easily explained by natural selection plus teleological factors, it being impossible otherwise to account for the complex structure of organisms. By the teleological factor Ward does not mean, as Martineau seemed to, the old view that each species was immediately designed and directly fashioned to occupy a fixed place in a particular plan of creation, but a factor, "analogous to that of Lamarck," which, involving sentient life in the satisfaction of needs, "is oper-

[29] *Naturalism and Agnosticism*, I, 140.

ative and essential throughout all biological evolution." [30] The presence of the self-preserving activity in human beings is indubitable, and Ward's problem once more is: Can mind be made coextensive with life (and eventually inorganic matter)?

The characteristic of life is its tendency to conserve itself. While organic evolution, therefore, is inexplicable if life be regarded as a mere form of energy or a *tertium quid* mediating between matter and mind, the study of mind reveals two principles which would render it intelligible. An organism differs from a machine both in its ability to start its own activity and also in the fact that its function determines the structure of its parts. If, then, we can borrow from human life the principles of self-preservation and subjective or hedonic selection and apply them to the actions of plants and animals, the variations of organic evolution can be explained. For now the organism, striving to preserve itself, selects (as human beings do) those parts of the environment and those variations which are conducive to its existence. The origin of species, accordingly, is owing not only to physical but also to psychical activities;[31] concentrated practice perfects functions and functions perfect structures. The growth from lower to higher organic forms is more easily explained also, for now we can suggest that animals, bent on self-preservation, find novel and better forms of life and develop and modify further the organism already preserved.[32] "The creature is bent only on filling its skin; but in doing this as pleasantly as may be, it gets a better skin to fill, and accordingly seeks to fill it differently." [33] Thus, organic life is simply human life "writ smaller."

Whatever else the defects of pan-psychism may be, it is difficult to find a better metaphysical account of organic evolution. If knowledge of other human beings is based on ejective analogy with our own experience, why may we not interpret the activities of animals and even plants by a varying scale of psychical organization and ability? Ward, confronted with the facts of organic evolution, has given an empirical account

[30] *Naturalism and Agnosticism*, I, 288 ff.   [32] *Ibid.*, I, 298.
[31] *Ibid.*, I, 297.   [33] *Ibid.*

of it, not simply by appeal to the principle of continuity but by an extension of the same empirical method by which we come to the knowledge of other selves. The problem now is: Can the analogy of human experience be carried further into the organic world?

E. The Unity and Teleology of Nature

The uniformity or unity of nature for Ward is not an axiom which it would be absurd to deny; it is neither self-evident, nor a deduction from something that is, nor a brute fact. It is rather a postulate of our conative and cognitive nature. "The Unity of Nature is the ideal counterpart of the actual unity of each individual experience — an ideal towards which we first advance when intersubjective intercourse and reasoning begin. . . ." [34] Individual experience is first unified in accordance with conative interest, which is the basis of all the categories. The activity and passivity which the individual experiences in his personal and causal interaction with the "environment" is the basis of his interpretation of causality between objects. As a consequence of the development (by intersubjective intercourse) of (a) the experience of unifying interest involving agency and passivity, and (b) the analogous interpretation of the field of uniform events, we are led to postulate the regularity of nature.

Yet science, concerned only with sequence, sees neither transeunt action nor the efficient causality which we experience immediately in will. "There is nothing in it [science], therefore, that can possibly discredit that *prima facie* interaction of individual minds, of which the social fabric is a proof." [35] Activity is an ultimate of human experience which does not yield to intellectual analysis, which itself is an activity. The laws of nature are our formulations of events in accordance with our pragmatic and, consequently, theoretical interests. The discovery of the laws, not their fulfillment, lies with us, and the conformity of the formulae to the nature of things still remains to be demonstrated. Thus Ward finds that an

[34] *Ibid.*, II, 235.
[35] *Ibid.*, II, 242.

empirical view of the facts shows that "the whole notion of universal and necessary laws of Nature is, then, essentially a postulate," but with Kant he agrees that it is a postulate we *must* presuppose for the sake of experience or its own disproof.[36] In so far as nature is amenable to laws formed by human intelligence for the sake of human ends it may be called teleological. Yet, what can the constitution of nature be, if it is thus a realm of ends (from the human standpoint, of course)?

Here philosophy must supplement science. There is one warning we may take from the investigation so far. "From the reflective [teleological] judgment as *prius* to the mechanical judgment the way is easy; from the mechanical as *prius* to the reflective there is strictly no way at all." [37] Room may be found within the teleological scheme for mechanical process, but the initial assumption of mechanism leaves no hope for teleology. Now, since nature is intelligible, Ward argues, it is either intelligent itself, or there is intelligence beyond it. Again, human beings interact with nature or through it, so it is either causally efficient itself or there is a causality behind it.[38] The final answer is approached through an analysis of the ultimate meaning of cause.

Our laws of nature are based on the relations between things. However, the inert particles or atoms *of science* are all alike and the mere victims of the push and pull of circumstance. "If there are two things in the world entitled to exist separated by the whole diameter of being they are the so-called reactions of matter and the actions of mind." [39] Inertia, which means "incapability," is the contrary of both activity and passivity. "Matter does nothing, suffers nothing, and knows nothing, that is about all we can say about it in psychological terms. What wonder then that starting like Berkeley from experience, Leibniz should say, *quod non agit, non existit*." [40] That is, not only are the individuals of the historical world as we know it never identical, but "the only things of which we

[36] *Naturalism and Agnosticism*, II, 250.
[37] *Ibid.*, II, 272, 273.
[38] Cf. *ibid.*, II, 265.
[39] *Realm of Ends*, p. 509.
[40] *Ibid.*

have positive knowledge are subjects with intrinsic qualities, things that are something in themselves and for themselves"; and "the only *causes* of which we have positive knowledge are minds: these have a nature of their own and hence can interact, determine, and be determined." [41] Since we know best the interaction of mind with mind, "this must be the basis of our interpretation if we are to understand at all." [42]

It is on this empirical basis that Ward suggests, with Leibniz, that for physical atoms and their laws be substituted very elementary spiritual existences with determinate, psychical natures whose teleological interactions with each other form the ground of our natural laws. [43] In Spinozistic terms, the essence of each finite being in this historical world is its *conatus* towards well-being, and it is of such *conatus* that the natural world is the manifestation. "What is nothing for itself is nothing in itself." [44] Accordingly, Ward concludes that reality is constituted by a plurality of mental units varying widely but continuously in the scale of mental differences.

But this pan-psychistic pluralism is only the first step toward Ward's final theism, though he did believe that theism could not be established if spiritualism did not supersede metaphysical dualism. Ward says: "Pluralism, as such, I have confessed, 'can never furnish anything deserving to be called a philosophical justification of itself.' " [45] To this we may add: ". . . I am not and never have been a pluralist; though I hold and have always held, that experience, from which speculation must and therefore always does start, is for us primarily an interaction of the Many." [46] In order to know why Ward was never satisfied with absolute or nontheistic pluralism, we must understand the pluralistic explanation of nature and its laws.

F. PLURALISM AND ITS LIMITS

It cannot be too strongly emphasized that Ward was not merely invoking an abstract principle of continuity in order

---

[41] *Naturalism and Agnosticism*, II, 279.
[42] *Ibid.*   [43] Cf. *ibid.*, II, 280; *Essays*, pp. 233, 234, 242.
[44] *Essays*, p. 234; cf. also *Realm of Ends*, p. 21.
[45] *Realm of Ends*, pp. 200, 497.   [46] *Ibid.*, p. 95.

to extend the analogy of human experience into the very depths of the inorganic world. This principle is set to work as a further justification of the more important idea that nothing could exist which, in Platonic terms, could neither affect nor be affected. This, in terms of concrete experience, means that the inorganic world must be composed of an indefinite (and not Leibniz's less empirically conceived infinite) number of active beings. Now Ward quite frankly admits that in thinking of these beings as conative, cognitive, and emotional, the pluralist is in difficulty, for in the inorganic world there are no signs of preference and striving such as those found in the vegetable, animal, and human kingdom. Ward also realizes that he must account for natural law in terms of these very elementary spiritual beings. His task therefore is to show how, in a world where there are no signs of preference, natural law is explicable by the activities of striving beings.

Here Ward's empirically derived conviction that existence must be active is supplemented by appeal to the law of continuity.[47] The result is the postulation of monads at the bottom of the existential ladder which are conscious only of momentary pleasure and pain and motivated simply by their impulses of self-conservation. Thus, the beings of the inorganic world operate entirely on hedonistic principles. The whole of reality may now be described as a realm of ends, provided that "end" includes the unforeseen goal as well as the foreseen. It so happens that this lowest realm is the basis (though there are levels even within it) of the vegetable and animal kingdoms and that together they both form the means of subsistence and intercourse for the human kingdom on which they themselves do not depend.

If we now remind ourselves of the prevalence of custom and of the constancy which makes possible the statistical calculation of the activities of large human aggregates, we can easily account for the existence of natural law. And we need not, as does science, account for law by disregarding the quality of things in favor of quantity. We may rather conceive of

[47] Cf. *Realm of Ends*, p. 62.

natural law in terms of the habits formed by these bare
monads, which are probably influenced merely by their aver-
sion for pain. For, in the thinking of the pluralist, the notion
of chaos is unmitigated nonsense, and he consequently starts
with an *inchoate* state of definitely characterized monads
whose very definiteness automatically reduces the number of
possibilities of action. That is, each monad has a law of his
being, as it were, and not an external law imposed upon him.
Nor is there any *prius* of law to which he must conform. He
must be himself, and himself he must be, and on these "rocks"
is the natural order built. "At the start then the order that is
to be has still be become: everything is inchoate but nothing
chaotic. . . ." [48] Natural law is the outcome of the strivings
of these lower monads to maintain themselves in an environment constituted by the unique natures of other monads, all
of whom settle at convenient levels and desire novelty probably in accordance with the degree of their psychical com-
plexity and capacity. "All nature . . . is regarded as plastic
and evolving like mind: its routine and uniformity being explained on the analogy of habit and heredity in the individual, of custom and tradition in society; while its variety is
attributed to spontaneity in some form." [49] Habit is the result
of original spontaneity, and consequently on the pluralistic
view not only are there no laws prior to events, but laws are
themselves the result of the contingency which is at the core
of things in the conations of the monads. Harmony for the
pluralist is *to be* achieved.

This contingency is not chance, since every action is motivated, and there is always selection of that part of the environment most conducive to self-preservation. "The tendency at
any moment is simply towards more life, simply growth; but
this process of self-preservation imperceptibly but steadily
modifies the self that is preserved." [50] The essential difference
between man and the lowest monad is that though both are
motivated by the best *modus vivendi*, the monad is the victim
of comparatively blind impulse, while man is conscious of the

[48] *Ibid.*, p. 71.   [49] *Ibid.*, p. 74.   [50] *Ibid.*, pp. 79, 80.

ends he desires. Man himself, however, advances by trial and error "from animality to rational personality through inter-subjective intercourse," [51] since reason develops only in society. But the whole natural development is not merely the unrolling of the cosmic scroll on which all is already laid out, for there is novelty, the creation of new and unpredictable features (or epigenesis) all along the line of evolution.[52]

Pluralism cannot, therefore, be condemned for inability to explain law. On the other hand, there are difficulties in it which the theistic hypothesis would alleviate without giving up the essence of pluralism. To be sure, the application of the principle of continuity beyond man would lead to the hypothesis of a society of higher types of being which, to some extent, control and modify the destiny of human and subhuman species. Such an hypothesis would indeed account for the natural beauties which cannot be explained by sexual selection and "utilitarian principles" alone.[53] And the pluralist, searching for unity, might go further and postulate a Supreme Person, who, though ultimately a finite *primus inter pares*, might be so different in kind (as well as degree) that he would have more immediate communion with his fellow men,[54] and would have intellective intuition rather than discursive and symbolic thought, while time in some sense would have to be real for him. This postulate, however, seems to be the result of a search merely for unity, and since we are not told what empirical facts are explained, the principle of continuity would be used abstractly. This is perhaps one of the reasons why Ward is unsatisfied with pluralism, for his theistic

[51] *Realm of Ends*, p. 93.

[52] Cf. *ibid.*, p. 471; and see below, Chapter VI, pp. 250 ff. Time is taken much more seriously by Ward than by Pringle-Pattison, as shown by this doctrine of contingency — which Pringle-Pattison thought meant either nothing new for the whole or chance — but in considering the relation of time to God, since Ward allows for only a functional relation of a supratemporal God to time, he is consequently not far removed at this point from Pringle-Pattison.

[53] See *Realm of Ends*, p. 213. Once more the principle of continuity is used for empirical explanation and not abstractly only, for Ward seems to be stressing the compatibility of such a spiritual order with pluralism and is not himself convinced that there is enough empirical evidence for one.

[54] See *Realm of Ends*, pp. 193, 194, 234 ff.

hypothesis has explanatory work to do. His main objection to pluralism at its upper limit is that more than a mere *primus inter pares* is needed to account for the order of the astronomical *uni*verse and not a multiverse.

But there are difficulties at the lower limit also, for how explain the awakening of the "slumbering monads" [55] which constitute the lowest ideal limit of the pluralistic universe? And, further, how account for the mutual and complementary development which results in the closely woven continuity from the inorganic to the organic and the conscious world?

Finally, pluralism "is sadly far away from the heart's desire," [56] unless there is "also some principle of 'conservation of value' tending to prevent rational, self-conscious spirits from lapsing back into merely animal souls." [57] In other words, pluralism needs some argument to make evolution worth while, for if evolution is to get anywhere and not merely be a series of cycles, there must be immortality for conscious beings, in which metaphysical identity is not lost and the values already attained become the basis of further achievement. This, it seems, is what Ward means concretely by the conservation of value, namely, the possibility that all "fresh evolution" start from its past achievements and not in less favorable conditions, owing to the "personal continuity between the old constituents and the new." [58] "In a word, without such spiritual continuity as theism alone seems able to ensure, it looks as if a pluralistic world were condemned to a Sisyphean task." [59]

What the exact implication of "ensure" in this last quotation is we do not know, but the sense in which theism can ensure the conservation of values an empirical theism must define. Ward is accordingly ready to deal with this general problem and define more exactly the way in which an omnip-

[55] *Ibid.*, p. 197.
[56] *Ibid.*, p. 214.
[57] *Ibid.*, p. 213. The point before this was that pluralism needed some doctrine of "metempsychosis" to prevent a similar lapsing back of the organic into the inorganic. Cf. *ibid.*, pp. 212 ff.
[58] *Ibid.*, p. 214.
[59] *Ibid.*, p. 215. Cf. below, Chapter V, Section H.

otent, omniscient, perfectly good, transcendent and yet immanent God (the theistic hypothesis) is related to the world of souls. His argument against pluralism so far has shown the necessity of a cosmic Mind in some way responsible for the present cosmos. The next step is to see what modifications theism makes in pluralism in order to give "both unity and reason" to the scheme of things.

G. God and Creation

The doctrine of creation itself implies that "theism is not simply the possible crown and completion of pluralism," but modifies it. For now the transcendent Being is not beyond the many but "is related to them in a way in which none of them is related to the rest: they do not simply coexist along with it, they exist *somehow* in it and through it." [60] Ward is perfectly frank in conceding that "there is nothing in all our physical experience that *compels* us to admit" that the world is the result of a creative act, but "on the other hand there is nothing that would justify us in denying it." [61] The implicit argument here, we take it, is that when a notion is neither empirically justifiable nor empirically unjustifiable, then the empirical philosopher may accept it, provided it seems justified by the rest of his empirical theory. Now the nearest analogy we may find to God's relation to his world is the creative activity of an artistic genius who spontaneously embodies his spirit in the work he loves, and yet is distinct from it. But even this analogy breaks down, because the work of art is after all a "relative creation" within the world, and there is an "impassable gulf" between this and the "absolute creation" of the world itself. "The one [the work of art] presupposes experience previously acquired, the other is coeval and identical with the divine experience itself . . . [and] any analogy drawn from our experience must be inadequate to such an experience. . . ." [62]

Ward's conception of the relation between the world and

[60] *Realm of Ends*, p. 231 (italics mine).
[61] *Ibid.*, p. 232.
[62] *Ibid.*, p. 240.

God is, we see, similar to Pringle-Pattison's. With the latter he agrees that creation cannot mean transeunt causation, since that involves an impossible alien datum. Furthermore, as Pringle-Pattison insisted, "God is God only as being creative." [63] Creation is neither a change in God nor a change in anything already existing; it simply refers to the dependence of the world on God.[64] God would be nothing without the world, and the world nothing without God, "the ground [not cause] of the world's being, its *ratio essendi*." [65] Again: "If creation means anything, it means something so far involved in the divine essence, that we are entitled to say, as Hegel was fond of saying, that 'without the world God is not God.' " [66]

Thus far it might seem that Ward had lost all transcendence, but he explicitly rejects any Spinozistic notion of *"Deus sive natura,"* [67] or any attempts to identify the world with an ubiquitous knower. Though, on analogy with our experience, will and presentation may be attributed to God's experience, this cannot mean that either precedes the other, for creation "is at once 'pure activity' and 'original insight,' idea and deed, life and light." [68] "God is transcendent to it [his creation], for it is not God, but his utterance and manifestation; and yet, because it is *his* utterance and because he ever sustains it, he is immanent in it, it is his continuous creation." [69] Thus, Pringle-Pattison and Ward are at one as to the relation of God to the world. Both insist that God is nothing without the world and that he is transcendent though not temporally prior to it, statements which to us at least seem completely contradictory as they stand. For them, God's immanence does not mean that God is nothing but the world, and his transcendence does not mean that he could be conceived to exist without a world or what Ward calls "the Many." [70] Ward, in spite of his recognition that Nature is the "prelude to Mind," [71] does not say explicitly whether this Many includes human beings as well as monads constituting the physical world, nor

[63] *Ibid.*, p. 234.
[64] *Ibid.*, p. 233.
[65] *Ibid.*
[66] *Ibid.*
[67] Cf. *ibid.*, p. 234.

[68] *Ibid.*, p. 240.
[69] *Ibid.*
[70] Cf. *ibid.*, pp. 141 f.
[71] *Ibid.*, pp. 262, 264.

whether God could be God without human beings. In any
case, one may be willing to grant the idea of creation, even if
"it is impossible . . . that experience should directly give
rise to it at all," [72] but it is difficult to believe that God both
transcends and yet is nothing without the world. For if God
transcends the world he cannot literally be *nothing* without
it, unless he is simply the sum of its parts, a notion foreign to
the rest of Ward's thought.

The difficulty may, however, be removed if a distinction is
drawn (not a separation made) between God's ontological being and his moral being. It might then without contradiction
be said that God's moral being,[73] for example, his goodness,
would be diminished without the world, though his existence
as an ontological person is still conceivable. Of course this is
the very distinction which Pringle-Pattison and Ward would
not accept, since God ultimately for them always existed as
the *complete* realization of the highest values, which in turn
constitute permanent characteristics of his ontological nature.
We should no doubt be accused of falsely hypostatizing the
distinction between God's ontological nature (a thinking, feeling, willing unity of consciousness) and his moral nature (the
realization of certain ideals by the ontological nature). But
we nevertheless persist that a more correct conception of
God's moral nature, fortified by the following hypothesis,
would save us from such an accusation. Perhaps it will be
best to outline the suggested alternative first.

If by God's moral goodness is meant the consistent willing
of the Good, which, as both Ward and Pringle-Pattison would
agree, is the creation of a world in which free beings might
achieve moral character, then we may hold that God's *goodness,* materially (as opposed to formally) conceived, is nothing
(that is, impossible) without the existence of the world and
men. God's moral goodness formally conceived, however,
would not be affected by his failure to achieve his end. It
would then be intelligible to say that God's material goodness
is nothing without the world and man, though his ontological

[72] *Realm of Ends*, p. 232.
[73] This would involve God's social being, so far as we know.

being is still possible and not structurally dependent on the existence of the creation. For God to be creator of the world and man does not necessarily mean that he could not or did not exist before his creation, much as his moral and social being depended on the creation of the world and man. God, before the creation, would still be (at least) a *unitas multiplex* of will, cognition, and feeling, though all of these are dependent for their further development on the existence of the world and man if we assume the truth of pan-psychism. This implies that the creation of the physical world (assuming the truth of pan-psychism), as well as of man, was an event in time. To this view Ward would object for two reasons.

First, as he and Pringle-Pattison insist, God is inconceivable apart from the world. But we may simply suggest: (1) that they themselves have insisted that God is *more* than just the world (or other than a determination of the world), and if this means ontologically transcendent it is contradictory to say that God cannot exist apart from the world. All that the statement can mean is that God's achievement of his good purpose is impossible apart from the world. (2) Leaving aside the creation of the physical world for the moment, their views must take account of the fact that human selves are, if science is to be trusted, additions to the history of the cosmos, and that God, consequently, must have existed before their appearance. Human beings, therefore (unless time is ultimately unreal as Pringle-Pattison tried to maintain), are not necessary to God's ontological existence, though by hypothesis they are necessary to the *fulfillment* of his moral purpose, if not to the moral purpose as such. On this view we can still say that God's goodness, that is, his good will, is as eternal as he is. This, to be sure, does not tell us how creation is possible, but creation we admit, with Ward and Pringle-Pattison, is something empirically inconceivable, yet not only not necessarily absurd, but the rational justification of transcendence and human free will.

(3) But if God's ontological nature is possible without man, is his existence possible without the physical world? We

shall soon give reasons for denying the pan-psychistic view of the physical world in favor of a view which equates the world with God, though not God with the world. Now, however, we may suggest that if the creation of human spirits out of nothing is possible (and this is only our way of saying that we do not know how creation takes place, but that so far as our knowledge does extend it is a *new* fact in the history of God), then the world, too, may be said to constitute a new fact for God without any greater intrinsic difficulty than the admission of creation itself. For Ward creation out of nothing means that God had no external datum; for us it means this and more, that a God existed whose purpose to create a world [74] and man preceded the actual creation in which that God is continually immanent as its source. God purposed to be a Father before he became a parent, and though his children depend on him, the fact of his *fatherhood* (and grandfatherhood), but not his existence, depends on them. To hold otherwise is to empty God's transcendence of even a minimum of meaning. On this view, to be sure, the idea of creation still remains a mystery, but the contradiction of a transcendent being whose existence is nevertheless dependent on his creation is avoided. But Ward's other objection, to which this brings us, must be faced.

Second:

> There is equally little to support the view of creation as an event that occurred at a finite date in the past. . . . Whatever the reason or motive for creation may have been . . . it seems "absolutely inconceivable," as v. Hartmann put it, "that a conscious God should wait half an eternity content without a good that ought to be." [75]

To this it may be answered: (1) whether we like it or not it does seem that God did wait "half an eternity" before human beings were created, even though we have no reason to suppose that God was content with this state. (2) God, it is con-

---

[74] Equating the inorganic world with God, as we do, the only meaning creation of the world has for us is the production of that physical order most conducive to human values and moral growth. See below, Chapter VI, pp. 244 ff.

[75] *Realm of Ends*, p. 233.

ceivable and we suggest, did not have enough power to remove the obstacles *within* his own nature which prevented him from fulfilling his purpose to create (the world) and man. This hypothesis does not destroy God's moral goodness, but it does limit his power and indicates that the obstructions, though impeding him, did not overcome him. The nature of this ἀνάγκη which needed persuasion (in Platonic terms) will be described in Chapter VII, but it is mentioned here because it does render intelligible the fact that man at least did not appear sooner on the cosmic horizon. (3) Ward's idea that creation involves no external limitation but self-limitation on God's behalf "seems [as he says] to imply a prior state in which it was absent whereas a limitation held to be permanent — as we hold creation to be — suggests some ultimate dualism rather than an ultimate unity." [76] Interestingly enough, Ward defends himself against this implication of temporal creation by a mathematical illustration which by its very nature as logical cannot suffice here, for a logical relation is always one of logical implication rather than one of the dynamic, alogical causality needed here if real creation and human freedom are to be preserved. As defense against ultimate dualism, Ward adds: "We do not say that God comes into being with the world, but only that as ground of the world he limits himself: duality in unity is implied here as in all experience, but not dualism." [77] This does indeed save Ward from the accusation of dualism, but it is difficult to see how he is saved from the implication that self-limitation was a temporal coincident with the creation of the world and man, for whose sake the limitation occurred. Nor does it suffice for an empiricist to deny temporal creation by saying: "Such an objection is in keeping with our ordinary experience confined as that is to temporal processes, but it is not applicable to the notion of an absolute ground. . . ." [78]

But much as we object to Ward's positive case for the rela-

[76] *Ibid.*, p. 243.
[77] *Ibid.*, p. 244.
[78] *Ibid.*, pp. 243, 244. Cf. below, Chapter VI, pp. 247 f.

tion between man and God, we can heartily endorse his
defense against pluralism. Creation, inexplicable though it
be, does carry Ward beyond the "incomplete and unsatisfy-
ing" yet inconsistent totality of the interacting Many of the
pluralist. "A plurality of beings primarily independent as
regards their existence and yet always mutually acting and
reacting upon each other, an ontological plurality that is yet
a cosmological unity, seems clearly to suggest some ground
beyond itself." [79] As Ward says, the very fact that we are the
result of creation makes it impossible for us to have a clear
idea of it. And to anyone who questions "the use of a hypothesis that can never be directly verified," [80] Ward correctly answers that "this objection rests on a complete
misapprehension as to the function of philosophy," which,
unlike the particular sciences, deals with experience as a
whole. "But if the idea of creation will carry us further
[than radical pluralism], and if nothing else will, then that
idea, it is maintained, is rationally justified though it be not
empirically verified." [81]

H.   THEISTIC MONADISM AND PERSONALISM

1.   WARD'S OBJECTIONS TO PERSONALISM

The pluralistic metaphysics, Ward has shown, must be
modified by the theistic view of creation, but his next step is
to show that the theistic cosmology is rendered more intelligible if supplemented by the pluralistic theory of interaction.
Both views insist that ultimate reality is actively spiritual,
but Ward opposes to the usual theistic hypothesis (that
reality in its entirety is ultimately a society of persons) the
pluralistic alternative that reality is constituted by a scale
of spiritual entities, ranging from the barest monad to the
highest type of person existing, which have the same bond of
relative independence and dependence to God as do persons
on the theistic view. Ward's position, therefore, will be called,

[79] *Realm of Ends*, p. 241.
[80] *Ibid.*, p. 245.
[81] *Ibid.*, pp. 245, 246.

as he himself named it,[82] *theistic monadism*, and the theistic view he criticized, *personalism*. To the latter Ward is sympathetic, though he believes it to be too complicated. The specific view that shall be defended against Ward's criticism is that modification of Berkeley, Lotze, and Malebranche (of whom Ward is speaking) held by Borden Parker Bowne and his critical disciples, A. C. Knudson and E. S. Brightman.

For personalism (to substitute this name for what Ward calls theism) God, as Ward says, is not only "the creative and sustaining activity, whereby the finite Many [persons] exist," but also "the continuous mediation whereby they are brought into living relation with each other." [83] Two passages from Ward summarize the view concisely.

According to the cosmology of theism, in short, the physical world is simply a system of means provided for the sake of a realm of ends: it is only to be understood as subservient to them, and apart from them is alike meaningless and worthless.   .   .   .   .   .   .[84]
The creative activity [of God in creating persons] is then, the theist holds, only the condition of, not at all conditioned by, the mediating activity; and the unity and purpose of the former as a realm of ends involves and determines the law and order of the latter as a system of means.[85]

One comment is required, as well as further elucidation. It is doubtful whether the personalist will dogmatically say that the physical world is "meaningless" and "worthless," or *merely* "subservient." For him the physical world he sees is a joint product of his own active response to the direct stimulation of God, but he does not suppose, or need not suppose, that it is simply a system of means, for it may exist for God in a different way and for a purpose hidden from mankind. Personalism is pantheistic so far as the world is concerned, for it holds that Nature *is* God's energizing. There is no mediator between persons and God or God and Nature. Not Nature but God is the direct medium between persons. That is, on the occasion of one's willing to speak, God varies his

---

[82] Muirhead, ed., *Contemporary British Philosophy*, II, 25.
[83] *Realm of Ends*, p. 248.
[84] *Ibid.*, p. 252.
[85] *Ibid.*, p. 253.

energizing so that those physiological and physical processes take place which result in sound for persons. The medium of interaction between persons in every instance is God's activity in accordance with willed requests.

Now Ward is ready to admit that the order of the physical world and therefore the possibility of science is intelligible on this system, but he asks: "Does the idea of creation necessarily imply what we may call a unified and systematic occasionalism?" [86] This, Ward grants, is a possible explanation, but, other reasons aside, he finds "the assumption of a twofold divine activity," [87] of creation and mediation, a "needless complication." He consequently suggests the panpsychistic hypothesis in its place. We have already indicated that mediation, in the sense that the world would not otherwise exist apart from man, is no necessary aspect of the personalistic metaphysics. We may now add a minor objection that Ward's version of pan-psychism, even if tenable in its entirety, complicates the problem of creation in that God creates both the monads of the physical world and persons. On the personalistic hypothesis God, being identical [88] with Nature, creates persons only and not the physical world. Let us turn, however, to a consideration of the pan-psychistic alternative.

The pluralist tries to explain interaction without appeal to "subsidiary aids" by suggesting that between the spiritual individuals in every stage and between different stages there is mutual understanding or sympathetic *rapport*. This contact, at its highest level, is best illustrated by the relation between two kin spirits, but it "tails off rapidly in our intercourse with strangers, and tends to dwindle away altogether as we pass to creatures further and further removed from us in the scale of being." [89] It is essential to be clear about this important notion. Ward is trying to avoid the obviously inadequate scientific conception (which Lotze exploded long ago) of the transfer of forces and influences, between individ-

---

[86] *Realm of Ends*, p. 253.   [87] *Ibid.*, p. 508.
[88] This does not mean that God is not more than nature.
[89] *Realm of Ends*, pp. 253, 254.

uals, for this "is no longer applicable even as a figure to personal intercourse. The doings and sufferings of persons are both alike immediate; what brings them into relation is a 'sympathetic *rapport*' or *interest that rests upon cognition* [italics mine]." [90] Social intercourse rests upon the mutual knowledge of attitudes, feelings, and intentions, "displayed or announced," which lead to coöperation and to new feelings and intentions based on knowledge. Here "no physical constraint whatever directly enters," and phrases like *noblesse oblige* express the sort of thing meant.[91] If we discard physical things, the objections which Lotze pressed against transeunt action "do not apply to personal interaction based on mutual *rapport*." [92] Sympathetic *rapport* needs no go-between. In other words, if the monads are given windows to each other and God, then intermediation is not necessary.

We are now confronted with two hypotheses. The one invokes sympathetic *rapport* between monads whose windows are open toward God and man, and the other invokes a great Providential Exchange to whom all persons have access and through whom all interaction takes place. In considering them, let us note Ward's further objections to personalism.

First, to assemble similarities, pan-psychist and personalist both agree "in holding all real existence to consist in experients and their experience." They agree also in the analysis of experience into "presentation, feeling, and action." The occasionalist, however, interprets presentations, Ward complains, "as subjective modifications, assumed to be due directly to the divine activity," and thus "becomes hampered with all the epistemological difficulties of what is known as subjective idealism," which makes the "existence of the external world such a hopeless problem," by confining the windowless monads to their own worlds.[93] But one need answer only that personalistic occasionalism is not necessarily confined to the view of presentations as subjective states or modes of the subject. On the contrary, the personalist, accepting Ward's view of the presentational continuum, regards presen-

[90] *Ibid.*, p. 218.
[91] *Ibid.*, pp. 218, 219.
[92] *Ibid.*, p. 219.
[93] *Ibid.*, p. 259.

tations not as "a relation among monads," but as a relation be-tween God and persons, God being the source of stimulation.

To say, secondly, as Ward does, that "natural realism" is a simpler and prior explanation of the facts and that, after all, occasionalism would never have been heard of had Descartes not dichotomized the world is equivalent to saying that from the viewpoint of common sense occasionalism is a "needless complication." [94] A complication it may be (provided that it necessarily involves "a distinct medium of intercourse"), but to say it is needless is to say that there is no problem of interaction. And Ward himself, having scrutinized his own view with admirable empirical objectivity, finally concludes:

> Nevertheless, since we cannot actually verify the indefinite regress which the existence of bare monads implies, and since we cannot show that the indirect mediation of finite intercourse is not a fact, we have no means of deciding empirically between the two alternatives. The most we can say is that the pluralist alternative is the *prior* as well as the simpler, and it seems adequate.[95]

Before further analysis of the pluralistic hypothesis, let us note another of Ward's arguments against personalism, which, though tucked away in a footnote, plays, we believe, a very important part in Ward's rejection of personalism. "Physical catastrophes," Ward says, "are a serious difficulty for the theist on this view," [96] for now they result from the direct activity of God. Pan-psychism, in other words, seems to enjoy the advantage of explaining natural evil by attributing it to the activity of monads independent of God. Whether pan-psychism actually does offer a more adequate explanation of evil remains to be discussed,[97] but we may now turn to a preliminary problem and ask whether Ward's sympathetic *rapport* does explain interaction.

2. PAN-PSYCHISM CRITICIZED

Before we consider the meaning of *rapport* among the lower monads, let us evaluate its adequacy in human experience. Is not sympathetic *rapport*, which is supposed to be substi-

[94] *Realm of Ends*, p. 260.   [95] *Ibid.*   [96] *Ibid.*, p. 261.
[97] Cf. below, p. 122, and Chapter VII, for a full criticism of this alternative.

tuted for interaction, only a name for a kind of interaction different from the metaphorical transeunt action or passing of influence of the materialistic metaphysics? There is little doubt that Ward would agree, but his appeal to it arises from a demand for direct interaction between monads rather than from the indirect action involved in personalism; and he thinks that he finds such direct interaction in human intimacies especially. We suggest, however, that this not only introduces an inconsistency into Ward's theory of the knowledge of other selves, but also is an inadequate account of the experience concerned.

It must be noted that Ward attributes our knowledge of others to ejective self-analogy in the interpretation of certain modifications of our presentational continuum. What reason then is there to suppose that sympathetic *rapport*, which he expressly defines as interest based upon cognition, operates in any more direct manner? If sympathetic *rapport* is based on the indirect cognition of analogy, how can it be more direct? Is not the difference Ward has in mind really one of amount of knowledge rather than of the kind of interaction involved? When I see a body similar to mine, as in Madame Tussaud's famous gallery, I, interpreting only physical phenomena, immediately say: "there's a porter." But as soon as I receive no answer to my question, I begin to suspect that this figure is one of the remarkable wax effigies. If, however, I receive a grammatical, intelligent, and courteous answer, though in all of this I am aware of *nothing but* the words, facial expression, and general demeanor, I begin to classify this body among my categories of men. His attitude as well as his existence are inferences guided by my own experience; the attitudes I cannot understand among men are those which find too little corresponding to them in my own experience. On the other hand, when a dear friend, long known and well loved, confides his trouble, how often I can tell more from his facial expression than by his words; but in every instance, understanding is limited by my own experience, the friend's ability at self-expression, and my capacity for reading his countenance, a skill which is the result of a long training in the correlation of his words and behavior. To be sure, so many times, especially when two persons are filled with emotion, one often says: "You don't have to tell me." Then there seems to be a unique relationship, where words are not only unnecessary but impossible, and yet the very words, "I know how you feel," show that similar emotions have been called up (though very often in such cases investigation would show that the judgment was quite mistaken). The point, however, is that even here there is analogical or indirect knowledge, and the *feeling* of "sociality" and sympathy which results from one's feeling that he is (for example) seeing the other person's soul in his eyes is *psychologically* immediate, but the knowledge, correct or incorrect, is *epistemologically* mediate.[98] Sympathetic such experiences are, but the "suffering together" or sympathy is not the result of direct *rapport* between souls. They are considered "direct" and immediate epistemologically only because we "don't stop to think about it." It is queer that Ward, of all men, should have erred thus, so queer that one feels certain of his own misinterpretation until after continued scrutiny of the evidence. But unless Ward is to hold two theories of the knowledge of others, sympathetic *rapport* must be taken to be only an extension of indirect ejective analogy charged with emotion. If so, Ward does indeed not avoid the problem of interaction either on the human or (even more) on the subhuman levels. Furthermore, this criticism affects other aspects of Ward's metaphysics, as we shall now discover, as we pass to the difficulties in the pan-psychistic theory of the physical world.

For if, as we have seen, sympathetic *rapport* involves at least memory, what can it mean in bare monads with momentaneous awareness devoid of memory? Again, if direct knowledge is out of the question even for fully conscious monads, how can these bare monads interact harmoniously enough to explain natural law unless they are *so* made? Ward could justly answer this second question by saying that God created certain hedonic creatures whose spontaneity and search for

[98] The importance of this distinction is very great in religious experience, as we shall see.

satisfaction could operate within certain limits, thus allowing for the amount of contingency reflected in the statistical laws which are really human formulations of the habits of these hedonic creatures. That is, though a *perfect* harmony is not pre-established, sufficient harmony is pre-established to make statistical laws possible, and the creation of *perfect* harmony is left to the creatures themselves. There is nothing *inconceivable* about this explanation.

But is the first question answerable? It is part of the larger question: Has existence for self, or individuality, any meaning for the lowest monads described as bare? Let us examine Ward's description. As already indicated, if every mass point of the physicist were transformed into a unique conative being, the conception of the stripped, naked, slumbering monad would be approximated. In our own psychological experience we approach an analogy to the structure of the bare monad when we pass to the ideal limit of pure sensation, divested of memory. Consequently, this monad "can only react immediately and to what is immediately given" [99] and, having no memory, can "gain nothing by experience," [100] and therefore cannot deal in different ways with its directly experienced environment. An indefinite number of such monads "would provide all the 'uniform medium' for the intercourse of higher monads that these can require, without any need for divine intervention as occasionalism assumes." [101]

The greatest difficulty one confronts on this view is that, memory having been denied the monads, a type of experience we really know nothing about is attributed to them. Limited to gurgles of pleasing sensation, indeed, moved simply by the desire to avoid pain, so elementary that perhaps a response similar to the reflex action of the human knee-flex (apart from the consciousness of it) might be applied to it, what meaning does "being for self" have for one of these creatures? Without memory they are plainly victims of the rest of their comrades (for there is no other environment for them), and

[99] *Realm of Ends*, p. 257.
[100] *Ibid.*
[101] *Ibid.*

"conation" becomes, as Ward says, mere blind impulse. Since, for such beings, living catch-as-catch-can, learning is impossible, the uniformity resulting from their jostling experiences can be the consequence only of a dull similarity contrary to the uniqueness Ward ascribes to them.

Furthermore, even contingency, as distinguished from chance, is meaningless for these creatures, because monads without memory cannot be aware of the fact that they *are* more comfortable when they are more comfortable. Hence either their actions are owing to the chance winds that blow in that sphere or, since Ward would immediately repudiate chance, the only other alternative is that God is directly responsible for their activities and consequently for the statistical harmony that does exist. But since the monads' natures are such that, though conative, they cannot learn to change their relation to their environments, and since they are not responsible for their own created natures, the responsibility both for statistical order and for physical evil no longer falls on them but on God. Pan-psychism is, therefore, no better off than personalism at this point.

The truth seems to be that a psychical atom is really no more intelligible (or empirically conceivable) than a physical atom. The use of words such as conation, sensation, psychical, and others, which do have specific and concrete meaning at a higher level, lends a certain deceptive plausibility to elements which have really lost all empirical meaning. Furthermore, since there are no signs of striving in the inorganic world, the extension of the principle of continuity so that a "psychical" nature is attributed to its constituents is not empirical. The contortions through which Pringle-Pattison passed in trying to attribute the characteristics of human purpose to God are here repeated, though in reference to the lowest plane of existence. But empiricism cannot transcend human experience at either end, and the empiricist must not be deceived by the connotations of words which have really lost their concrete empirical denotations. Empiricism may be set aside when no other more empirical hypothesis will do, as was the case with creation, but here another alternative is possible.

3. A SYNTHESIS OF PAN-PSYCHISM AND PERSONALISM
SUGGESTED

We have tried to show, first, that pan-psychism does not explain interaction, but gives it the name sympathetic *rapport* which, second, is untenable as meaning direct knowledge, and third, that monads without memory cannot have such *rapport* and are really nonempirical entities. Pan-psychism accepts interaction as an ultimate, inexplicable fact but tries to conceive it spiritually and not physically. In so far as sympathetic *rapport* means spiritual stimulation by one soul of another, there is no a priori objection to it and no empirical verification for it, but under no circumstances can direct knowledge be based on direct *rapport*, whatever that be. For knowledge, presupposing direct interaction, is interpretative and mediate. If bare monads, as described above, were acceptable, there would be little reason for not accepting pan-psychism, especially since interaction or metaphysical causality seems to be an inexplicable ultimate on any nonlogical view of reality.

The personalist, after all, does not explain interaction. Unable to accept either the pan-psychistic medium of intercourse or the material world (which the pan-psychist also rejects), he is necessarily confined to the providential, mediating activity of God. But in this alternative he has merely shut the window of the monad to other monads and opened it toward God. Interaction between God and man has still been left unexplained, and at first glance it certainly seems arbitrary to protest against interaction between finite monads and affirm it between God and man. If the personalist should argue here that there is no reason why *God* cannot so interact, since he is God, then we should disavow this ontological form of argument. On the other hand, the attribution of interaction to God as *Creator* of these finite monads is not arbitrary, for now, it is implied, interaction is possible only between Creator and created. At least, such would be our stand. Interaction is an ultimate and is most intelligible between Creator and created.

In rejecting the pan-psychistic view of the natural world we have not, however, put aside its explanation of organic life, and here we would enlarge or modify our personalism. In the organic world, there is evidence of being-for-self (in varying degrees from the amoeba to the ape), in the self-preservation which is the basic characteristic of life and mind, and of this the empirical personalist must take account. This may not result in the clear-cut view of reality supposedly implicit in the statement that persons constitute ultimate reality. But even in such a proposition the broadest definition of the word *person* is assumed, and this universal does not express the degrees of development between the individuals subsumed under it, all of whom have some degree of volition, feeling, and thought (which is the minimum definition of the word *person*). Those living human individuals devoid of memory and other "normal" functions are called "abnormal," but what is really meant is that a different degree and type of mental organization exist "in that body." Therefore, unless the word "personal" is to be restricted to individuals with certain kinds of bodies, we have in many human bodies not much more *personal* organization than exists in higher animals. Thus, leaving concomitant bodies aside, we might say that mental organization varies in degree and type to such an extent that in many instances the line between the "person" and the higher animal is difficult to draw. And once having landed in the animal kingdom, we find degrees of organization extending down to plant life. Hence, the whole organic realm may be said to represent different stages in mental organization.

But we would not base our argument simply on an indication of the possible continuity of the normal mental organization of persons, through abnormal or subnormal developments, with the animal kingdom and with plant life. Only an expert psychologist-biologist-philosopher might argue with authority along these lines. Yet pan-psychism, in considering evolutionary variations and developments the result of the conative activities of lower types of mental organization, does make organic life more intelligible.[102] For there is no reason a priori

[102] Here Ward's reasons for making mind coextensive with life are accepted. In other words, monadism in the organic world is intelligible and enlightening.

why there should not be such a scale of being. If, then, the activities of plants and animals are in some sense analogous to human behavior, why should we not extend our interpretation by analogy to the activity of other types of bodies than the human and postulate as much mental organization as reasonable analogy allows? To be sure, the nearer we come to inorganic nature the more difficult the conception of being-for-self becomes, but given the slightest iota of memory in the most elementary form of plant life where adaptation (striving) to the physical environment is observable, and the difficulty is not insuperable. If the theist can think of God as an idealized person (but not, we insist, with a nature completely transcending the fundamental characteristics of our own), may not his imagination work backwards similarly? On this view physical nature is still the energizing of God's will, which is the medium of interaction between a scale of beings from the most perfect human personality to spiritual beings with an almost negligible specious present and memory. And is not such a view more consistent with the facts of experience and the personalistic method of interpreting the objective continuum in terms of self-experience?

I. WARD'S ARGUMENT FOR GOD'S GOODNESS

So far Ward has shown that pluralism must lead to the postulation of God in order to explain the ontological order of the world. But we remember that he also insisted that if pluralism is to account for the conservation of values, it must indicate a moral Unity which "ensure[s] a teleological unity for their varied ends, in being . . . the impersonated Ideal of every mind," [103] the ultimate end of ends. The argument at this point is neither clear nor consistent, but we may begin by indicating the more empirical elements in Ward's argument.

Reflecting on the empirical nature of good and evil, Ward finds that there is no principle of evil, that evil lives simply by deceiving persons, that left to itself it would die, while good grows by its multiplication.

But there is no unity, no principle of evil (or of error) and no permanence of evils (or of errors) to set over against such conservation of values

[103] *Realm of Ends*, p. 442.

(both intellectual and moral) as we find. Such evils flourish only disguised *sub specie boni*: . . . The good like the true then tends to 'prevail'; and herein lies the essence of moral progress.[104]

Evil has no solidarity, and the fact that progress *has* been made shows it is not insuperable.[105] Now, from the foregoing, the problem of evil notwithstanding, we would suggest that Ward might well have concluded that the personal Ground of the universe was not evil.[106] The philosopher, after all, must meet the problem of goodness as well as the problem of evil. And we, borrowing from Plato, may add that not only has evil neither solidarity nor principle, but, in so far as it succeeds at all, it does so by presupposing a certain amount of good. As Plato indicated, for an adventure of plunder to be successful there must be loyalty and honesty among the thieves. A universe so organized that goodness intrinsically succeeds and is the only basis of any lasting achievement may not be one in which we can be *absolutely* certain that God always hits the mark, but it certainly provides a basis for moral confidence and optimism. But we continue with Ward's theory of value and the remainder of his argument which is not, we believe, adequate.

Ward, having investigated the connection between feeling and value, is so impressed with their interrelationship that he concludes: " 'The value of an object' then, we may say with Meinong consists (*besteht*) in the fact that a subject takes, could take or at least reasonably should take an interest in that object." [107] In his *Psychological Principles*, Ward also points out, as he discusses the development of moral ideals in the individual, that from the very dawn of life "spontaneous sympathy" not only coexists with self-interest but indeed precedes self-development and "egoistic reflexion." [108] The essential point for our discussion, however, is that valuation, "like the analogous theoretical advance, . . . begins with what is

---

[104] Muirhead, ed., *Contemporary British Philosophy*, II, 52. Cf. *Realm of Ends*, pp. 374 and 446.

[105] Cf. *Realm of Ends*, pp. 133–137.

[106] See below, Chapter VII, pp. 259–265.

[107] *Psychological Principles*, p. 388.

[108] *Ibid.*, pp. 396, 397.

only 'psychologically objective' — temporary and individual values: permanent and universal values, the axiological objective, it reaches last of all." But since psychology cannot touch the problem of "the epistemologically objective," he does not there go into "the sanctions of ethics." [109] In other words, our valid moral ideals arise from the rational criticism of private valuations in the light of intersubjective valuation. On this view consistently developed (as in Ward's natural epistemology) the objectivity of values does not mean their independent existence in God's mind, or elsewhere, but simply their validity for human individuals existing in this universe. If the objectivity of knowledge based on intersubjective intercourse is its over-individuality, then the same holds for values (at least on Ward's view of the origin of value); and the temptation to hypostatize validity, as Tennant points out, must be overcome in both the physical and moral realm. That Ward ultimately fails to do so in the realm of values is clear particularly in his last essay, entitled "The Christian Ideas of Faith and Eternal Life."

Speaking of the "common intellectual world" made possible through intersubjective intercourse he says:

> Of this world the lowest or sensory level of experience gives no hint and the lower animals never get so far. *And yet it is there.* Then, may there not also be a yet higher — we may call it a spiritual world — which mere intelligence cannot discern? Nevertheless we may have hints of it from other sides of our being, for intellect is neither the only nor the highest of human "faculties." And surely we find such hints — truths that live to perish never, noble deeds long done that never die, things of beauty which are a joy forever! All these have a meaning and value for us, which are quite beyond the purview of science.[110] Yet none the less they too are there; and we have come to call them "the true, the beautiful and the good" — eternal values, for they are not temporal events. And again the intelligence which enables us to express this appreciation does not explain it, and is not its source.[111]

Thus, Ward, joining hands with Martineau, Pringle-Pattison, and Taylor, has hypostatized value, impersonate it as

[109] *Ibid.*, p. 389.
[110] Here Ward refers in a footnote to W. R. Sorley, *Moral Values and the Idea of God* (1918), pp. 286 ff., with whom we shall deal in our next chapter.
[111] *Essays*, pp. 354, 355.

he may in a spiritual God. Turning to the *Realm of Ends,* we note a similar line of argument.

Implicit in the last quotation is Ward's Kantian contention that the proof of God lies in our practical natures, that there is no theoretical proof. Ward distinguishes between faith and knowledge, belief in God being the result of the former, which he defines, not as cognitive "but rather primarily as just conative and eventually volitional." [112] It is a matter of "personal trust and confidence" in that which is not completely proved theoretically. But recalling Ward's conception of the process of experience and learning, we realize that knowledge was always the handmaid of an adventurous trust which led beyond present achievement and often resulted in the development of new powers as well as greater knowledge of the self and the environment. On this account, Ward concludes, it is well that knowledge should leave room for faith.

Ward develops his arguments by reminding us that we are now not dealing with individuals originally or incorrigibly psychological hedonists, that the self to be satisfied is rational and moral. Though, in his *Psychological Principles,* Ward defines the primitive conscience as a "higher phase of self-consciousness" [113] resulting from intercommunication, he now speaks of conscience as having authority even when it is disobeyed, as "a power in it [the actual world] working for the righteousness, in which alone the world finds its own meaning and its supreme ideal." [114] Man has "spiritual yearnings" also which faith seeks to satisfy,[115] and religious experience, though private, is not to be left out of account. It is, then, with a religious and morally sensitive individual that we are now to deal, and not the primitive specimen who sold his bed to buy his breakfast. *This* person's postulates or trust may lead to worlds he knew nothing of before. "Humanity already has yearnings and aspirations that the fleshpots of Egypt — material and temporal well-being — can never content; is it, compelled by these longings for higher things,

[112] *Essays,* p. 349.
[113] *Psychological Principles,* p. 369; cf. p. 395.
[114] *Realm of Ends,* p. 373.
[115] *Ibid.,* p. 441.

destined to wander aimlessly in the wilderness for ever unsatisfied?" [116] Unless there is a good God and immortality,
this is, Ward concludes, the result, but fortunately we may
believe in God (and, therefore, immortality) for the following reasons.

We have seen that psychologically and historically an "un-
scientific trustfulness," a *"credo ut intelligam"* [117] pervades
experience. Thus, continues Ward, theistic faith is "only
the full and final phase of an ascending series, beginning in an
instinctive belief in the relatively better and ending in the
rational belief in the absolutely Good, with its corollaries,
the existence of God and the life hereafter." [118] But, surely,
the leap to the "Absolutely Good" from the "better" must be
justified (even though science cannot deny it),[119] for the
Absolute is not separated from the relatively better by degree
but in quality, and, as Tennant remarks somewhere, *relative*
implies *correlative*, not *absolute*.

But Ward comes to closer grips with his problem when he
holds that belief in God, though "a practical position . . .
is none the less deserving of the title rational " [120] in the sense
that only then does the world process have a purpose or meaning, a meaning impossible to define apart from man, the
highest value we know. To be sure, Ward continues, the
meaning of the world is not to be interpreted by man's whims
or mere desires. "A good deal depends surely upon the rationality of the desires" to which we would have the universe
respond. But the moral ideal that "places the highest good
of each in the highest good of all," which "the best of men
. . . regard as absolutely binding and yet — because self-imposed — as absolutely free," [121] this ideal is certainly not unreasonable. However, the difficulty arises that, the world
and man being what they are, the realization of our ideal
of good will is impossible. To this objection Ward capitulates

[116] *Ibid.*, pp. 425, 426.
[117] *Ibid.*, p. 416.
[118] *Ibid.*
[119] Cf. *ibid.*, p. 417.
[120] *Ibid.*, p. 418.
[121] *Ibid.*, p. 420. Here, we note, Ward agrees with Martineau rather than
with Pringle-Pattison.

too easily, in the light of his remarks about the solidarity of goodness, and answers: "if man stands alone and if this life is all, the objection is hardly to be gainsaid." [122]

But then we are confronted by a serious dilemma. Either the world is not rational or man does not stand alone and this life is not all. But it cannot be *rational* to conclude that the world is not rational, least of all when an alternative is open to us that leaves room for its rationality — the alternative of postulating God and the future life.[123]

If the word "rational" in this quotation means the same thing in each instance, the argument is tautologous and begs the question. (Furthermore, the empiricist, for whom the rationality of the universe is to be demonstrated, cannot prove a certain contention by appealing simply to the rationality of the universe.) But the *rational* we have italicized evidently means reasonable in the sense of "most coherent," and that sentence really means: But it cannot be coherent to conclude that man is alone in the world when by postulating God we can avoid this conclusion. However, the very contention to be proved is that the facts of the world indicate man is not alone. If the rest of nondivine reality in relation to man rendered his ideals impossible to realize, if man in other words *were* alone, as Ward at this point seems to admit, there would be no hope of finding the hypothesis of God coherent. Once we admit that the world and man *here and now* are such that we can say "it is good" only by appealing to a good God and not to either of his creations, we have taken the foundations from any empirical argument for God's goodness. Whether man will be alone or not in the future can only be argued by reference to the present and the past. If reference to the past and present could show man to be alone, then there would be no basis for argument. At the bottom of this reasoning also is the fear that morality loses its vitality if it cannot be assured of the future, a point we find developed as Ward offers the hypothesis of God as a solution for the problem of egoism and altruism.

Theism does not, Ward argues, render egoism and altruism

[122] *Realm of Ends*, p. 421.
[123] *Ibid.*

compatible by providing sanctions, but by making unselfishness rest on a living faith in a God who has "a definite moral ideal as an eternal purpose, which finite wills alone might strain after and never realize." "To any other being I may decline to say, Thy will not mine be done, but not to God, if I believe in him." [124] But once more the argument goes around in circles, for if one can believe in such a good God and know his will, of course there will be no refusal to be unselfish! Such self-denial rests on the very confidence the grounds for which must be established. Though one may grant Ward's conclusions, his argument "from faith" seems simply an argument from faith not rationally justified. One final word must be said about religious experience.

As already indicated, Ward recognizes the existence of religious experience, but he does not believe it can in itself be used as evidence for God, and, in any case, he is looking for "evidence . . . of a purely objective and scientific kind, not merely evidence which could satisfy only persons with certain subjective convictions lying outside the purview of science proper." [125] Yet the presence of religious experience in which one is conscious of a higher spiritual being, which is believed in not through ejective interpretation but because of a subjective certainty of unity, cannot be denied. But, to repeat, this "inward conviction . . . is for *the purposes of our discussion*, to be classed as faith, not as knowledge, in so far as it is — epistemologically, though not psychologically — subjective, incommunicable and objectively unverifiable." [126] The veracity of religious experience is in the last analysis to be judged by "good works" which constitute the ultimate justification for faith in God.

J.   Estimate and Summary

This examination of Ward's theistic monadism reveals the greater consistency of his empiricism as compared with that of Martineau and Pringle-Pattison. Indeed, Ward's psycho-

[124] *Ibid.*, p. 422.
[125] *Realm of Ends*, p. 186.
[126] *Ibid.*, p. 452. This position will be developed by Tennant.

logical penetration and philosophical insight constitute him one of the greatest British thinkers and empiricists. It is only at the very end of his argument that this empiricism falters unconsciously, led astray perhaps by the strong imperative of moral experience. He is least empirical as he argues for the objectivity of value. Had he defined the objectivity of value as well as he had defined the objectivity of knowledge, his empiricism might not have flagged. As a matter of fact, it is around this problem of the meaning of objectivity as applied to value that the argument for God's goodness has centered. As we turn to the theism of W. R. Sorley, we shall confront this problem again and find moral realism at its best. But let us first summarize the salient points in this chapter.

1. Beginning *in mediis rebus*, Ward finds that experience (a) is a unified complex of conative, cognitive, and volitional activities which (b) always involves a dualism of subject and object, and (c) striving for a better adjustment to its environment (d) develops itself, a common world, and custom, through intercourse with other selves and nature.

2. The mechanical scheme is applicable, and then not strictly, to only a part of nature, and breaks down completely in the face of organic evolution. The latter is most adequately explained if mind is considered coextensive with life, for then variations and developments may be explained by the success or failure of conative creatures to preserve themselves.

3. The unity of nature is not an axiom but a postulate arising from the experience of self-unity and the interaction of subject and object developed by intersubjective intercourse. The ultimate "reals" of nature are psychical monads.

4. Pluralism accounts for law by the development of habits in the hedonic monads which were originally in an inchoate state of being. But pluralism, in failing to account (a) for astronomical order, (b) for the awakening of slumbering monads, and (c) for the conservation of values which alone makes evolution meaningful, needs to be modified and developed by the theistic hypothesis.

5. Theism modifies pluralism by its doctrine of creation, which though empirically neutral is justified rationally as

the best explanation of the order of the world made possible by the immanence of a transcendent God in his creation. But the doctrine of a transcendent God that cannot exist apart from his creation is contradictory, and the following suggestion was offered.

6. The creation (of persons especially) is a new fact in God's experience, and it is the achievement of God's purpose, his Fatherhood, which is impossible apart from creation, rather than his ontological being, within which there is an obstructing element that retarded the fulfillment only of God's purpose.

7. Sympathetic *rapport*, one kind of interaction, (a) does not yield direct knowledge and (b) is meaningless among memory-less monads whose individuality is empirically inconceivable and whose structure makes contingency among them unintelligible. The result is that the uniformity and catastrophes of the physical world must be owing directly to God's activity.

8. Personalism does not explain interaction but justly confines it to the Creator and created, but personalism should, in the interests of greater consistency and empiricism, be modified to include the pan-psychistic view of the organic world.

9. Ward's argument for God's goodness in so far as it rests on empirical grounds is acceptable, but his moral argument hypostatizes validity, and begs the question in assuming the rationality of the universe to prove that the Good is ultimate.

CHAPTER V

WILLIAM SORLEY'S MORAL ARGUMENT FOR GOD

A. SORLEY'S INTELLECTUAL DEVELOPMENT

WILLIAM RITCHIE SORLEY (1885–1935) received his collegiate training at the University of Edinburgh, where he studied under Professors Blackie, Calderwood, Tait, and Campbell Fraser. His friends among the students included A. S. Pringle-Pattison, R. B. Haldane, D. M. Ross, George Adam Smith, and R. Adamson. Smith later became Sorley's brother-in-law, and Adamson his colleague at Aberdeen. After taking his degree, Sorley spent three years in the study of theology at New College, Edinburgh, though his interest in theology led him, not to ordination, but to two more summers of study at Tübingen and Berlin. The results of these studies were published soon after he left Edinburgh, where he had been the Shaw Fellow, to study at the University of Cambridge. First was the article, published by *Mind* in 1880, "Jewish Mediaeval Philosophy and Spinoza," which was highly praised by Professor Zeller of Berlin for both its method and its conclusion, that the essence of Spinoza's thought was not to be found in the medieval Jewish philosophers who influenced him. The second essay, which won the Hulsean Prize for 1880, was published the next year as a book, entitled *Jewish Christians and Judaism*. Both these early studies no doubt supplied the training required for the construction of his later volume, *A History of English Philosophy*, the best historical treatment of British thought to date.

At Cambridge, Sorley came under the influence of James Ward and Henry Sidgwick. Though Ward ultimately had the greater effect upon Sorley, Sidgwick also was a source of stimulation and aid. Tennant writes interestingly:

To Sidgwick and his lectures Sorley went. And, as he had already been arriving at convictions opposed to some of those which he would hear his teacher expound, we can understand the remark, said to have been made by Sidgwick, that Sorley's attitude in the lecture-room suggested "a well-bred atheist listening to a sermon." In a memoir which Sorley subsequently wrote he spoke of the powerful influence, both intellectual and moral, which Sidgwick exerted on his pupils, and of the training which they received from him in the philosophical temper of candour, self-criticism, and regard for truth; and he ended with the words "there are (in Cambridge) not a few who feel that the wisest and justest man they have ever known has passed away." [1]

This same spirit of painstaking research, as well as a joyous regard for truth, was evident even on the surface of Sorley's own teaching. Our personal experience of this scholar corroborates Tennant's statement:

> Though Sorley was as reserved as he was modest he could, all through his long career as a teacher, put young men at their ease with him by his simplicity in manner and induce them to talk to him as to an equal. He would insist on his students' "putting things through their own minds," as he expressed it; he could always welcome their criticism of his own views and arguments. . . ; and, for all his kindliness, he could on occasion be frankly outspoken and prompt to deal with any sign of affectation or conceit. [2]

Sorley's high regard for Ward is evidenced not only by his own thought but also by the fact that Ward was appointed to the Gifford Lectureship, as was Royce, while Sorley was occupant of a chair at Aberdeen, and by his coöperation with Professor Stout in selecting and editing some of Ward's important essays in a volume (which includes an excellent memoir of Ward by his daughter, Olwen Ward Campbell) entitled *Essays in Philosophy*. Sorley became a colleague of Ward in 1900 when he succeeded Sidgwick as the Knightbridge Professor of Moral Philosophy, the chair he held until his resignation in 1933.

Sorley's teaching previous to his final return to Cambridge was done at the University College of London (1886–87), as Professor of Logic and Philosophy at Cardiff (1888–94), and as Professor of Moral Philosophy at Aberdeen (1894–1900). Wherever he went, the impress of his enterprising and courageous spirit was felt. It is no surprise that Edinburgh

---

[1] *Proceedings of the British Academy*, XXI (1935), 395.
[2] *Ibid.*, p. 398.

conferred on her worthy son the honorary degree of LL.D. in 1900, or that in 1905 Sorley was elected a Fellow of the British Academy. A man of many interests extending from literature to politics, Sorley represents an ideal which many in his own profession might well emulate, at least if philosophy is to be the leaven of everyday life.

There can be no doubt of the main trend of Sorley's philosophical thought. His rather short-lived sympathy for T. H. Green's idealistic theory of knowledge may be associated perhaps with the fact that his first important ethical essay, on "The Historical Method," was published along with the contributions of such men as Pringle-Pattison and R. B. Haldane in the volume, dedicated to Green in 1883, entitled *Essays in Philosophical Criticism*. In this essay at the beginning of his career, Sorley gave early indication of the direction of his thought by insisting that the validity of knowledge and of ethical ideals is not shaken by the historical account of their development. The historical method "implies categories of which it can only trace the historical manifestation, leaving the investigation of their logical position and nature to the theory of knowledge or to the theory of action." [3]

His interest in the significance of evolution for ethical theory found further expression in Sorley's next work, *The Ethics of Naturalism*, but it is in *Recent Tendencies in Ethics* (1904), that the trend of his own thought begins more definitely to converge on doctrines whose final development constitutes the burden of the Gifford Lectures. That the universe is unintelligible apart from man, that the canons of evolution supply the rules of living but not the ethical standard of good living, that "the moral concept . . . cannot be distilled out of any knowledge about the laws of existence or of occurrence," [4] that a nonsensuous and nonintellectual yet real moral experience is part of the data of a comprehensive philosophy, that there must be a criterion for judging

[3] A. S. Pringle-Pattison and R. B. Haldane, eds., *Essays in Philosophical Criticism* (1883), p. 125.

[4] *Recent Tendencies in Ethics*, p. 131. Unless otherwise stated all references in this chapter will be to Sorley's works.

conflicting ethical systems, that the ultimate unity of reality
is one of ethical purpose (and not a mechanistic or rationalistic one) — these ideas form some of the more important conclusions of his early studies.

The general philosophical significance of the theory of
evolution is discussed in a brilliant and penetrating paper,
"The Interpretation of Evolution," read before the British
Academy, November 24, 1909, on the fiftieth anniversary of
Darwin's *Origin of Species*. The main substance of this and
Sorley's numerous other essays is expressed in *Moral Values
and the Idea of God*, for the writer the most critical and able
exposition of the moral argument for God in late British
thought, a work which towers above Pringle-Pattison's *Idea
of God* in force and clarity as well as in philosophical objectivity, and in all of these and other respects seems superior
to Taylor's *Faith of a Moralist*.

In these Gifford Lectures Sorley developed his belief that
the argument for God does not depend, as his teacher Ward
had maintained, on a spiritualistic metaphysics. True as it
may be that, as Ward says somewhere, Sorley's metaphysics
is a "systematic occasionalism," his idealism is grounded on
the metaphysical objectivity of value in a Supreme Mind,
whose ethical purpose is expressed in the reality of finite
persons to whose moral development life and the physical
environment are instrumental. This leaves no doubt that
ethical personality is the highest category for Sorley.

Though far from the opinion that his is the sole or necessary approach to belief in God, Sorley's own results are
reached "without bringing into consideration . . . religious
experience," [5] and a word may be said here on this point.
Sorley does not believe that religious experience can be ignored in a "final philosophical view," yet, allowing that
"religious experience is not allied with one form of theory
only," he still believes that "its most perfect development"[6]
is consistent with ethical theism. At all events, Sorley would
insist that the "philosophy of religion must bring . . . [the]

[5] Muirhead, ed., *Contemporary British Philosophy*, II, 266.
[6] *Ibid.*

special results [of the religious consciousness] into relation with the results of metaphysical and ethical philosophy before it can regard its answer as complete to the questions of the significance and validity of religious experience." [7] It is the moral life which most justifies confidence in a personal God.

Consequently, our main concern in this chapter will be with Sorley's moral argument for God, and other aspects of his thought will be treated at relevant points in the exposition of Tennant's philosophical theology.

B. THE PROBLEM

The fundamental thought underlying the whole of *Moral Values and the Idea of God* is that no adequate view of reality is possible without the just evaluation of the contribution of moral experience. This method reverses the traditional procedure of philosophers, who, deducing an ethical theory from a nonethical view of ultimate reality, presupposed that values ought not, or would not, make any difference to an impartial view of the facts of experience. But Sorley has two objections to this latter approach. First, all philosophers who disregard moral values in working out their metaphysical theories are really not interpreting the whole of experience. Second: "At certain points these theories all pass from propositions about reality or what 'is' to propositions about goodness or about what 'ought to be.' They make a transition to a new predicate; and the difficulty for them lies in justifying this transition." [8] That is, merely by thinking one cannot appreciate value any more than one can see a table merely by experiencing value. Both perceptual and valuational experiences are ultimate nonrational factors which together ought to be the data of a comprehensive metaphysics. "The 'reasons of the heart' are themselves facts in the life of mind, and are based on the more elementary facts of appreciation or experience of value." [9] Instead of a metaphysical ethics, Sorley pro-

---

[7] "Does Religion Need a Philosophy?" *Hibbert Journal*, XI (1913), 578.
[8] *Moral Values and the Idea of God* (3rd ed., 1930), pp. 8, 9.
[9] Muirhead, *op. cit.*, II, 248.

poses an ethico-theoretical metaphysics which endeavors to discover whether the "ought" contains a clue to the "is."

Thus, from the very beginning, Sorley's approach is empirical. Accordingly, though insisting that philosophers cease regarding the "ought" as an idle epiphenomenon of the "is," he is quite emphatic in holding that the "ought" and the "is" are different experiences and that the former cannot be derived from the latter, though, as a part of experience, it may shed light on its ultimate constitution. Thus, speaking of Rationalism and Naturalism, Sorley writes: "Their exposition has made clearer than ever the distinction which they so palpably ignored — the distinction between 'is' and 'ought,' between existence and value or goodness." [10] Reversing the procedure of the scientist, Sorley, on the other hand, considers first the realm of values in abstraction from the realm of existence as such (apart from value); then, having developed a theory of value, he investigates the relations of the two systems to each other. Before turning to Sorley's description of ethical values and their place in experience, we may simply remark that the temptation will be to overlook instances in which value and existence inextricably modify each other.

C. The Varieties of Value

Just as the interpretation of nonvaluational facts presupposes an investigation of the realm of experience which contains those facts, so the study of the relation of value to reality must presuppose a knowledge of the values experienced by consciousness. Accordingly, Sorley devotes two chapters to an investigation of the varieties and meaning of value respectively.

In his axiology, Sorley distinguishes values by their objects (Happiness, Truth, Beauty, and Goodness, for example), and draws formal distinctions between intrinsic and instrumental, permanent and transient, catholic and exclusive, and higher and lower values. Values for him exist only in and for consciousness. Furthermore, the superiority of permanent values

[10] *Moral Values*, p. 15.

(like knowledge, art, and morality) to transient values is based on their *independence of material conditions*, and the permanence of personal life itself. The higher values are catholic because *man and the universe are so constituted* that the attainment of truth, or goodness, or beauty by one self does not preclude the possession of each by others. The limited amount of material goods, on the other hand, renders their catholicity impossible. Since moral value, the willing of the best, is possible under all circumstances, it is the most catholic value.[11] Finally, in the comparison of values, the idea of scale must be relinquished for that of system. For, suggestions of quantitative estimates of value either rest on the illegitimate hypothesis that positive value belongs to pleasure only, or they leave ambiguous the nature of the ultimate value which is supposed to remain identical under the varieties of its manifestations.

In this connection, let us emphasize, before passing on, that every distinction among values is grounded by Sorley upon what is taken to be a truth or possible truth of reality, that material things are transient and limited, that personality may be permanent, and that quantitative distinctions between values are inadequate. Thus, the importance of values is for us dependent on certain intrinsically nonvaluational facts.

D.   The Meaning and Nature of Value

Before attempting a more detailed analysis of Sorley's theory of value, we may first state his general position.

Sorley discredits the attempts of psychological analysis or of social history to invalidate the possible objectivity of value. "Morality begins with judgments about good and evil, right and wrong, and not simply with emotions. . . ."[12] In this respect the moral judgment is on the same level as any other judgment of experience, for it refers to something beyond the mental state of the subject, and, therefore, its emotional or other antecedents can no more invalidate it than they can other judgments of experience. Furthermore, moral

[11] Cf. *Moral Values*, p. 49.
[12] *Ibid.*, p. 69.

values do not merely indicate the objective relations on which
they are founded, for in themselves the relations have no
value; rather, in becoming values do these relations take on a
new and living, and not merely conceptual, relation to mind.
Though our value-judgments are based on our apprehension
of qualities, "when we predicate worth or value we assert
or imply that the object is worth being or ought to be . . .";[13]
our assertion is one not only of existence but also of moral
approbation.

Sorley's position and our own in relation to it may be
clearer if we employ several distinctions. First is the distinction between *value-claim* and *true value*. As Brightman defines them,[14] the first means anything a person is interested
in, and denotes the truth that the value of a thing for a person
arises in his desire for or want of it. A thing has true value,
however, when it *ought* to be desired. The first is descriptive
and for Sorley instrumental, while the second is normative
and ethical. In the light of this distinction it is clear that
Sorley means by an ethical value-judgment a judgment that
something is truly valuable. The term "value" for him is
normative in denotation, and consequently a value-judgment
has as its subject-matter something which ought to be, whether
or not it is desired or has been desired.

Second, it is evident, as Sorley holds in the latter part of
the third chapter, that value does not consist in the objective
relations of things to each other. In either of its meanings,
value involves another relation to the subject of the things
in the objective relation, and that is why we ourselves maintained [15] that value was a dynamic relational quality created
by the existence of a new relation between the thing and the
subject. This new relation, we should hold, must be at least
one of desire for the object; but any value-claim for the person in earnest with life becomes the matter for the specifically
moral evaluation, which involves the consideration of the
value-claim in relation to the person's ideals, or approved

[13] *Ibid.*, p. 77.
[14] Cf. E. S. Brightman, *Religious Values* (1925), pp. 15, 74.
[15] Cf. above, Chapter III, p. 71.

plans of action. Thus, if we begin with existential relations, the specifically moral judgment is of a dynamic relation two removes from them, the first new relation (introduced by the existence of desire) being value-claim, and the second (introduced by the evaluation of the value-claim through considering its relation to the ideal) being true value. This explicates and is not inconsistent with Sorley's view that value involves a new relation of things and their relation to the subject, though, as we shall see, the relation here indicated between value-claim and true value does not recommend itself to Sorley. We may now proceed with our exposition.

Further delimiting the meaning of value, Sorley rejects, for reasons similar to those just given, views which identify value with the qualities or properties of an object as such, though, as he insists, "our judgment of value is indeed *based upon* an apprehension of qualities — the colours of the sky or the volitional attitude of the man." [16] Sorley continues: "But it [the value-judgment] is not merely the assertion of these qualities or of another quality in addition. When we predicate worth or value we assert or imply that the object is worth being or ought to be." [17] That is, whereas the addition of a quality to an object is conceptual only, the attribution of true value to it "has a definite bearing upon existence," [18] in the sense, we take it, that every effort must then be bent to realize the existence of the object or attitude so valued. Therefore, "value is not reduced to an existential proposition; but the notion of value always implies a relation to existence. . . ." [19] What the exact relation to existence is remains to be seen when we discuss the chapter "Relative and Absolute Value." The relation now to be considered is that between value-claim and true value, or what Sorley calls the judgment of value.

The main contention, to which other considerations are subsidiary, is, we have seen, that "the objective character" [20]

[16] *Moral Values*, p. 77.
[17] *Ibid.*
[18] *Ibid.*, p. 78. A. E. Taylor would confirm Sorley on both of these points. Cf. *Faith of a Moralist*, I, 37 ff.
[19] See *Moral Values*, p. 72.   [20] *Ibid.*

of moral judgments cannot be denied on the basis of psychological or historical analysis. The word which cries for definition in a discussion of this sort is "objective," and we must stop immediately and outline the more important meanings.

(1) All experience is objective (as Martineau, Pringle-Pattison, Ward, and Sorley hold) in that there is a dualism of subject and object, regardless of whether the judgment is finally true or untrue. Following Tennant's painstaking methodology, we shall denote this objectivity (or mere objective reference), which all other meanings presuppose, and which is psychological rather than epistemological, by an *o* (as in object). Such objectivity is purely private and affected by all the idiosyncrasies of the subject.

(2) The word "objective" may also be used epistemologically (as Ward,[21] and Tennant, following Kant, use it) to mean the opposite of private experience, namely, to denote the object (now written *Object*) of common or over-individual discourse. This Object may include values as well as phenomenal "things." The point is that the discussion of objects (of private experience) reveals fundamental similarities in them which are not therefore owing to the peculiarities of the subjects and issues in the definition of the Object. This meaning *presupposes* the definition given by G. F. Stout, which emphasizes the control of the subjective processes of cognition, feeling, and willing, by the nature of the object. "Subjective activity is always a process of experimentation: the result of the experiment depends on the object." [22]

(3) A third meaning of the words "object" and "objective," in contrast to the second, which is epistemological and phenomenal, is metaphysical. This meaning denotes the quality commonly called objective, that is, as characterizing or being the metaphysical entity which is the source of the (second) Object and *may* be the source of the (first) object. This third meaning Tennant denotes by the Greek ω, but we shall speak of the *metaphysical object* and *metaphysically*

[21] Ward, *Realm of Ends*, pp. 122, 123.
[22] Baldwin, *Dictionary of Philosophy and Psychology*, II, 192. Cf. also Eisler, *Wörterbuch der Philosophischen Begriffe.*

objective. These definitions are fundamental, and views of the objectivity of value may be classified in relation to them. Those already considered belong in this class, in the sense that values have their ultimate reality in God's nature. Before classifying Sorley's view, we must study it further.

As already indicated, our philosopher, though admitting that genetic and descriptive psychology sheds important light on the genesis and development of moral approbation, denies that such investigations can have anything to do with the validity of moral judgments. Considering two such theories, he says: "In all moral experience there is something which cannot be simply identified with pleasure or desire, but contains a *differentiating fact which makes it moral* and not merely pleasant or desired." [23] Here we are reminded of Martineau's insistence that moral obligation is a unique and *sui generis* experience, though Sorley takes fuller account of the emotional and social factors involved. [24] Sorley's objection to the reduction of moral approbation to pleasure and desire is that the essence of morality consists in the *choice between* pleasures and desires. (Hereafter we shall speak only of the desire theory, for the pleasure theory may be reduced to it.) Moral ideas, or true values, provide a standard in accordance with which preference is given to certain desires over others: "to the permanent over the transient, to the social over the selfish, to the spiritual over the sensual." [25] But the important point is that the moral judgment or preference "is not got out of the desires themselves [or their objects] but is an appreciation of desire founded upon objective discrimination." [26] What the object of "objective discrimination" is, we are not told. Since it cannot be either objects or desires, it must be the perception of a value-object in no degree constituted a value by its being desired, but felt to be obligatory as the standard by reference to which desires receive their moral evaluation. Desire may be an experience concomitant with the moral value-judgment, but the moral quality of the total experience is imparted to it by a non-

[23] *Moral Values*, p. 57 (italics mine).
[24] Cf. *ibid.*, p. 59.
[25] *Ibid.*, p. 63.
[26] *Moral Values*, p. 63.

conative and a non-desired (not undesired) element, whose validity is unquestioned at the time.

Resuming our analysis, we may say that, on Sorley's view, men in our present stage of development begin with certain value-judgments of the type "this is good," which, though appearing "in the midst of emotional and impulsive experiences . . . is not itself either a feeling or a striving." [27] No matter what the ancestors of the moral judgment may be, the genetic psychologist must begin working with this present mental fact, and Sorley correctly insists that the very quality, "oughtness," must not be allowed to fall through the cracks of analysis. (It must be noted that for Sorley not only moral judgments but moral emotions also are *sui generis*.)[28]

These moral judgments, however, may be wrong in any given instance, "but the assumption of the value-judgment is always that there is a value which may be predicated of this or the other situations." [29] That is, the judgment "this is good," like the judgment "this is a book," may or may not be correct, but it presupposes that there are true values in the world, just as the latter presupposes that there are books, the question now being whether *this* is one of them. The claim either judgment has to truth is not affected by its psychological antecedents. The claim of a value-judgment "is not that the subject desires a certain object or is pleased with it, any more than the judgment of sense-perception means that he has certain sensations." [30] Thus for Sorley, value-claims, though concomitants of true value, have no intrinsic connection with true value, but the judgment of true value (though it may be wrong) is a judgment independent of them and one by which they are criticized.[31] The judgment of true value is first objective, but it claims to be valid of a value or moral order independent of the subject and over-social or absolute, that is to say, independent of all human subjects. It would be correct to say that values belong to the class of subsistents

[27] *Ibid.*, p. 69. [29] *Ibid.*, p. 68.
[28] *Ibid.* [30] *Ibid.*, p. 72.
[31] Once more Taylor would agree with Sorley. Cf. *Faith of a Moralist*, I, 44 ff.

or validities, which are not existent though they are "implicated in reality" or "valid *of reality*." "We say of them not
that they exist, but that they are valid; but their validity
cannot be separated from their implication in reality." [32]
That is, they are not "simply ideas in the mind"; nor are they
"entities with a separate existence of their own." [33] For this
kind of object there is no place in our classification of the
meanings of "object." But since Sorley, in a later stage of
his argument, finds the home of these values to be God, we
may well say that true values are metaphysically objective,
for they have their being, independent of all human desire
and cognition, in God who is their source.

E.   CRITICISM OF SORLEY'S VIEW

Though we shall try to show that man's values are not mere
subjective fancies, that they do have a cosmic Ally, we do
not believe that the position represented at its best by Sorley
can be maintained. We hold that it rests on a defective analysis of moral experience and an inadequate theory of moral
knowledge. Such an analysis of our consciousness of ideals
with the analogy of natural knowledge in mind leads, we
shall see, to a confounding of epistemological and psychological issues, and to a misinterpretation of the source of the
authority of ethical ideals.[34] Views already suggested will be
developed as we proceed.

If our analysis is correct, the moral consciousness of the
individual is for Sorley a *perceptive* function that compre-
hends moral objects,[35] which may be concomitant and even
identical with objects of desire but are not reducible to them.
A value is not a moral value because it is desired, but it
derives moral significance because of its relation to something
which ought to be desired. Now, the perplexing element underlying Sorley's discussion is his use of the terms "judgment

[32] *Moral Values*, p. 188.
[33] *Ibid.*
[34] Cf. my article, "The Authority of Ethical Ideals," *Journal of Philosophy*,
XXXIII (May 7, 1936), 269–275.
[35] The word "object" will be used in none other than its epistemological
sense, and, therefore, not for "thing."

of value" or "value-judgment," "moral experience," and "moral idea" as synonyms. Does not this confuse an epistemological and a psychological issue? That is, though moral obligation is expressed in judgments of value which would be impossible without ethical experience (just as sensational experience is the ground of existential judgments), can any number of value-judgments exhaust *the moral consciousness* or the feeling of moral obligation which underlies them all? We come directly to our point.

When Sorley says that moral experience cannot be reduced to pleasure or desire (or, we would say, to any other element of experience), we agree that the present fact of *moral obligation* must not fall through the cracks of psychological analysis, for one psychological fact must not be explained away by others. But, psychologically speaking, is the experience of moral obligation, of "ought," a cognitive experience? We refer to the experience as lived, *erlebt*, not as known. If our own interpretation is correct, it is a peculiar kind of compulsion rather than a cognition, though it may be accompanied by cognition. For, of course, we never experience "ought" apart from a specific object, and we consequently say "I ought to do this." Yet the "ought" itself is in no way a perception or intuition of a "this" or object. And our contention, therefore, is that what makes an experience moral is not the cognition of some unique moral object, irreducible to desire, but the presence of this *cognitively innocent* feeling of "ought." The "ought" is a compulsion to action, not to cognition, which is its logical antecedent. However, our philosophers, biased by the analogy of natural knowledge, conceive of moral experience as a cognitive functioning rendered moral by the fact that its object is moral (value). One need not wonder, therefore, at their insistence that the moral judgment is not one of desire or interest, that value cannot be defined in terms of desire. For certainly the experience of obligation cannot by any stretch of psychological analysis be reduced to want or desire. The "ought" is *sui generis*. But then, all one can say is that the "ought" in the judgment "I ought to do this" cannot be reduced to desire. Whether the "this" can be reduced to desire still remains a question. Certainly, the fact that desire is not intrinsic to the experience of moral obligation does not mean that desire is not intrinsic to the "this," or value.

Further introspection and analysis of the "ought" reveals, if we are correct, not an experience of mere compulsion which in itself would be unintelligible, but a compulsion or obligation to will the Good to the best of one's ability in the given situation. Moral obligation, as such, means "I must do whatever I consider good"; it is not a knowing of the Good. This moral imperative, in other words, gives no light on the nature of the Good, though whatever appears to the self as good (or better than any other alternative) in a situation always becomes imperative. Whatever the Good may be ultimately, so long as one considers any particular action good, whether it be head-hunting or contributing to the community chest, that action becomes obligatory, and only that action. This seems to be the psychology of the moral experience, and it must be kept logically separate from the epistemology of the experience.

Let the above contention be granted, and it follows that when I say "I ought to do this," the "this" must be the subject of a logically and chronologically prior judgment "this is good." If one is conscious of obligation to the Good, then the judgment "this is good" is immediately followed by the imperative command, "I ought to do this," as the conclusion of a moral syllogism. The full meaning of the statement "this is good" is not merely "this ought to be done," as Sorley holds, but "this is something good which ought to be done."

The epistemological problem arises when we consider what the statement "this is good" means apart from the moral imperative immediately evoked by it. It is suggested that "this is good" implies and presupposes on the part of the subject a notion clear or indistinct of what "*the* Good" is, so that the meaning of "this is good" turns out to be, "this, if realized, will help to achieve the Good." Hence, the problem of knowledge revolves about the question: What is the Good? Into this problem we cannot go, but we may address ourselves to the question of primary concern, namely: What are the *data* with which the ethical philosopher must begin? The *problem* is: Among the data of ethics are there, besides value-claims, judgments that claim to discern specifically moral characteristics (or objects) which are not tainted by, though possibly concomitant with, conation? Again, are there moral intuitions of the goodness of actions and events which are good independent of their being desired?

Sorley, as we have seen, insists that though the *appreciation* of value is a subjective, conative, and affective process, the true value apprehended has in itself no constitutive relation to these processes. To quote:

> The origin of the value-judgment may lie in the affective or creative experiences of the individual mind passing the judgment, but its reference is to something beyond that individual mind. The judgment does not mean I, the subject judging, experience pleasure or desire, but that something is good or beautiful or worth desiring.[36]

Just as our apprehension of things arises out of sensation, so our appreciations of value arise out of affective-conative experiences. The *experiencing* of value is subjective, conative, and affective, but the value itself is independent of these processes. Curiously enough, the examples which Sorley uses to illustrate the fact that there is the same reference beyond the self in value-judgments as there is in existential judgments are drawn from aesthetic experience, thus revealing the kind of analogy he has in mind. In any case, he rejects the view that value "consists in the relation which some context presented to a subject has to that subject's sensibility, thus producing pleasure, or to some desire or system of conative tendencies of the subject, to which it promises satisfaction." He insists, on the other hand, that these views in explaining "value as a relation to a subject" rest on a "confusion between the process by means of which we become aware of value and the value itself of which we become aware." [37] (We ourselves reject the reduction of value to pleasure.)

[36] Muirhead, ed., *Contemporary British Philosophy*, II, 250.
[37] *Moral Values*, p. 73.

Sorley, in other words, finds value-claims instrumental to, but not constitutive of, true value or what ought to be.

Two comments may be made. It certainly would be true that not every value-claim would be a true value, but it is possible that the Good may be discovered by a systematization of value-claims (rather than true values) organized according to principles Sorley himself has suggested, such as permanence, and catholicity, and that therefore particular value-claims would become true values, that is, good as helping to realize the Good. It must not be arbitrarily supposed that because value-claims are constituted by the desires of individuals that they have no reference beyond the individual, for conative and affective experiences do refer beyond themselves and are evoked by what is beyond. Consequently, if true value is defined in terms of criticized value-claims, it does not become either a purely subjective creation, or (necessarily) a provincialism of our planet, as Martineau would say, though the nature of the objectivity ascribed to value will have to be redefined (as Objectivity).

Secondly, it seems to us that Sorley, though he might correctly have rejected attempts to reduce *moral obligation* or the "ought" to desire, has misinterpreted the facts in rejecting the definition of *that* which ought to be done in terms of desire. Preoccupied, perhaps, with the belief that the objectivity of moral value could be saved only if moral cognition apprehended an object independent of the mental state and irreducible to desire, he wrongly objectified a characteristic *of the subject*, namely, moral obligation, which cannot be reduced to desire. The "ought," however, has no epistemological value, it is not a source of intuition, and there is, we suggest, no perception of a moral object which is not an object of desire. Value *is* constituted by the interest of mind in an object or action. The "ought" is harnessed to none other than objects of desire or value-claims when these are coherently organized.

To be sure, Sorley might justly inquire: Whence, then, the standard or norm by which to judge between objects of desire, or values? We have the space to indicate the answer only very briefly. A reasonable person, desiring to live, finds the realization of certain desires preferable to other desires because they give greater and more permanent satisfaction (in which pleasure may be an element). The objects of desire may range from sensuous pleasure to self-sacrifice, but the experience of these by the individual desiring them constitutes the data of ethics. The coherent systematization of these experiences of desired objects establishes the nature of the Good. As the total experience of the individual changes and grows from childhood to manhood, his definition of the Good may indeed change (as it has in the history of the race), for he discovers through experiment with values that what once satisfied no longer satisfies. In the individual's search for values the experience of great men and of the race may be a guide, but every judgment of value needs to be criticized by its relation to what he has hitherto deemed the Good. Man's ideals are nothing but the generalization he has made on the basis of values *actually experienced* in part, at least, by himself or others. The point to be emphasized is that at each stage in his moral progress man feels himself obligated to achieve what he considers to be the Good. Hence, if the Good at one time is nationalism, then the individual acknowledging this as the Good is by the very constitution of his nature morally obligated to support everything conducive to nationalism; but if his moral experimentation leads him to consider internationalism as the Good, he once more feels the imperative to work for its realization. The definition of the Good may be made, then, in terms of satisfactions of desire coherently organized, but the obligation to the Good is a *sui generis* experience of the self evoked by whatever the intellect judges to be good. In this way the authority of the Good is not reduced to desire, although the Good is.

Nor does the insistence that value is constituted by the dynamic relation between desire and an object or action embog one in subjectivism, according to which value depends on the individual mind alone for its existence. For any value-claim is not a statement about myself alone, but about myself in relation to the conceived constitution of others and the world in which we live. My judgment of true value is a statement of the fact that a certain object or action is such that in relation to my desires (which reflect my determinate, though growing, nature) it serves certain contemplated ends. Hence, my value-claims and my true values are *controlled* both by my determinate nature which my conative activities express, and by the nature of the environment, personal and natural, within which my nature develops and finds various degrees and kinds of satisfaction. If the self and the environment allowed all values equally there would be no distinction, for example, between transient and permanent values, and so on, as Sorley has well pointed out. A true value is also a statement about myself and the universe, for every time I achieve a true value (or a rationally approved value-claim) I must conclude that my nature and that of the universe are such that certain values I deem myself morally obligated to realize are accessible. This view does not make the conative life a mere subjective process leading to the recognition of value, but it makes value-claims play a part similar to that which sense-impressions play in our knowledge of the external world. Through their rational criticism (influenced by inter-subjective intercourse) we build a common world which we say is not identical with, but at least relevant to, the metaphysical world. In the same way, through the rational criticism of value-claims we build a common, phenomenal [38] valuational world which must be explained, for it is plainly relevant to human life in relation to nature; and the problem now becomes: Does it furnish any evidence for God? The difference in the point of view here presented from Sorley's may be brought out if we consider the criteria of moral value. We first summarize and then attempt an analysis and contrast.

F. THE CRITERIA OF MORAL VALUE

Sorley assumes the general validity of moral experience in order to make possible the criticism of one part with the

---

[38] A phenomenal valuational world is not one to be contrasted with or relevant to a metaphysical value world, as the word "phenomenal" might seem to imply. The same sentence defines what is meant.

assistance of the remainder, and urges that the work of thought is to produce systematic harmony in the content of moral experience. Accordingly, he proceeds to extract general principles from the data of ethical experience, which for him are particular "oughts." He finds, first, that every moral judgment claims objective validity, that contradictory judgments about the same value cannot be true, and that each judgment has universal rather than individual application. Second, though all moral judgments claim validity, they cannot all be valid because they are not mutually consistent. "Any moral judgment which is valid must be coherent with all other valid moral judgments: at least it cannot be inconsistent with any. Freedom from contradiction, coherence, and thus possible systematisation are criteria by which the validity of any moral judgment may be tested." [39] Since all particular moral judgments involve universal principles, the systematization of these may compel the rejection of the first expressions of moral consciousness, and in this way, by weighing each judgment against a system of judgments, we can discriminate between valid and invalid judgments. This same criterion of systematic coherence is used in deciding the validity of all our sense-perceptions, and we cannot consistently reject it in the former sphere and accept it in the latter. But when two or more systems are internally consistent, the problem of deciding between them can be solved only by choosing that system which is most comprehensive and penetrates beneath the conflict by including the greater value of both. So much for Sorley's view in general; we now turn to further analysis and comment.

Every value-judgment for Sorley presupposes that its subject ("this") exists, even though the existence of the thing is a contemplated postulate. "The moral consciousness is thus one aspect of the consciousness of existing reality or of something contemplated as existing." A thing must first exist in order to be good or evil. "But on the other hand the ground of its goodness lies in something else than its mere existence." [40] It is always the realization of the concept or idea that

[39] *Moral Values*, p. 96.   [40] *Ibid.*, p. 85.

forms the subject of the moral judgment. In other words, the moral judgment either approves something already existing, or it approves another contemplated relation or change of something existing, which, when effected, will render the conceived and unrealized good actual.

The problem however is: What is the ground of our approval of a contemplated change or relation? Is it the contemplation of a non-desired, or irreducible moral object, as the writers considered would have us think? Our contention has been that desire for that new relation (since it seems at the time to preserve or make life more attractive, this good being the implicit and inarticulate premise for action) is what gives it value-claim. And our further point is that a preference for another value over a present one (or a change in the present relation which would increase value) is the result of a conceptual idealization based upon present and past experiences of value. This preferred value, if approved as most conducive to what is supposed to be the Good (itself an idealization), becomes obligatory. In other words, the moral judgment proceeds on an assumption of existence, not because the true value now perceived *is* realized, but simply because the individual making the judgment has *had* a foretaste of the true value in his own experience of value-claims or has been told about it by others. The moral judgment is a judgment about the future based not on the cognition of a non-desired value, but on actual moral experiments, appreciations, and achievements in the past. The contemplation of a value's possible existence is nothing but an hypothesis about the person's future life — an hypothesis which is the result of his own moral experiments influenced by his past moral judgments and by the experience of others. Such a person believes that the value contemplated *can be* realized because it *has* already been desired and realized to some extent. Otherwise he could have no idea of it, for it is an idealization (for him at least) based on his own experience and that of others. There is no "ought" and there cannot be any "ought" to an inconceivable satisfaction, or one which has not even been experienced in part. The "this" which is the subject of the moral judgment is not a non-desired value-object which is claimed to be good. It is rather an object, action, or event evaluated by critical reference to a hypothetical state of existence considered to be the Good as a result of experience. Therefore, it is deemed morally obligatory. This does not mean that we always first desire objects, actions, or events, and then evaluate them morally, for actions may be desired originally because they are conceived to be conducive to the achievement of the Good. The main point is that we start with experienced value-claims, the critical examination and coherent arrangement of which yield the (growing concept of) the Good.

Sorley, however, begins at the other end, not with value-claims, but with "primary moral judgments," or judgments of true value, partly because he would hold that the above position reduces primary moral judgments to subjectivity, and also because the idea of a supreme Good is not "explicitly present" in our "ordinary moral judgments." (We have admitted that it is not explicitly present; neither is it more than an ever-growing hypothesis to which, however, we are always morally committed.) As Sorley himself says, he differs from the traditional intuitional moralists in advancing from particular "oughts" to the general principle, rather than in proceeding deductively from a general principle, and here his method is certainly more adequate than theirs. For him

The universal of morality is contained in particulars, and at first concealed by them. . . . Goodness is, first of all, recognised in a concrete situation. The moral judgment is in the first instance a perceptive judgment, as Aristotle held; and ethical science is based on these perceptive judgments just as natural science is based on the judgments of sense-perception. The data of ethics are accordingly the particular appreciations or judgments of good or evil passed in concrete situations. These are moral intuitions, in the literal sense, for *they are immediate and of the nature of perception, not the results of reasoning.* . . . Nor have they any infallible claim to truth. In this respect they are on the same level as the judgments of sense-perception.[41]

In contrast, our claim, to repeat, is that there are no *moral* intuitions, no moral givens, though there is irreducible moral

[41] *Moral Values*, p. 91 (italics mine).

obligation; that there is no *moral* consciousness, but a consciousness which views life's experiences of value-claim and
hypothetical true values as a whole, with a view to discovering
what is the Good for it (this being a matter of insight no different from that which is required for any kind of philosophical
truth). Such insight criticizes desires and their objects. It is
very important to realize that desires are not necessarily self-
centered or depraved, for the "life of desire" so much dis-
paraged is one of a "chaos of desires," or of particular evil
desires. The difference between Sorley's view and ours, therefore, is this. For him primary (true) value-judgments claim
validity, and the Good is known inductively by the coherent
systematization of "oughts." For us, value-claims assert validity, and the Good is inductively known by the coherent systematization of desires. This Good becomes obligatory, but
only those particular desires whose realization is conducive to
it are transformed from mere desires or value-claims to
"oughts" to be desired or true values. Hitherto, then, we have
sought to contrast and reconcile the most significant claims
of the moral realists or intuitionists, best represented by Sorley, and of the moral naturalist who reduces moral obligation
to desire as well as value. We must now reflect on several
other significant aspects of Sorley's theory.

One further question may first be asked about the validity
or universality of the value-judgment. Is the universality
claimed by the moral judgment parallel to the similar claim
of the judgment "this is a book," or is the claim of validity
and universality the common characteristic of both judgments simply because they both claim to be *true*? In other
words, it is suggested that the universality claimed by the
moral judgment is not uniquely and originally its own, but
one which it derives from its claim to be true.

It is also important to note Sorley's procedure in confirming
the truth of moral judgments. For him the particular moral
judgment always implies a universal. "When I say 'this is
good,' it is because of some character of the 'this' that it is
called good." [42] Sorley is here appealing to the fact that reflec-

tion upon a particular choice shows that it contributes to a more inclusive approved good; and, like Martineau, Sorley finds that though "two judgments upon some concrete situation contradict one another . . . this contradiction may not apply to the underlying grounds of the judgment, if these have been correctly analysed. These may, indeed, be largely identical and differ only in degree of comprehensiveness." [43] For example, reflection upon the savage's approval of his head-hunting would reveal the ground of this approval to be "tribal welfare is good," while the ground of the civilized man's condemnation of this good is the more comprehensive "common welfare is good"; but the idea both men approve is community welfare. In this way, Sorley finds that the particular intuition involves a broader principle.[44] The systematization of such principles according to the kind of objects to which they refer, as well as to their degree of generality, and so on, will "compel us often to reject the first expression of the moral consciousness, but yet without throwing doubt upon the *fundamental validity of that consciousness.*" [45] The very next sentence is: "In this way system becomes a criterion of moral validity." When a moral judgment conflicts with a system it is to be rejected, and if one system conflicts with another the more comprehensive is to be accepted.

Finally, Sorley finds that the history of moral ideas, though there has been change in particular applications, shows that "the higher [spiritual] life and the wider [social] life . . . these the moral judgment approves with a constancy which is almost uniform." [46] Our only comment is: Is this uniformity an achievement of a *moral* consciousness or of more penetrating insight into the consequences of certain desires, the learning of the laws which must be obeyed in order that man's developing physical, mental, and moral nature may be satisfied? At the risk of a digression, we shall enlarge on the pre-

[43] *Ibid.*
[44] Taylor would agree, but he does not explicitly give a criterion. Cf. *Faith of a Moralist*, I, 159 f.
[45] *Moral Values*, p. 99 (italics mine).
[46] *Ibid.*, p. 106.

suppositions involved in our view, all of which may be found scattered through Sorley's pages,[47] but not made central.

First, self-preservation we deem to be the primary law of all life. Second, the way in which and the extent to which different beings preserve themselves depend on their natural endowments and on the nature of the environment to which they must submit in various degrees, but which they may also use. Third, the individual bent on conserving himself never knows exactly what he wants or that he can fulfill his desire (and this fact we ordinarily express by saying that he does not know himself); but in any cool hour, at least, he is never satisfied with his present level of achievement and seeks novelty, though this *may* mean nothing more than a mere change. How often, indeed, do we want something without knowing what we want! Fourth, in the very act of fulfilling his wants he often finds, and *this is the real mystery*, that his nature is not satisfied (and, in satisfaction, we agree with Aristotle, pleasure is only an element; indeed, often when pleasure is being enjoyed one finds one is not satisfied). This means that without knowing it the individual has "grown," or, as Ward would put it, that in preserving himself he has modified the self to be preserved. This, we repeat, is one of the mysteries of existence; the individual knows not *how* it occurs, but he is sure *that* it does occur. Fifth, remembering that man, a conative as well as a rational being, is not intrinsically selfish, that his very instincts bind him in nonselfish ways to his human environment, one can see man as he develops changing his desires to suit a nature which has been changing. His problem is always: What is that form of adaptation to the physical and human environment which will be most satisfactory (the Good)? Sixth, we must also remember that one of the developments in man's nature was the consciousness that he *ought* to achieve the Good. Thus his problem as an individual is to discover those laws of his own nature (the necessity of intersubjective intercourse is presupposed in this discussion) and relate them to his physical and human environment. This means the sifting and criticism of private valuations, experimentation, learning

[47] The same may be said of Taylor's *Faith of a Moralist*.

from others, and, briefly, the construction of ideals which are Objective in the sense that they are true of him in relation to his environment. The ideals represent a re-evaluation of value-claims by reference to his present experience and nature, the natures and experiences of others, and the past experiences of both. During this whole process he does discover that certain values are more lasting and catholic, that the self he now finds it necessary to preserve, if he is going to be satisfied, is the higher and wider self. He becomes acquainted, in other words, with certain permanent laws of his being which must be obeyed (as faithfully as the law of gravitation must be obeyed for preservation in the physical sphere) if he is to live happily. Perhaps man began merely with the desire to live, but a Socrates soon realizes that death is better than not to live well. Hence, on our view, man's conviction that he ought to do the Good is permanent, but his interpretation of the Good develops with experimentation and insight. All man ever knows is a better (as our writers must admit, since they hold that the Ideal is ever imperfectly known). Man continues to consider the best, or the better-than-anything-else, the Good until the very process by which he achieves the better has in a mysterious way so developed his moral sinews and sensitivity that, on arriving at his supposed ultimate goal, he finds himself to be a mere pilgrim who can "tarry but a while" at this destination. For his very achievement leaves him unsatisfied in the light of a new ideal only now rising above the moral horizon.

The cause for this moral dissatisfaction and change, however, is not to be conceived similarly to the cause of changes in the physical world, for there our thought seems obsessed by the notion of pushes and pulls or external influences. Martineau and Pringle-Pattison, for example, seemed unable to account for moral dissatisfaction and change apart from the pricking of an immanent Good.[48] We would suggest, on the other hand, that our dissatisfaction is not caused by an (ill-conceived) Good which lured us on even though we saw it

[48] Taylor especially emphasizes this view of moral growth. Cf. *Faith of a Moralist*, I, 213 ff.

dimly. Rather do the facts seem consistent with the view that we find ourselves, as we proceed toward goals we had set, human beings with capacities of which we had not even dreamed; we discover that the ascent reveals hitherto unknown peaks of experience and new alternatives to be faced. The paradox and the mystery of life, as we have suggested, is this growth; but the pricking is our own, though we did not make it originally possible. Nor did we institute the spiritual laws which must be obeyed if we would find peace. *Our natures are such*, and they grow from within, in a personal and physical environment. Morally we are Leibnizian monads, and if our windows are open to the Eternal, the passage of influence cannot conflict with free will.

It is not worthwhile for our purpose here to include an exposition of Sorley's view that intrinsic value exists only in personality [49] and that all other value-judgments are of values existing only as instrumental to personal development. Let us instead turn directly to the important contributions of the chapter: "Relative and Absolute Value." It will be interesting to see the degree of harmony between the view just presented and Sorley's, the main difference lying again in the interpretation of value.

G. Relative and Absolute Value

Sorley once more returns to the attack on views which define value in relation to a subject. He, on the other hand, would say: ". . . what I mean when I assert 'A is good' is not that I like or desire A or even that I feel approval in contemplating A, but that this predicate 'good' does, as a matter of fact, characterise A." [50] Now we have already renounced any identification of value with pleasure, and we repeat that it is difficult to see why value is rendered subjective, when it is made relative to desire. For the realization of any desire, even that for pleasure, means not that the individual is capable of pleasure, but that something, the desired object, *gives him pleasure*; it

---

[49] Cf. *Moral Values*, pp. 118 ff. (Unless otherwise indicated, all other page references in this chapter will be to *Moral Values*.)

[50] P. 134.

is always a statement about his nature and the nature of his environment. The statement "A is good" means, on this view, not that "I desire A," as Sorley says, but that A's attributes are in accordance with an ideal recognized by myself also to be good, and therefore as having a true value for me.

There is no more reason, Sorley continues, for saying that value is subjective and relative because appreciated by us than for maintaining the relativity of ordinary facts, which are subject to similar conditions. There is a sense, however, in which values are relative though not subjective or divorced from reality. When we assert that a thing is right under certain conditions but wrong under others, we imply that goodness is not only relative to us, but also to the objective whole of which we are a part at the time. Yet goodness is not applicable to the abstract concept of the act or its class, but to a concrete existence or an existence contemplated as real. And since a person lives in a physical and social environment, his acts of goodness are to be judged relative to that environment and his own capabilities. Yet the relativity to circumstances is not complete, for though the latter determine the particular direction of the good man's attitude, they do not decide its general character. Thus, Sorley concludes: "We must not expect to find the permanent or universal principle in classes of conduct valid for all circumstances; it should rather be sought in the moral spirit or purpose which may inspire the most diverse conditions without being itself restricted to any." [51] The unconditional duty of life is to seek the Good; it is "a striving towards the realisation of the best conceived, though the concrete nature of that best may be far from fully defined." [52] (This, on our view, is the *only* meaning for the "moral consciousness.")

Though this principle is formal only and waits upon the primary appreciations of (true) value, it is not altered by the latter, nor by judgments based upon them. Hence, Sorley correctly holds that, though the moral universe is dependent on and relative to the actual nature of persons and things,

[51] P. 145.
[52] P. 148.

there is yet a unity of spirit which cannot be traced to external existential conditions. The moral life can only realize itself in the actual universe; it nevertheless exhibits a single principle throughout all its details, "a valuation in which the interests of the spiritual and social life are preferred to those of sense and self." [53] (Yet it must be realized that, if what Sorley has already maintained is true, we seek these interests because of their catholicity and permanence, which in turn are based on the nature of existence.)

Thus, moral judgments are objective not only because they claim objectivity in asserting a value which is found in a supposed or actual person, but also because, when correct, they exhibit universal values and display a common purpose and spirit which characterizes the good will. "In the third place, this common or universal element in goodness will be made clearer if we find that moral values are connected in such a way as to form a system . . . an organic whole to which the name of Chief Good may be properly given." [54] But since, as we have seen, the good is always good in relation to a certain whole (which whole in turn is good in relation to another whole, and so forth), the relations of each value-experience are limited only by the boundaries of the existing universe of value. We can, therefore, never determine fully the nature of the Chief Good, for its absoluteness lies in its own completeness. The search for the absolute has no more success in the non-valuational world. But there cannot be two absolutes, one of which is ethical. Hence: "We can form a conception of an absolute only as an individual reality which contains harmoniously within itself both the actual order and the moral order." [55]

H.   The Conservation of Value

So far Sorley has insisted: (1) that true values cannot be reduced to conative elements, (2) that the value-judgment claims "objective validity," which means for him both Objectivity and metaphysical objectivity, and (3) that reflection on value-judgments reveals fundamental principles of action

[53] P. 149.   [54] P. 150.   [55] P. 157.

the systematization of which becomes the task of ethics. A coherent interpretation of such value-judgments indicates that values are as metaphysically objective as are the existential objects reached by way of a coherent interpretation of sense-impressions. For Sorley the procedure is not: Are the values metaphysically objective? but rather: Which of the values claiming this objectivity are metaphysically objective?

Before considering the relation of his results to the interpretation of reality as a whole, our philosopher turns to the problem of the conservation of values, which is the "borderland between the purely ethical and the more metaphysical argument," [56] for it raises the problem of the permanence of value. An empirical philosophy of value must define the meaning and grounds for the conservation of value, and a few suggestions are advanced as we follow Sorley's discussion.

A close inspection of this chapter reveals Sorley's thesis, that the only ground for the faith in the conservation of values is the metaphysical objectivity of value. But he comes to his argument only after a preliminary discussion of the formation or discovery of ideas of value and the production of values. It is, however, more relevant at this point to discuss the conservation of values before turning to the main problem.

Tracing the development of moral ideas, Sorley holds, interestingly enough, that experiences of values lead to reflection about them, and the choice of one or another as the ideal.[57] Man "must have felt pleasure before he set his mind upon a life of enjoyment, . . . had some taste of intellectual effort and of the knowledge which is its reward, before he could speak of science as having the highest value." [58] This we have expressed by saying that man finds new forms of satisfaction corresponding to new developments and laws of his being. At this point, however, Sorley remarks that: "New experience may thus lead to new values — meaning thereby not the creation of values, but the discovery of them in directions formerly unexplored." [59] Now, if the word "creation" here means that we create the cause of our values or our own dispositions and the laws of their development, then, of course,

[56] P. 158.   [57] P. 161.   [58] Ibid.   [59] Ibid.

we do not create the values. But surely the additional valuation of the object by human beings creates a new relationship
and therefore a new value (or disvalue) over and above any
of the possibly already existent valuations placed upon it. At
least, potential value has become actual. We do not create our
values outright any more than we do our world. Nevertheless,
in both cases, unless the self is a *tabula rasa*, something new is
created, even though in our reflection after such creation, we
realize that these objects might have been so valued earlier.
The discovery of value, then, does not mean that we find what
was "there" without us, but that we find that certain desirable
relations to our world were possible even before we actualized
them. Even if there were an eternal realm of values, they
would have an additional value created by their relation to
our needs, as Sorley himself would seem to admit.[60] Sorley's
point that the rise of present intrinsic values is the result of
the modification and refinement of pre-existing values is the
very point we ourselves have stressed, and he himself *speaks*
of the production and creation of value.[61] But the crucial
question is: To what extent can man have assurance that the
values for which he has striven will be maintained and
preserved?

Man may produce values, but their conservation does not
depend entirely upon him.[62] If, then, we deny that Höffding's
axiom regarding the conservation of value is true and consequently suppose that "the forces of the universe cannot be
trusted to conserve values," [63] what empirical evidence is there
for the belief in the conservation of value? Sorley first considers the working of the law of compensation in nature, the
fact that the destruction of what at the time seemed to be institutions of high value is, on a larger view of the facts, a real
good to humanity. "In spite of many setbacks, the total conditions of the world at the present day are more favorable
than they were some thousands of years ago to the production
and preservation of values." [64] So far, so good, but Sorley finds

[60] Cf. p. 175.
[61] Cf. pp. 177–180.
[62] P. 169.
[63] P. 170.
[64] P. 171.

that scientific predictions about the future of our planet by
no means guarantee the conservation of our values, and he is
forced to look elsewhere for the support of this axiom. Yet,
before attending to the latter, it will be well to consider even
the compensatory action more carefully (though it must be
remembered that Sorley is not resting his argument upon it).

Say what one may about the compensation of values, one
fact seems quite true — that at least for those people before
whose eyes cherished institutions passed away nothing but the
destruction of value was felt. The fall of the tower of Babel
may have seemed a good thing to a succeeding generation, but
the broken hearts and thwarted aspirations it caused must have
left the builders with a sense of futility. One may answer with
justice that this loss, seen in the light of a future consequence,
might well be a good, and that a value rationally approved in
a particular past situation might be a decided disvalue in the
light of a present situation. But even so, can the estimate of a
value leave out of account the predicament in which it arose
and the process by which it was achieved? Whether or not an
unrealized true value for one generation turns out to be a
good for a new generation, the older generation found no
consolation for what it felt to be a genuine loss of value. Indeed, had many true values of former generations been
realized, would not our own level of achievement be greater?
Often those very values our ancestors realized for our sake have
been lost. Furthermore, whatever compensation the future
may have brought, it did not go at the time to them who suffered, and consequently the loss is never fully requited.

In the light of such loss and shifting of values from generation to generation (to the extent that what for one is the
destruction is for another the preservation of value), what
meaning can the *conservation of value* have? Can we say much
more (but this is much!) than that, despite the opposition of
the universe to the conservation of certain values, it still
allowed for continuation of many values and of their effects,
as well as for the creation and discovery of new values?

What has been said ought to warn us against the glib use of
the *conservation of values* to cover the wholesale preservation

of values we cannot specify concretely. Can we say that the
future will be good to many of our specific values: our homes,
our writings, our works of art? Can we say that even the present cosmos is congenial to many of our fondest ideals? And
since all values are instruments for the attainment of worthy
personality, the ultimate question, as Sorley says, remains:
Are persons, the bearers and producers of value, as well as intrinsic values to be preserved? As Ward [65] defined the conservation of values it meant the possibility of the realization
of moral ideals, and this involved the assurance of immortality. Yet what substantial empirical evidence have we for
immortality except a yearning and a hope that have pervaded
men's lives? The basis for the assurance of immortality is
ultimately the goodness of God, but can God's goodness be
established except in his relation to the actualized values of
mankind? The empirical data, we have seen, force us to interpret the conservation of value to mean that those values we
have experienced and do experience have been made possible
by physical nature and man. Other than this it can only mean
that value will not disappear from the earth. The assurance
we have that our *specific* values will be preserved is no greater
and no less than that of the scientist, who, reasoning from
probability, insists that his laws will hold as long as the conditions upon which they are founded remain constant. The
empirical data may not warrant faith in our own immortality, but they do justify faith that the values created and discovered by us will, by positive or negative influence, form part
of the basis at least for values to be created by other men. And
our point is that the conservation of value as here interpreted
cannot be explained unless the "powers that be" are friendly
to man.[66] Thus, for Sorley, as for us, confidence in the continuation (and improvement, one may add) of the conditions
necessary for the attainment and increase of value depends
upon the existence of a good and powerful God. The difference is in the nature of the argument for God's goodness, as
we shall see. Sorley's approach may now be further indicated.

[65] Cf. above, Chapter IV, pp. 107, 108.
[66] Cf. below, Chapter VII, pp. 263–265.

Whether the future will hold circumstances more favorable to the attainment of value a criticism of the scientific data will reveal. Having faced this problem, Sorley concludes:

> Accordingly, if we depend simply upon what observation enlightened by physical science can tell us of the prospects in store for human life, we are forced to conclude that the law of compensation will not hold indefinitely — that old values will in time cease to be replaced by equal or greater values. . . . Confidence in the permanence of values throughout its changes of form and object can only be justified on the assumption that the account given by physical science is incomplete. The confidence, therefore, implies a belief that the ultimate power in the universe is not indifferent to what man calls good. *It is impossible to hold, as Höffding does, to the faith in the conservation of values, and to justify this belief, without being led on to postulate a power and will that conserves them.*[67]

Whether values continue to exist in the future or not, today we live and enjoy them, and "if the world were to come to an end to-morrow, yet, to-day, beauty would remain better than ugliness, truth than error, good than evil." [68] This (which is the main ground, we contend, for belief in God's goodness), Sorley holds, "is sound so far as it goes," but he himself contends that the axiom of the conservation of value "is not the foundation of the objective validity of value." [69] On the contrary, he adds: "It is because values are objective that we are led to think that the universe, which upholds and contains these objectively valid values, will not carelessly let them go but will provide some means for their permanent realisation." [70] Thus, belief in the conservation of value can be justified only if we can find a home for present objective values in a good and powerful God. Hence, Sorley's argument for God's goodness rests largely, as we shall see, on the need for a personal embodiment of those values which are cognitively revealed to us. God's goodness cannot be firmly grounded, he would contend, on the actual amount of realized value, but on the fact that without Him the moral objective order would be unintelligible. We cannot affirm that Sorley's position rests *wholly* (instead of "largely") on the theoretical need of a source

[67] *Moral Values*, p. 172 (italics mine).
[68] P. 173.
[69] *Ibid.*
[70] Pp. 173, 174.

for the objective moral order, because Sorley's argument for God is not simply "a direct inference" from the validity of the moral order to God. For to reason thus, he says correctly, would be simply "to give the moral order a new name and not to have established the reality of a living self-consciousness as the ground of the universe." [71] Sorley's argument has a "wider range," for it is "founded not on the moral order by itself but on its relation to the order of existing things." [72] Before treating this final stage of the argument, we may briefly indicate pertinent past progress.

Value, Sorley found, resides in the concrete existent. Now, the values which we ascribe to physical things are not values in the strict sense, but only a means or instrument to intrinsic values, which belong to persons only. With regard to these intrinsic values, there are only two possibilities for Sorley. "Either they are objective, or else they have no reality outside the mind of the subject who affirms them." [73] (Our difficulty was really in accepting this disjunction as complete, since there is a sense of "objective" that Sorley does not take seriously enough, namely, epistemologically Objective.) Sorley's point, in itself acceptable, was that "the grounds for denying the objectivity [or Objectivity, for us] of morality are equally grounds for denying the objectivity of knowledge." [74] The problem now narrows down to the relation of these objective moral values in particular to the rest of reality or the causal series.

I. VALUE AND REALITY

That Sorley is not oblivious of the difficulties in making the journey from "ought" to "is," is evident from his statement that though the actual performance of a good action is an instance in point of the transition from goodness to reality, yet since we often apply the term "good" to *not yet existing* things which may, indeed, never exist ". . . it is clear . . . that there are obstacles on the way from 'ought' to 'is,' from goodness to existence. . . ." [75]

One might expect Sorley to overcome this obstacle by

[71] P. 479.   [72] *Ibid.*   [73] P. 498.   [74] P. 499.   [75] P. 184.

arguing that the idea of the good involves its existence, but Sorley has little respect for the ontological argument. It cannot be denied, however, he maintains, that ethical ideas always have existential connections: (a) as elements in personal consciousness realized through volitional activity in the character of persons, and (b) in their claim to objective validity which is not invalidated by their being ideas. But the crux of the problem at issue is: Are the principles or laws which moral reflection formulates of any avail in interpreting reality? [76] The usual answer is that, since moral laws are only partly obeyed by reality, they cannot be used to interpret the whole. Here we note that Sorley is approaching the same problem which Pringle-Pattison faced in his second answer to Hume. We are acquainted with Pringle-Pattison's answer: Man's reach, he insisted, as well as his grasp, gives a clue to reality, and the Ideal within man urging on his progress is really the voice of God within him. How will Sorley deal with the problem?

Sorley admits the difference between goodness and the actual, but he denies the conclusion drawn from this that since reality as actually observed is a mixture of good and evil, therefore principles of goodness cannot be used in the interpretation of the whole actual system. First, Sorley answers, ethical ideas *have* entered in and influenced the actual cause and effect system through their presence in persons who have based their actions upon them, and this may continue in the future to a much greater extent. So far Sorley cannot be gainsaid. But, second, he goes on, apart from such causal efficiency of ethical ideas, moral principles "do not depend for their validity upon their presence in any particular minds," and as such have validity "which may be compared with the objective validity of the laws of nature." [77] In being valid, like natural laws, they are implicated in reality; for validity, Sorley agrees with Ward, implies reality.[78]

[76] Cf. p. 186.

[77] P. 188.

[78] It is interesting to note at this point, on the nature of the objectivity and validity of ethical principles, that Ward's two pupils, Sorley and Tennant, part

Now Sorley is quite correct in his insistence that the presence of ethical principles in minds does not invalidate them any more than the same fact invalidated natural laws. This, however, cannot be taken to mean that there can be laws without minds. For example, before the law of gravitation is accepted, it is shown to be the most reasonable hypothesis allowed by the facts. If later it is found discrepant with new facts we say that *our* law, *our* formulation, and the actual occurrence in nature do not harmonize, but not that the law of the activity in nature itself (which we have not yet discovered) is wrong. Natural laws are valid of physical reality as long as they serve to interpret the physical data correctly, but because they are always our formulations of what is going on beyond us, they may be wrong, and in any case, reflecting our capacities and needs, they are far from photographic copies. Moral laws are constructed in the same way, by the systematization and coherent organization of the facts of value, so that the moral law also rests on the promise that so long as this kind of natural world and human nature exists, the law holds. The difference, as Sorley states it, is that the moral law is not always realized in existence, as the natural law is, for if it were, there would be no need for "ought." Nevertheless, do we not think that our formulation of the principles of human behavior in relation to *this* environment is such that if applied it would fulfill the conditions for approved happiness? Are not our moral laws scientific in the sense that they represent generalizations about the value-experiences of mankind which become obligatory for the serious moral agent? The real difference, therefore, is that moral laws cannot be depended upon to operate independently of human volition, because they do not belong to a mechanical system and thus cannot be so completely verified. Nevertheless, they are *our* formulations; they are hypotheses (based on the facts of man's present and past experimentations with value-claims and true values) regarding the kind of actions man must perform to

company, the former agreeing with Ward; but as to pan-psychism, Tennant favors Ward, and Sorley does not, while both disagree with Ward that theism cannot be established without the acceptance of spiritualism.

live meaningfully and happily. They are not cognitions of an independent realm, but idealizations of the actual laws which our experiments (more inclusive than cognitions) reveal.

Sorley, on the contrary, finds that ethical principles apply to persons who live not under law only but also by the "conception" of law. And this is so because he thinks of this law as independent of man but to be realized in man. "The law which the person recognises as valid for his life is that which tends to the end in which personality is conceived as reaching its true good." [79] This law, however, does not depend for its validity on its presence in man's mind. Nor are moral principles valid of man in the same sense as physical laws are valid of the physical universe, that is, as constituting its actual order. For "a person is not merely what he does, but what he is capable of doing. The law which is valid for him must exhibit its validity by appealing to his rational consciousness without restricting his freedom." [80] Hence, for Sorley physical principles are valid for physical things and moral principles for persons. This is certainly conceded in what has been said. But the important point, at least not brought out by Sorley, is that the moral ideal, though never fully realized (as a natural principle would be), *is* nevertheless approved because it *has* commended itself to man even when *partially realized*. It is based, not on a criticized intuition of an objectively valid value, but on an approved experience. It is not true, or it is only partially true, on this view, to say simply that "ethical principles are valid for persons," [81] for ethical laws are valid *of* persons in interaction with this kind of physical world and this kind of personality. The laws would be different, conceivably, for angels in a celestial kingdom. Ethical principles have a footing in both the personal and the material world. And though, as Sorley says, "physical principles are valid for material things," [82] ethical principles are valid of persons in their relation both to each other and to a physical world. (We cannot add "in relation to a spiritual world," for that remains to be proved.) They are not gained by contemplating a

[79] P. 190.
[80] P. 189.
[81] P. 190.
[82] *Ibid.*

quasi-Platonic realm, but are rooted in the experience of ourselves and our environment.

But Sorley comes to closer grips with his problem after a necessary digression,[83] the fundamental thought of which is that the unitary self knows existence directly (and not by way of "mental modifications"), and has an active, practical, as well as cognitive interest, in accordance with which it unifies its experience. "The distinction of thing from thing is largely our distinction, imposed for our purposes. . . ." [84] Further-more, he believes that "relations belong to reality as much as things do," [85] and that without relations things would not be what they are. Values, which are relations manifested in per-sons rather than things, are no less objective than other rela-tions. Yet one might insist that this does not prove the point; for, since the values actually realized by persons are only part of reality and constitute only a small part of the value we wish to realize or may ever realize, we cannot say that all values are a part of reality. Thus Sorley is confronted, as he admits, with the "real difficulty" of his position. Even if one grants the truth of Sorley's theory of moral knowledge, on the validity of Sorley's solution of this problem rests the success or failure of passing from the "ought" to the "is."

Sorley contends that passage from the "ought" to the "is" would be impossible *if* it were legitimate to take a cross section of human life as representative of the whole, but he believes it is not legitimate because persons cannot be understood by their achievements at any moment: "their nature is to be realizers of value." [86]

We do not get an adequate understanding of the world — which is a world of persons — if we judge it simply by its manifestations at any given moment. . . . We have to take into account what at any moment is only ideal, if there is ground for regarding the realization of that ideal as the completion of personality.[87]

[83] One of the most profitable parts of Sorley's work is his discussion of the self and its knowledge of things, but there is fundamental agreement here between Sorley and Tennant, whose thought will be discussed in Chapter VI, and differences will be indicated there.

[84] P. 226.

[85] P. 229.

[86] P. 232.

[87] P. 237.

Since, then, we cannot understand persons without knowing their ideals, these "ideals, accordingly, may be held to belong to reality as much as do the persons whom they express." [88] But does this follow? Would Sorley admit that because mechanism is true of a part of reality, it is also true of human beings? Why then should ideals, admittedly applying to persons only, belong also to reality *as a whole*? Furthermore, there is no way of knowing beforehand whether the ideal will complete personality, *unless* we argue from experience, or past experimentation, rather than from cognition as such. The main difficulty comes out more clearly if we consider Sorley's position in greater detail.

Each person, Sorley holds, realizes his own deficiencies and approves the goodness of others "because his consciousness, his nature, is in sympathy with the value which he sees, even when he fails to reach it himself. It is the *anima naturaliter moralis* that speaks." [89] Here the argument begins to be cloudy, and it must be followed carefully. It is not clear whether the person's *nature* is dissatisfied, a nature which he takes to be "his better self," or whether his nature is dissatisfied *because* he is conscious of, or has a cognitive relation to, an ideal which he finds obligatory. Sorley continues: "He has affinity [a word like Pringle-Pattison's "organic," which needs careful definition] with the ideals he approves even when he fails to follow them; the values are his values, and have their root in the nature which he shares with his social environment." [90] It begins to be evident that man's dissatisfaction with himself arises from an energizing, we may say, within him of an ideal whose presence his cognition realizes. However, the very nature of an affinity demands that it rest not on a cognitive relation (which it supports) but on a structural similarity that, in this instance, gives rise to the ideals which are the basis *in* oneself *for* the affinity with the ideals approved in the beyond. An affinity testifies to some sort of underlying union between the objects which have an affinity for each other. Hence, in this case the affinity of man and ideals must rest on some substructure which supports that affinity. But

[88] *Ibid.*   [89] P. 232.   [90] P. 232.

Sorley has proved no such basis for affinity and seems simply to emphasize the cognitive relationship between man and his ideals, and the existence of ideals beyond as the *ground* for their cognition by the person. Accordingly, a person's values seem to be "his," not because he has experienced them in part and approved them as being obligatory upon him, but because they operate within him so that he *sees* them and himself in their light. This doctrine is like Pringle-Pattison's and similarly begs the point to be proved, namely that there is an independent, though not humanly realized, moral realm which we know and know correctly as the source of our ideals. It also confirms our other writers in suggesting that moral dissatisfaction, instead of arising from the growth of the self, is externally provoked. There are two other considerations to be dealt with in this connection.

Moral values, Sorley holds, belong to reality in two senses. In the first place, they are independent of the achievements of moral persons or even of recognition by them. "Whether we are guided by them or not, whether we acknowledge them or not, they have validity: they ought to be our guides." [91] But why ought moral ideals to be our guides? Sorley, no doubt, would answer in part, at least, that unless they do give guidance, our natures will not be satisfied.[92] But then it would seem that we accept them because we find our natures satisfied in so far as we obey them, and not because we merely perceive them. As we have already said, there is no obligation to inconceivable (because not experienced) values, and to ascribe validity to them is meaningless. A realm of values valid whether man realizes them or not and yet valid "for" man is certainly difficult to conceive in empirical terms. Rather are values valid *of* our natures (and hence *for* our natures) because, having applied them and experimented with them, we find that they do give satisfaction in proportion to the extent they do inform and have informed our lives. We do not know how to test or arrive at their validity otherwise.

In any case, validity is meaningless apart from the knowledge relationship. We can understand how an unrealized

[91] P. 238.   [92] Cf. p. 237.

value which coheres with a whole system has validity, but for a value we know nothing about, and which has no place in our system, to be valid is to relegate validity beyond the realm of knowledge. There may be values for God which are valid for him and in accordance with which he controls the universe, but they have no validity for us until they become at least experiences whose further realization we approve. Since, then, validity of ideals is meaningless apart from the knowledge relation, and since completely unrealized ideals could not be man's guide, the validity of ideals refers to the applicability of idealizations (hypotheses) of man's experience to his true nature and happiness (which can be discovered only by actual experimentation). Ideals have imperative reality, not because they already exist in a realm of their own, but because they are conceived by us as a result of experience to be the best for us; and they, therefore, become obligatory.

The second point may be made as we emphasize the way in which Sorley makes the transition from "ought" to "is." Summarizing his position, Sorley states: "What is implied so far is that the validity of moral values — seeing that it is not derived from their acceptance by persons for whom they are valid — must have another source." [93] Since they must belong to the universe in some way, Sorley contends that because moral values "characterize personal life as completed or perfected" and are "factors in the fulfillment of purpose," they express "the limit towards which the nature of persons points and presses," [94] and are therefore as real as the persons, who, indeed, do not create the moral values in accordance with which they complete their natures. "That is to say, the objective moral value is valid independently of me and my will, and yet is something which satisfies my purpose and completes my nature." [95] By thus insisting that values are intrinsic to the development of human purpose and personality, Sorley makes a connecting bridge between these two types of reality and passes from the "ought" to the "is." But even this transition is impossible unless man is akin to reality independent of him, and unless there is an affinity between his mind and the

[93] P. 238.   [94] P. 239.   [95] Ibid.

values independent of him and his will and yet necessary to his development. Thus, when, for example, we ask:

> What is it that impels the philosopher to his unresting search for truth? . . . [Sorley answers] Because there is a natural affinity between his mind and the truth he seeks. He is not yet wise, for the truth has to be sought; he can never become completely wise, for there are hindrances to the full view of truth which mortal nature can never finally overcome. But he is not altogether ignorant; if he were he would have no impulse to philosophy; he can recognize the truth when he sees it and he is unsatisfied in its absence; and this shows that his mind is allied to truth and has kinship with it. Therefore the philosopher does not need to wait for truth to come to him from the outside.[96]

The value-realizing process throughout seems to be that man, driven by dissatisfaction, first sees the Good and then tries it (just as he sees a chair and then sits on it) and finds it satisfactory. But experience, we suggest, belies this description, for man cannot know the Good apart from experiencing hypothetical goods from which he projects his ideal. The only objectivity Sorley seems to find conceivable is that which pervades natural knowledge, and he therefore thinks of metaphysically objective goodness as being the cause of man's knowing the Good. Then, like Pringle-Pattison, he is forced to make the veracity of man's knowledge depend on a "kinship" between man and that independent realm. For him, in our mere act of perception we know the relevance of an independent realm of ideals to our lives. Yet it is a fact that even for Sorley intuitions must be tested by the remaining facts of our experience, and our decision as to which ideals are metaphysically objective depends on their relation to our natures, not on any number of mere cognitions or moral presentations, as it were. Our natures ultimately decide which ideals are relevant to us; we can decide only by rational criticism of our moral experiments. What we know are our own natures, not moral objects independent of them and relevant to them, these being really hypostatizations of valid, constructed ideas. Sorley's attempt to prove the existence of ideals not realized in man's experience leads him to suppose that persons participate (cognitively) in metaphysically objective ideals which, strange

[96] P. 234.

to say, are not, as we should expect, in persons, but in a Person. And this brings us to a final difficulty.

If, as Sorley says, "nothing is ultimately of worth for its own sake except persons or some quality or state of a person," [97] in what sense can there be metaphysically objective moral values except in persons who have completely realized these personal values? This is another way of stating the difficulty which has haunted these pages, that if the Good is the Good *for man* it is impossible to see how the Good (whose existence *depends upon* man's realization of it and only his) can be metaphysically objective, independent of man and yet valid of him. Ideals which are of man and for man cannot be independent objects existing in and for themselves, as it were. If they are, what does it mean to say that self-sacrificing love, one of man's ideals, is independent of him, that courage and loyalty are valid guides for man's life but not dependent on him for their reality? The trouble is, as already suggested, that man's ideals or idealizations, arrived at by critical examination of his experience, have been hypostatized and then made responsible for his knowledge of them. What our writers have really been trying to substantiate is the goodness of God. For the metaphysically objective values, they contend, do not exist disembodied and immutable, like Plato's earlier Ideas, but have "life and motion" in the personal activity of God. These philosophers really mean that mutual love and loyalty, courage and temperance are God's *purposes* for man. It is God's love for man which is the metaphysically objective, cosmic counterpart of man's duty to love his fellow man and God. Because goodness is metaphysically objective in the sense that it expresses God's purpose, our goodness must follow the cosmic plan; goodness is not a mere provincialism of our planet, nor the inexplicable sport of atoms evolving fantastic patterns within the brain.

This, we repeat, has been the aim of our writers, but they have been dominated by the eye-analogy, by the notion that our moral knowledge is owing to stimulation of a moral realm independent of us (similar to the independent natural realm),

[97] Muirhead, ed., *Contemporary British Philosophy*, II, 253.

though in some sense present to us. But how can God's or any-body's love be in any way a presentational object, any more than their minds can be? Our thesis is that we can no more know *the love* which God purposes than we can know the purposing itself, except by inference grounded in analogy with our own experience and substantiated by the facts about ourselves and our world. We can know only what we deem to be the effects of his loving purpose. If we *infer* (rather than directly know) his intelligence, we can know his goodness only by inference from the nature of the world and man and their interconnection, for which he is ultimately responsible. In other words, we know God's ideals only on analogy with our own, instead of possessing special knowledge of a metaphysical realm of moral values which then needs to be personalized in God to be intelligible. Our authors have mistaken the mix-ture of moral restraint and attraction which our own natures provide (in the ultimate feeling of obligation to the best) for the external control felt in sensation.

That the pathway is from man (and the world) *by inference* to God is well illustrated even in the work of Sorley. After our philosopher has discovered the moral realm to have its home in God, he is confronted, strangely enough, upon defini-tion of the idea of God, with the problem (reminiscent of Plato's difficulty with mundane objects such as mud): Which virtues may be attributed to God? We say "strangely enough" because there is no reason, on this view of the objectivity of moral values, for denying and every reason for supposing that loyalty, courage, temperance, and other human ideals are not all metaphysically independent and in some sense the causes of our knowing them. When this objective realm is given a home in God, however, most of our concrete moral values, such as those just suggested, seem to disappear as such. For example, Sorley finds that "Courage, for instance, and temper-ance are human virtues which we cannot attribute in anything like their human form to the divine nature, for they postulate obstacles on the part of sense or of impulse to moral perform-ance." [98] Most human virtues are the "excellences" of a being

[98] *Moral Values*, p. 489. (The remaining references in this chapter will be to the same work.)

with both a sensuous and a spiritual nature, and, consequently, they cannot be applied to a purely spiritual being. The only virtues, therefore, which can be applied to God without complete loss of analogy (and empiricism) in human experience are Wisdom and Love. Even then, however, his Wisdom is not only greater but different from human wisdom in being intuitive rather than discursive, and his Love connotes at least "the will to the good of others and the will to communion with them." [99]

Is this not a large concession to our fundamental thesis that moral knowledge is not attained by reading off or knowing any independently valid realm, but that it is a generalization of the experiences of mankind, which have Objectivity, rather than metaphysical objectivity as the source of our knowledge? If temperance and courage do not have analogous cosmic counterparts, do they therefore become mere dreams and cease to become obligatory or rational? The answer is that they are Objective rather than metaphysically objective, that they apply to and express our natures, that they are descriptions of our moral satisfactions. And the same may be said for all human moral ideals. Their objective validity does not depend on their existence independent of man; they have Objective validity, and whether or not they express God's purpose for man cannot be decided by mere cognition of a metaphysically objective order. We do not behold a metaphysical moral order imperfectly; rather have we not even begun to exhaust the meaning of human personality and its capabilities. If God is love, he is not love because we merely know or feel it, but because his works show it; or at least without the evidence of the latter we should seriously doubt the former even if it were possible to feel it. In morality, if anywhere, we are bound in our knowledge of an independent Moral Reality by analogy with experience of ourselves.

But we must now go back and consider the remainder of Sorley's reasoning. For his argument favoring the metaphysical existence of values (incompletely realized by us), as established by man's affinity with those values, is only part of the argument for God. The next step is the consideration

[99] P. 490.

of whether "the meaning which the world expresses in its temporal process" [100] is brought to light by the moral values which have validity for and are manifested in persons. Sorley's procedure is synoptic, since his empiricism [101] demands that the whole be not lost sight of in analysis.[102] But his empiricism also demands that any particular synopsis be subjected to "empirical tests" (or coherence).[103] A synoptic view will require, he rightly holds, that the causal and the purposive orders of existence be harmonized, that the relation of moral values to the realm of existence be seen as a whole. God for Sorley is not merely the explanation of the realm of values, but he is also the explanation of the connection of that order with the natural or causal order. Let us study the method and content of Sorley's proof.

J. The Moral Argument

Before passing on directly to the moral argument for God, we may well make reference to Sorley's remarks on the teleological argument, though we must omit consideration of his remarkable analysis of the ontological and cosmological proofs.

The theory of natural selection renders the "old-fashioned teleology" obsolete, but natural selection itself, Sorley holds, is only semimechanical, since it assumes *vital* nonmechanical processes, like heredity, the tendency to variation, and self-preservation.[104] Furthermore, natural selection cannot explain the rise of "wider interests and their growing ascendancy" which have no direct relation to life-preservation. Though the old teleology be rejected, "we must nevertheless admit that there is adaptation (not accounted for by natural selection) between our reason and the actual cosmic order — a design greater than any Paley ever dreamed of." [105] Nor is the adaptation characteristic of the intellect alone, "but also of morality and the whole world of intrinsic values." [106] That there is a fundamental truth in these contentions cannot be denied, for it is on a wider teleological argument that the

[100] P. 291.
[101] Cf. p. 288.
[102] Cf. pp. 239–260.
[103] Cf. p. 268.
[104] Cf. p. 325.
[105] P. 326.
[106] Ibid.

reasoning for God must rest. Yet one cannot but notice Sorley's failure to bring out the creative contribution man has made in the achievement of truth and morality. Enough of the theory of natural selection is admitted to allow for the struggle in the organic world for self-preservation. Man may have created (not completely anew of course) new organs, but once his intellect appeared, it seems ultimately, on Sorley's view, to play the part of a mirror for a metaphysically objective order of truth and value. Man's intellect and conscience seem to be parallel to that objective order, and his knowledge is always of a pre-existent metaphysical object. "The order of truth which the intellect *discovers* and the order of moral values which reason *acknowledges* are objective characteristics of reality, and they are *reflected* in the mind of man." [107] Thus our previous interpretations are confirmed. As in the thought of Pringle-Pattison, much as the mind is asserted to be creative, the whole process of its creativity is assumed to play no greater part than that of an eye, and what we have called the eye-analogy dominates the discussion.

But, to continue, any argument for the goodness of God must face the problem of evil. And Sorley, like Martineau, is forced by dysteleological facts to use the moral argument for God in order to prove God's goodness. One would suppose that if the existence of evil can invalidate the teleological argument for God, it can invalidate any, but Sorley does not think so. Let us, then, follow his reasoning.

Sorley objects to postulating God, as Kant did, to bring together the moral and nonmoral realms. "It would seem as if . . . neither nature nor morality . . . by itself stood in need of God; and as if, if they had happened to be in better agreement with one another, God would have been equally superfluous." [108] On the other hand, the causal system and the moral realm are not two different worlds but different aspects of one reality. The problem is to find what general view is justified when both systems are taken into account. Since Sorley has already proved that the moral order is an objectively

[107] *Ibid.* (italics mine). Cf. also p. 268.
[108] P. 335.

valid order, belonging to the nature of reality, what is needed is "to vindicate the position that the world is a moral system, or that goodness belongs to the cause or ground of the world. . . ." [109] The argument, therefore, must turn on the answer to the empirical question: Is the rest of reality instrumental to the realization of the moral order, and therefore an element in *one* moral purpose? Our hypothesis about the world's purpose must take full account of both the moral and the natural realm. Accordingly, Sorley tries several hypotheses.

The view of the world's purpose as the production of happiness among human beings is rejected, owing to the facts of evil. It is clear that an ethical conception of ultimate reality is impossible on a hedonistic ethics, for the world is imperfectly adapted to man's desires for pleasure. And if the moral criterion demands due proportion between merit and happiness, we are again at a loss. Such a view "leaves out of account the consideration that individuals or selves, and the community of individuals . . . are all of them in the making. . . ." [110]

An ethical view such as Sorley's, however, which holds that selves, in willing the good, are "fashioners of their own characters," is not open to the same objections, for the "world will be contemplated as providing a medium for the realization of goodness. . . ." [111] This view sees difficulty and suffering as the basis of the character of free persons. ". . . An imperfect world is necessary for the growth and training of moral beings. If there were no possibility of missing the mark there would be no value in taking a true aim." [112] Sorley, however, like Ward, is not confident that the relation of natural forces to moral ideas does justify the inference of the goodness of God, and therefore he adds: "All I have argued is that our experience is not inconsistent with such a conclusion." [113] His whole point is that the structure of the world as we know it, because it does not make impossible the good will, at least destroys the argument that goodness cannot be at the heart of reality. (But it would seem that the good will is possible, since it is absolute, no matter what the

[109] P. 337.   [110] P. 342.   [111] *Ibid.*   [112] Pp. 343, 344.   [113] P. 346.

ultimate relation of value and reality is.) On the other hand,
Sorley concludes this part of the argument thus:

> I do not say that experience of the relation of natural forces to moral
> ideas and moral volitions justifies of itself the inference to divine good-
> ness at the heart of all things. The mere fragment of life with which
> we are acquainted is too scanty to bear so weighty a superstructure.[114]

Thus we see that the goodness of the cosmic Purpose is not
disproved by the relation of the nonmoral and moral realms.
However, though the relation of the world to moral ideas is
consistent with cosmic goodness, the actual achievement of
goodness is insufficient proof of God's goodness. Consequently, Sorley is once more forced to appeal to purely cognitive grounds for the affirmation of goodness at the core of
reality.

This admission is not discouraging for Sorley, who is confident of his remaining grounds. To repeat, his attitude seems
to be that if actualized values were all the evidence there is
for God's goodness the argument would indeed be weak.
But for those who, like ourselves, have no recourse to cognitive grounds for final proof of cosmic goodness, the stone
which the builders rejected will have to be the cornerstone.
A universe in which man has through the ages been able to
develop a moral character, in which both the good will *and*
goodness have been experienced sufficiently to convince serious men that there are spiritual laws of human happiness,
such a world (though more has to be said about evil) is no
more explicable apart from the hypothesis of God than the
falling of bodies is explicable by a law which is the adverse
of the law of gravitation. We argue not from cognitive
relationships between ourselves and a so-called objective
goodness, but from those experiences without which the cognitions would at best be only interesting psychological phenomena. If the argument for God's goodness cannot be built
on what has already happened, what ground have we for
supposing that our cognitions of the objective values Sorley
speaks of are true or relevant to our moral struggle? Unless

[114] *Ibid.*

experimentation, based on even such cognitions, did not satisfy our natures and produce that harmony and peace which indeed passeth understanding, the cognitions themselves would be of no use to us in our attempts to achieve that harmony. We must now, however, consider Sorley's "other reasons for saying that goodness belongs to the ground of reality." [115]

From this point on, we must realize that our philosopher is grounding the argument on his assumed proof of the metaphysical objectivity of moral values. The problem for solution remains: In what way can the existence of metaphysically objective values be conceived? From everything Sorley has said so far one might well think of the realm of immutable Ideas of the early Plato, but, like the Plato of the *Sophist*, Sorley must (not embody) but "ensoul" them in the mind of God. Sorley and Rashdall are at one in this "specific moral argument." God is now to be conceived not only as the ground of the orderly world and man, but also as the source of that extra-material world of abstract truths which man discovers, and which found in God "their home when man as yet was unconscious of them." [116] Certainly their eternal validity could not exist except in a soul! Thus the last step in the argument:

> Further, persons are conscious of values and of an ideal of goodness, which they recognise as having undoubted authority for the direction of their activity; the validity of these values or laws and of this ideal, however, does not depend upon their recognition: it is objective and eternal; and how could this eternal validity stand alone, not embodied in matter and neither seen nor realised by finite minds, unless there were an eternal mind whose thought and will were therein expressed? God must therefore exist and his nature must be goodness. [117]

If we inspect this argument closely, we notice that a word has slipped in which can be accepted only if it is analytically implied in the words "objective validity." We refer to the word "eternal," undefined, but probably meaning everlasting and immutable. Two pages later we are again told that since the valid (but unrealized and incompletely apprehended)

[115] P. 346.   [116] P. 348.   [117] P. 349.

ideal "cannot be valid at one time and not at another," it "must be eternal as well as objective." [118] Hitherto we have been given to believe that moral values are dependent neither on our recognition nor on our realization for their existence. But the same might be said about the existence of other persons without entailing the further predicate of eternity. On empirical grounds there is no reason for supposing that metaphysical objectivity involves eternity (though neither would there be empirical grounds for the generalization that objectivity did not involve eternity). However, once any objective realities are characterized by eternity, a God (defined as eternal) is needed to explain not only their objectivity but also their eternity. On the other hand, it is at least conceivable that the original objectivity to be explained may have been pre-existent to human perception but not eternally pre-existent. The trouble is that Sorley now is beginning to argue not only from what he has established but also from what the traditional conception of God involves. The objective realm is colored by God's presupposed eternity before it is proved that he is its source; the argument oversteps itself and is unempirical. Notions like absoluteness and eternity seem to go together, and Sorley, like Pringle-Pattison and Rashdall, is trying to ground value in the very nature of ultimate reality. As the quotation Sorley borrows from Rashdall puts it:

Only if we believe in the existence of a Mind for which the true moral ideal is already in some sense real, a Mind which is the source of whatever is true in our own moral judgments, can we rationally think of the moral ideal as no less real than the world itself. Only so can we believe in an absolute standard of right and wrong, which is as independent of this or that man's actual ideal and actual desires as the facts of material nature.[119]

This brings us to another point. Does not reflection on these quotations and the substance of his thought make the following formulation of Sorley's answer to Hume a fair one? "I have an idea of goodness which is valid and eternal, whether I realize it or not, and since such goodness is not

[118] P. 351.   [119] P. 347.

fully realized in man and is irrelevant to matter, it must belong to God." In the last analysis, have we gone much further than the Cartesian cosmological argument, which is further reducible to the ontological argument? The only line of reasoning which would save Sorley from this conclusion is that this ideal of goodness in the life of man was concomitant with and owing to experiences (not mere cognitions) of goodness, that it is a rational description of man's satisfactions in volitional action.

Indeed, the main facts with which Sorley is dealing may be expressed alternatively, with less theoretical and empirical difficulty, in three statements. First, the only absolute in the ethical realm, as Sorley maintained, is the good will. Second, a moral standard can be "independent of this or that man's actual ideas and actual desires" [120] by being Objective and not metaphysically objective (in the same sense that the sun as scientifically defined is independent of private, psychological objects of individuals). Third, *obligation is absolute* to this (Objective), common, moral ideal which, like the phenomenal world, is *relevant* to, not the copy or imitation of, the metaphysical world (in this instance, man, the world, and God). The consciousness of the ideal of goodness is, then, not owing to a supposedly metaphysical object causing us to have the idea, but is a complex construction *based on the actual experience* of many minds, though never completely realized in any one or any group as a whole.

But the fact that the ideal of goodness is not realized in the world underlies Hume's objection to the assertion of God's goodness. And it is because Pringle-Pattison, Ward, and Sorley unfortunately grant his objection that they are forced to fly for refuge to a cognitive rather than an experiential ground for affirming the (eternal) goodness of God, though they add that Man's progress is impossible apart from this cognition. Furthermore, in order to safeguard the validity of this cognition, both Pringle-Pattison and Sorley beg the question at issue and, without sufficient grounds, postulate a kinship between the world and man. Granted even this

[120] P. 347.

kinship, their argument is weakened by the fact that both admit not simply that men "have not achieved agreement with it [the moral ideal] in their lives," but also that "even their understanding of it is incomplete." [121] Thus, for these philosophers also, man, at any stage in his development, can only hope that *his conception* of the ideal is relevant! In contrast, on our position the cognitive objectivity of our ideals does not depend upon their presence in God's mind, but we should insist that a world in which the Objectivity of ideals and knowledge is possible is inexplicable apart from a Being who willed their possibility in his initial creation of the world and man.

This point is important, and it may be reviewed from a different perspective in connection with further remarks Sorley makes about his moral argument.

This argument, Sorley asserts, may be maintained even if the objective validity of abstract truths is denied. For example, one may insist that if we can discover the laws of nature as relations already embodied in nature and not look to God to account for them, and if we do not need God to account for mathematical or logical relations (for these may be considered abstracts from the actual order), why look to him for the validity of ethical ideals in the external world? Sorley answers that the case is different with moral values, for the validity of moral laws can neither be verified in external phenomena, nor found by observing nature, since they hold for persons only.[122] "Other truths are displayed in the order of the existing world; but it is not so with moral values," [123] since "their peculiarity consists in the fact that their validity is not in any way dependent upon their being manifested in the character or conduct of persons, or even on their being recognised in the thoughts of persons." [124] Therefore the moral order must be regarded "as the order of a Supreme Mind, and the ideal of goodness as belonging to this Mind." [125]

It is evident that one's agreement or disagreement with

[121] P. 351.
[122] Cf. pp. 349, 350.
[123] P. 351.

[124] P. 350.
[125] P. 352.

Sorley ultimately depends on his ability to accept this theory of value. Having stated our objections, we must now suggest an alternative. Briefly, is not the ethical system we hold that formulation of the approved conceivable actions which may exist between persons and between persons and nature, and which we think to be most reasonable in the light of both the nature of persons and of reality? That is, our ethical ideals, we repeat, are a reflection of what we take reality, our own and the world's, ultimately to be. And since we cannot hold that they are eternal in the mind of God for every conceivable existence, and that they are objective because our act of knowledge in itself reveals their validity, we can say no more than that they have validity for us only when we are conscious of them and that they are valid only of this kind of existence (since they arise from it in the first place). In other words, we are holding that the Objectivity of the moral law is relative to the nature of the personal and natural epoch in which we now live, in the same way as present natural laws hold for this epoch. The ideal of the Good is the rational interpretation and description of man's volitional experience, as we have already said. It is independent of individual men, but it is not independent of man. We deny the distinction Sorley makes between validity or objectivity of moral principles and natural law. The Objectivity of both natural and moral law depends upon the coherence of physical law with the facts of nature, of moral principles with the combined facts of the physical and the personal world, the difference being that now we are looking for the laws of prospective behavior which we may continue to initiate. For example, when in this particular world we treat other persons as ends and not simply as means we find that such actions eventuate in satisfactory and harmonious living. Hence, the law of love is based on an analysis of human experiences with such action, and its truth is to be further demonstrated in the lives of men through their volition. The validity of ethics depends upon the coherence of our interpretation of ourselves in relation to each other in this physical world, not upon complete realization, and the validity of any natural law as we formulate it depends *not* simply on the fact that it works, but on its adequacy as a comprehensive or reasonable and fertile hypothesis.

Because Sorley minimizes and misinterprets the exact relation of values to man and the world, he leaves a gap between the moral and the natural, and thus has to seek objectivity in a different way. He finally makes the objectivity of morality depend on God, and, in order to avoid possible cross-purposes and mistaken cognitions between our minds and God's, he resorts to man's kinship with the universe to save the day. The thought of this work is that the existence of God may be arrived at through a full realization of the interconnection of natural and moral law, and of the meaning of objectivity in both realms. God is needed to explain not only the Objectivity of moral law, but the Objectivity of natural law as well. Humanism is not to be rejected because it does not explain the objectivity of values in Sorley's sense, but because the Objectivity which values do have cannot be explained by the clash of atoms, because the possibility of "scientific" salvation (even if the latter were granted) cannot be explained without a good God. Man does not create completely even value-claims; he must be grateful for a constitution and a world which makes them possible.

K. Summary

The following theses summarize the salient points in this chapter:

1. Since there is no legitimate transition from the "is" to the "ought," a comprehensive philosophy must take both into account. Sorley proposes to evaluate the contribution of moral experience to a synoptic view of reality, which will regard the moral and the causal realm as coöperative parts of one system.

2. Moral experience cannot be reduced to other psychological elements. Though moral judgments are not infallible, their objective validity is not affected by historical and psychological analysis, and they may be tested by their coherence with a system of values.

3. We held, however, that, though the "ought" (which in itself is cognitively innocent) cannot be reduced to the "is," moral values are not subjective even if they are reducible to value-claims whose coherent systematization leads us to the Good, which is obligatory.

4. We also insisted that value-claims (not primary value-judgments) claim validity, and that the Good is known through an inductive and coherent systematization of value-claims (not of "oughts"). This Good, when discovered, immediately becomes obligatory, and, accordingly, those particular desires the realization of which is conducive to the Good are transformed from simple desires to "oughts" to be desired, or true values.

5. Moral judgments are objective for Sorley not only because, like existential judgments, they claim objectivity, but also because, when correct, they exhibit universal values and display a common purpose and spirit which characterize the good will. But there is no absolute good apart from the good will. Here we agree except for the underlying theory of value.

6. For Sorley, belief in the conservation of value can be maintained only if there is a source and ground of the metaphysically objective values, for it is not justified by the amount of realized value in the world. But we suggested that the present enjoyment of values and whatever conservation there is, indicate the existence of a cosmic Friend.

7. The metaphysical reality of values incompletely realized by man is made to depend by Sorley upon a cognition, guaranteed by a gratuitous kinship with the universe, of a realm independent of man's cognition and yet valid for him. But validity here is meaningless and hypostatized.

8. For Sorley the causal realm, as a necessary condition of moral character, is consistent with but insufficient proof of God's goodness, and he therefore turns to the objectivity of value to complete the argument. But if the argument for God's goodness cannot rest on

achieved values, we should be led to doubt the truth of
our cognitions of a moral realm and its relevance to
our moral struggle.

9. The metaphysical objectivity of moral values is another way of expressing God's goodness, but since
(a) the Good *for man* cannot exist independently of
him as the cause of his knowing values, and (b) human
moral ideals cannot be attributed to God in their entirety, our values are really Objective, and God's goodness and love are inferences, based on human analogy,
from his relation to the world and man's moral
struggle, as are his other attributes.

10. Because persons are conscious of a metaphysically objective realm of values, this realm, since it cannot exist
either by itself alone, in persons, or in matter, must
exist in God. But Sorley's reasoning at this point may
be ultimately reduced to the ontological argument.

11. The alternative view is that values are Objective and
that this Objectivity, which is based on the idealization
of actual experiences of value and not mere cognitions,
cannot be explained without the hypothesis of a good
God who willed their possibility in his initial creation
of the world and man.

CHAPTER VI

FREDERICK TENNANT'S TELEOLOGICAL ARGUMENT
FOR GOD

A. TENNANT'S INTELLECTUAL DEVELOPMENT
AND WORK

THE religious beliefs of Frederick Robert Tennant (1866–) did not differ from those of the orthodox laymen of the Church of England during his undergraduate years (1885–89) at the University of Cambridge. The first two years at Caius College were spent in the study of physical and biological sciences; and in the last two years Tennant concentrated on chemistry and physics. In 1889 Thomas Huxley, exploiting the biblical criticism of Walter Baur and Friedrich Strauss, was challenging orthodox beliefs in England. Aroused by this attack, Tennant began his search for a *rationale* of religion which could profit from all legitimate scientific conclusions as well as withstand criticism from all avenues of learning.

The years 1891–94 were employed in the teaching of science at the school Newcastle-under-Lyme, where Tennant's own precollegiate training had been received, but the end of this period found Tennant qualified, as a result of private study, for ordination in the Church of England. After three years (1894–97) in parish work, Tennant became chaplain of his own College at Cambridge, and it was during this period that he turned to philosophy in order to reconcile the demands of science and theology. The ultimate and finest fruit of this course of preparation was to be *Philosophical Theology* in two volumes.

Previous to his appointment as University Lecturer in Philosophy of Religion at Cambridge in 1907, Tennant had continued his ministry in Norfolk, and it was on the strength of earlier theological writings that he was called to Cambridge. From 1913 to 1931 he was Lecturer in Theology, and in 1931

he was invited to give the Tarner Lectures which resulted in
the publication of *The Philosophy of the Sciences*. At the
end of the present academic year,[1] Tennant will retire from
active duties as a Fellow of Trinity College and Lecturer in
the University of Cambridge.

Ward, McTaggart, and Sidgwick were Tennant's teachers
at Cambridge, but it was Ward who finally recommended
himself most to Tennant and who was Tennant's fast friend
at Cambridge. It was not, however, until after fifteen years of
teaching, during which Tennant, expounding the merits and
demerits of different philosophical views, was slowly reaching
his own standpoint, that he found himself very near on many
points to Ward. It must be noted that Ward's contribution
to Tennant's thought is in natural epistemology and psychology. Of Ward's *Psychological Principles* Tennant says:
"I myself regard it as the greatest single work, of any age, on
the human mind." [2]

The appearance of Tennant's *Philosophical Theology* extended his influence from the purely theological realm (for
he already was a recognized authority in the Church of
England on the problem of sin) to the philosophical. Yet
it must be said, unfortunately, that in England an amazingly
small number of professional theologians and candidates for
the ministry agree with C. D. Broad that "they could not be
better employed than in studying Dr. Tennant's work." [3]
The indexes of too many recent books in religious philosophy
have too few references or none to Tennant's work. On the
other hand, a growing interest in Tennant's philosophical
thought is noticeable especially among younger American
thinkers.

In Tennant's two volumes, *Philosophical Theology*, the
student may find the structure of theism supported by a thorough, yet concise, investigation into the main problems of
philosophy. *Philosophical Theology* "takes reading," as Ten-

[1] 1937–38.
[2] *Philosophical Theology*, I, vii. All references, unless otherwise stated, are
to Tennant's works.
[3] *Mind*, XXXVIII (1929), 95.

nant himself once said, but in no other work in late British philosophy of religion can one find a clearer, more exhaustive, and more painstaking exposition of the argument for theism. The first volume on "The Soul and Its Faculties" is a whole in itself, and is the logical, psychological, ethical, and metaphysical preparation which, in a Spinozistic phrase, leads the student by the hand to the theological investigation of the second volume on "The World, The Soul, and God." There are some men who are emotionally predisposed to religious beliefs; there are others whose responses are impossible without intellectual conviction. In Tennant's work the religious-minded may find cogent reasoning to which they may tie beliefs that are otherwise apt to wander, like Plato's statues of Daedalus, in the face of difficulty; while the intellectual may at least find "a sustained application of the empirical method" in reaching theism "from universally accepted data and under the constant control of facts and sciences. . . ." [4]

Before proceeding to the exposition of those views most relevant to Tennant's own theological conclusions, we gladly acknowledge what the reader has already noted, the influence of Tennant on our own thinking. The unity of his work, as he himself says,[5] is in the use of the empirical approach to the problems of philosophy and theology. In this respect the influence of Tennant added weight to that of Edgar S. Brightman of Boston University. Of this method of empiricism Broad, to whose adverse criticisms we shall attend later, says: "If a system of speculative philosophy cannot be established by Dr Tennant's method, I agree that it is still less likely to be established by any other." We can also agree heartily when Broad continues: "Dr Tennant's method at least ensures those who use it against nonsense, enthusiasm, and credulity; it leads to a form of theism which is intellectually and morally respectable and in practice inoffensive. . . ." [6]

[4] *Philosophical Theology*, II, 247.
[5] *Ibid.*
[6] *Mind*, XXXIX (1930), 483, 484. Unless otherwise stated, our own view may be identified with Tennant's in what follows.

B. THE EMPIRICAL METHOD

The data of philosophy for Tennant are the presumptive knowledge gained from every aspect of experience, whether already criticized and organized by the sciences or not. Knowledge about the actual world can be most adequately obtained by trying to fit not facts to theories, but theories to facts. Consequently, the method Tennant employs is not logical and deductive, but proceeds from actual experience and is inductive, though of course this does not mean that deduction is not involved in inductive procedure.

The task of synoptic philosophy is to render experience coherent through further analysis and synthesis than is open to the various sciences. The problem is: What is the procedure which will allow us to take the least for granted? Since the *ordo essendi,* issuing in the *ratio essendi,* is concerned with the logical presuppositions of present presumptive knowledge, it is interpretative of the known rather than critical of the means by which knowledge was gained. The *ordo cognoscendi,* however, takes less for granted, since it investigates the procedure by which the structure of knowledge is built. In other words, if philosophy is to proceed empirically and cautiously it must proceed to the logically prior through the psychologically prior. Thus, a philosophy (a) controlled [7] by the presumptive knowledge of common sense and science which is the data for further philosophical criticism, and (b) employing the *ordo cognoscendi,* takes less risk of being led astray, for it sets out from fact and keeps close to fact (or knowledge with the minimum of theory attached), than would a philosophy which employed either the *ordo concipiendi* or the *ordo essendi.*

This thesis may be put and developed in another way. If philosophy is to seek knowledge of the whole through examination of the presuppositions of the sciences and common sense knowledge, it would be careless if it did not investigate the nature of knowledge itself. Now, if we concern ourselves only with the discovery of the logical presupposi-

[7] Cf. *Philosophical Theology,* I, 4.

tions of knowledge, we risk the possibility of overlooking
the light which the genetic study of the knowing process
might throw on the nature of knowledge. However, the
genetic psychology here involved must be supplemented with
analytic psychology. Though Tennant says so explicitly nowhere in his works, he has admitted in conversation that if
the results of genetic psychology should conflict with those
of the analytic, the latter are naturally to have priority, since
they constitute the data from which genetic psychology must
proceed.[8]

Tennant is quite conscious of the heresy he has committed
in supposing that the development of the knowledge process
has anything to do with its validity. But it is a misunderstanding of Tennant's method to suppose that he states this
contention dogmatically, before investigation. He insists,
rather, that nothing is lost and much may be gained by proceeding on the very plausible assumption that the evolution
of man or his relationship to the environment may bring
added insight into the nature, scope, and significance of
knowledge. Actually he thinks that man's thought would
never have been identified with Thought, or the world considered completely rational if the "plebeian" origin of reason
had been known; but the use of the genetic and analytic
methods does not foreclose these possibilities. Furthermore,
if the epistemological or logical analysis of knowledge is
followed, then invariably it is forgotten that nonlogical elements are involved in all knowledge, as Kant's rationalism
illustrated. Historically, "the analytical genetic method"
would have been a safeguard against the extension of ideas
far beyond the context in which they were born.

It is only by tracing the development of the knowledge-process that
we can ascertain the nature, scope and limitations of the product. So
the facts established by psychology concerning individual experience
must be the first quest. No less is meant than that the *ordo cognoscendi*
is the sole route that possibly may lead to a *known ordo essendi.* . . .[9]

Thus Tennant joins Ward and Schiller, and all three develop the methodology prescribed for philosophy by Locke.

[8] Cf. however, I, 18.   [9] *Ibid.*, I, 11.

One final objection may be met. There are those who would join Martineau (and one is reminded of Hegel's criticism of Kant, or of Whitehead's criticism of attempts to measure the limits of the mind) in holding that it is impossible for knowledge to criticize itself, since some certain and universal knowledge is presupposed in the very investigation. Tennant would admit that the laws of thought are preconditions of knowledge, but he denies that the knowledge otherwise presupposed needs to be any more than the presumptive knowledge whose presuppositions are not necessary principles which hold "no matter what." Rather are these so-called necessary principles "human postulations" whose practical efficacy has been such as to render them highly probable. Indeed, presumptive psychological knowledge, in this particular instance, may turn an "imperfect eye" upon itself as a process of knowledge and proceed to criticize, clarify, and render coherent even presumed knowledge about itself. And in so doing, the critic need "presuppose nothing but the fact that, by performing certain mental operations on confused opinions, clearer conclusions emerge which are stable beliefs capable of commanding general assent." [10] Consequently, the certainty alleged to be presupposed in the criticism of knowledge "can be replaced by the security of high probability of belief which passes for knowledge because of its serviceableness in enabling us to cope with life: which serviceableness bespeaks some relationship, however indirect and subjectively initiated, with the ultimate nature of things." [11]

C. The Mind as Knower

We cannot hope to do justice to Tennant's disinterested psychological study of the concrete knower, a study paving the way for epistemology, but presupposing no specific epistemological or metaphysical conclusions. We can only repeat the more relevant portions of what Tennant states more fully and clearly.

[10] *Philosophy of the Sciences* (1932), p. 41.
[11] *Philosophical Theology*, I, 41, 42. (References in notes 12–28, following, are to *Philosophical Theology*, vol. I.)

Analytical psychology must begin with the fact of consciousness, "our prime datum." Investigation soon reveals that, having a wider denotation than awareness, consciousness refers to an indefinable and ultimate qualitative feeling which is present in sensation, perceiving, enjoying, or thinking, and is logically and psychologically prior to knowledge. This feeling Tennant denotes by the word *erlebnis*, but each individual must ultimately find it in his own experience. The "first principle of psychology" is "that there is a unique kind of *erleben* which simply is and 'shines by its own light' . . . [and] is presupposed in the sophistry by which it is explained away." [12]

The very meaning of consciousness leads to the second fundamental principle of psychology, that there is no awareness apart from a subject and an object. Consciousness is a unique duality in unity, and all attempts to fly away from the subject of experience are effected by its wings.[13] Further analysis reveals three subjective elements in the activity of consciousness: (a) feeling, or pleasure and displeasure; (b) conation, which presupposes feeling but is irreducible to either feeling or cognition; and (c) active receptivity or attention, presupposed by feeling and conation and the condition of cognition. "Psychologically regarded, experience is *rapport, not timeless or static logical relation*, between subjects and objects; experience is not only change, but also interaction." [14] This conscious activity is ultimate and underivable, and it is to be expected that attempts to find it *logically* intelligible, as Bradley's thinking illustrates, should declare it to be contradictory. The partition of activity presupposes it. Before turning to the psychologically objective element in experience, we may summarize: the presumptive facts of experience would be impossible unless a subject is capable of pleasure and displeasure, desire, and active attention to objects which evoke both.

Of the object involved in all experience, it may be truly said, without begging metaphysical issues, that psychologically its *esse est percipi*. "To venture out of this ego-centric pre-

[12] I, 16.   [13] Cf. I, 18–24.   [14] I, 29 (italics mine).

dicament . . . involves for the metaphysician, whether realist or idealist, a leap in the dark, a venture of faith, such as may or may not be justified by the consequences." [15] The object of experience is not a state of the subject but "before the mind," "over-against a subject." [16] The most important species of all objective experience is the impressional sensum (or sensation as differentiated from the act of sensing), from which, and this is to be noted carefully, the imaginal is derived. The following quotation also needs close attention:

> The presentation, order and nature of impressions, in so far as involuntary or non-selective attention is concerned, are thrust upon us willy-nilly: that is what renders the impressional psychologically ultimate and inexplicable. The analytically simple data of all knowledge as to our actual world, are thus posited for us, not by us: they constitute an irrational surd which pure thought cannot eliminate.[17]

There are, however, no pure sensa, for thought and sense are together from the first. There is *nothing* in the understanding which was not in sense, *except* the activities (a) of retention, which involves interested activity and is the basis of recognition and memory; (b) assimilation of sensory residua with new impressions; and (c) differentiation of the sensory continuum.

Perception merely develops the "germinal perception" of the act of sensing, and Tennant stresses the point that pure objectivity and subjectivity are mythological; "there is nothing perceptual that is not subjectively fused; and tinged with the incipiently or implicitly conceptual," as well as with human interest. The result is that the percept always has a foot in both the objective and subjective worlds.[18]

The reader may have been wondering what this psychological analysis has to do with the empirical argument for God, but an understanding of Tennant's psychology is the necessary preliminary to the understanding of elements in his theology which are often rejected without reference to the psychology on which they are based. The following point derived from stated facts will be used to explode certain contentions whose strength lies in overlooking it. The perception

[15] I, 34.   [16] I, 35.   [17] I, 36.   [18] Cf. I, 45.

of an object is so immediate psychologically that we are unaware of synthetic activities and conclude that the whole experience is unanalyzable and simple, and unconditioned by previous experience. Reflection on that perception, however, soon reveals neither simplicity nor immediacy; and, consequently, a distinction must be made between psychical or psychological immediacy and epistemological immediacy. We need to remember that the psychological immediacy does not involve the epistemological immediacy.

The synthetic activity of the subject, however, is controlled by the "unalterable relations" between the sensa themselves. Hence the creative activity of the subject is limited to choice of the qualities of the objective continuum which shall constitute a unity *for the self*, a choice limited in turn by the determinate nature of the subject. The body is epistemologically the most important object of perception; for constituting, as it does, a constant group of sensa, it forms a constant background for all other sensa. By analogy with it we build up our notions of permanence and unity, while from the consciousness of our own voluntary activity in the face of resistance we form the first idea of cause (as Martineau held). Hence, substance and cause are not rationalistic Kantian categories, but products of the interaction of the retentive, attentive, and differentiating mind with a permanent group of unique sensa which it comes to regard as its own body. These categories are built up by the interested mind and become the instruments of the mind in the construction of its world. Substance and cause "are derived from life, not from logic; they are regulative while they are constitutive; they are both anthropic and mundane," and, "suffered by the sensory data into which he [the subject] reads them, they are tools for fashioning a phenomenal world in some respects after his own likeness." [19] Unless we realize that our thought-forms are born in the humble context of a conative self in *rapport* with a world, we tend to assert that these categories are originally independent of sense and absolutely necessary to *all* thinking. On the other hand, they

[19] I, 50.

are "regulative instruments" developed by the mental self. In this way, it seems to us, the essential truth of Kant's critique, the contribution by the mind of regulative forms which make orderly experience possible, is upheld and given a more adequate psychological foundation.

As already indicated, the "impressional core of all perception" for Tennant is "the primary reality and the objective source of all knowledge as to the existent." But he is careful to state that this need not mean "that all that exists is perceptual or even possibly perceptible," though it does "affirm that no other analytic data are indubitably known to science [systematic study]." [20] This is the ground for Tennant's rejection of the "thought-given existents" of the rationalists and the nonsensible and nonintelligible existents of some mystics. The main reason why Tennant ascribes actuality or reality (not Actuality or Reality) [21] to the impression or percept and not to the imaginal is that the subject is controlled by impressions which are psychologically independent both of each other and of previous impressions and images, while the imaginal is an outgrowth from the impressional and not similarly controlled. "There is nothing in the complex image of a non-actual thing, such as a mermaid, that was not previously 'in the senses.' " [22]

Now the imaginal is the ultimate source of ideas (though, of course, "there is embryonic conception implicit in the simplest perception") which constitute a further abstraction from the "that" of impressional experience.[23] The idea or concept is free from the here and now of the impressional and its concrete filling, but it "still has reference to actuality." [24] Yet because it has left the impressional core behind, an idea is not actual or real. "But an idea will be *valid of*

[20] P. 51n.

[21] The capitalized words, such as Reality or Time, always mean the epistemological or common, as opposed to the purely psychical, as indicated in the last chapter.

[22] P. 52.

[23] It is impossible to include the details here as elsewhere, and the reader must be referred to *Philosophical Theology*, I, Chapter IV.

[24] P. 63.

the perceptual *in which* it was implicit, and *from which* it has been abstracted; just as a frame will belong to, fit and suit, the picture it once enclosed." [25] Consequently, and this is one of the most important points in Tennant's thinking, "validity is not to be identified with reality, but is rigorously to be distinguished from it." [26] Any of our concepts may transcend the impressional context, and for this reason we must be careful not to extend them unconsciously beyond the context for which alone they are valid. Universals, consequently, can exist only *in rebus* for Tennant, and validity is not reality; our concepts are keys *we* make, but the lock to which we fit our key is not man-made.

So far, however, only the experience of the individual, apart from his all-important relation to other individuals, has been discussed. Each individual ultimately lives in his own private, impressional, and imaginal world which could not exist without him. This private experience is presupposed by all intercommunication between selves which brings to the individual the consciousness that his world has elements in common with that of other persons. Knowledge of the self, other selves, and the world develops *pari passu*.

D. The Self and the Soul

Knowledge of other selves, for Tennant, is mediated by ejective analogy with ourselves and presupposes some self-consciousness, which, in turn, is mediated by the identification of the self with organic sensa and the body.[27] Self-knowledge develops, as already stated, *pari passu* with knowledge of others. Furthermore, refinement resulting from this contrast with others leads to the notion of the pure perduring ego, as distinct from the empirical self, or the pure ego *plus* its states, relations, and objects.

Tennant has two objections to the theory that this pure ego is known by direct acquaintance. The essence of the position opposed is that there can be no indirect knowledge about the *I* unless there is direct knowledge. Tennant objects, first, that introspective acquaintance presents no *quale* of

[25] P. 63.   [26] P. 64.   [27] Pp. 70–74.

the *I* such as we find in impression. "Hence, the quality-lessness, or transparency, of the ego suggests that it is known only by, or as, idea. . . ." [28] Tennant admits that this is not a "conclusive refutation," but we venture that it is no refutation at all. For, we should insist, it is the unique *erlebnis* with its own peculiar, inexpressible characteristics that each person can know only for himself, which is the ego. To be sure, in no one specious present is the whole self or ego given, but we construct our knowledge of the self from our experience of the specious present. This does not mean that we have indubitable and direct knowledge in every instance of introspection, but it does mean that our knowledge of the whole ego (as contrasted with the complex of feeling, willing, and thinking in any specious present) is based on the coherent interpretation of its expressions. In holding that "the idea of self is founded upon an immediate experience of self as a unity or whole of life," [29] we are in agreement with Sorley at this point. [30] As he says, our experience of ourselves is deeper than intellectual sympathy, it being an immediate apprehension "which is lived in the moment that it is known, although it is preserved in memory and clarified by reflexion." [31] In other words, in the very *erlebnis* of momentary experience one is conscious of one's self, and his knowledge of himself grows as the nature of the self is unfolded in its activities. It is important to note that on this view the experience of ourselves always contains more than we can or do articulate; there is a penumbra we experience but of which our knowledge is not clear; we know *that* it is there and that it is *ours* but cannot say *what* it is. [32]

If this is true, we must admit that we never know exactly what we are, not only because we are creatures of growth,

---

[28] P. 77.

[29] Sorley, *Moral Values*, p. 263.

[30] Sorley, however, agrees with Tennant that there is a pure or noumenal self as the ground of the phenomenal or empirical ego. Orally he has said the self is *that* which thinks, *that* which feels, and so on. Cf. *ibid.*, p. 204n.

[31] *Ibid.*, p. 260.

[32] This last sentence Tennant would grant. Cf. *Philosophical Theology*, I, 78.

but also, as psychological disputation indicates, because we may gain mistaken self-knowledge. Hence, any particular experience of ourselves is subject to coherent criticism. And these foregoing considerations remove the basis of Tennant's next criticism. "If the I be apprehensible to itself with (*ps*) [epistemological] immediacy, it is strange that all sentient beings are not fully self-conscious. . . ." [33] We have not asserted epistemological immediacy of the *whole* ego as such, and we have held that knowledge of the whole ego is not given all at once but is constructed out of the past and present experience and knowledge of ourselves.

Thus we can hold with Tennant that we do not "sense" the self, that the (whole) ego is not revealed "apart from its acts, states, and even objects," that it is not "a simple presentation of the present moment." [34] Against him, however, we hold that the ego *is* its acts and states, the immediately known data from which we construct our notion of the whole self. Tennant's distinction between the noumenal and the phenomenal or pure and empirical ego is not granted. We thus come to the essential difference in the two views. Tennant, it would seem, must hold to immediate knowledge of the empirical or phenomenal self through which the pure ego is mediated and indirectly known, but we suggest that there is no other self than the experienced and known self. Let us consider Tennant's main reason for holding to his distinction.

The noumenal self is needed, Tennant argues, to render intelligible the presentation of consciousness in self-consciousness, or the fact that I know that I am knowing. The act of knowledge involves subject and object, but the knowledge of the act of knowledge involves another subject or possessor. This underlying self is not given presentationally or phenomenally but is the inferred bond which gives unity to the phenomena of consciousness. A unity is needed to unify not simply any act of cognition, but subjective states as well; "every single 'content' of the empirical self's experience, every single drop in the 'stream of consciousness,' must have

its subject." [35] Now we certainly do not deny that our awareness of ourselves in the act of knowing is impossible, unless
there is a unity of self-experience, but it is difficult to see
why the self that *knows it is knowing* is noumenal. What
seems to be given in the specious present is the whole fact
"I know that I know," not the fact that "I know that Me
knows." It is only when we review this experience intellec-
tualistically that we differentiate between the "I knowing" and
the "Me knows." We are consequently led to consider this
unique experience of self-knowledge and experience in the
light of our other cognitive experiences, wherein the distinction between the noumenon and the phenomenon is necessary, owing to the activity of the self which knows the
non-self. The unity of a specious present in which I know
that I know *is* the (former) *I* conscious that *it* is having a
certain experience of itself or of another object. This view
is consistent with the following conditions any tenable theory
of the self must meet.

Any theory of the self must explain the temporal continuity,
unity, and order of the mental life, as Tennant holds. Change
is impossible unless there is an ego which persists through it,
and the distinction of experiences and retention are precon-
ditioned by an abiding ego. The specious present, Tennant
correctly holds, is a "saddleback" and contains "the residuum
of the past, and anticipation of the future experience"; [36] each
specious present is continuous with and overlaps other specious presents, but all distinctions and transitions would be
impossible unless the abiding ego perdured. Against all serial
theories of the self Tennant insists: "Without appeal to the
marvellous or else to the abiding ego, it is, however, no easier
to unify two momentary experiences than a life-time of
them." [37]

We are not anxious to defend any of the theories Tennant
rejects. We agree that: "Apart from its [the mind's] abiding
subject, the individual mental life, or stream of consciousness, is no stream, no unity; and when the stream is abstracted from him, it is no wonder that he cannot be found in

[35] *Ibid.*, I, 81.　　　[36] *Ibid.*, I, 83.　　　[37] *Ibid.*, I, 87.

it, and that he 'transcends the facts.' " [38] But we deny that the soul or pure ego is Actual, that it "cannot be phenomenal" since "it is that to which phenomena appear." [39] We agree that it is "the one ontal thing that is assuredly known," [40] but we deny that our knowledge concerning the essence of the soul is *entirely* inferred. As we have said, and as Professor Edgar S. Brightman [41] states with greater force, the whole self is all the consciousness which we are able to connect, by the complex experience of self-identification, with the basic category of all experience, the "datum self," or the self as grasped in the immediate consciousness of the specious present. The whole self, then, is Actual, but it is Actual (epistemologically) because it has been actual (psychologically) in the self we know indubitably in the specious present.

To repeat, the fundamental fact in our view is that in any specious present we experience ourselves as complex conscious wholes of conative, volitional, and cognitive experience. There is unity, continuity, and order in the specious present or the datum self. Given this unity of consciousness in the specious present, we should hold that the self grows from within in response to its environment, though at certain stages it may be its own stimulus. In any specious present the self is pregnant with the past, with influences received from the non-self, and with its conative straining toward the future. Its problem is to keep its unity in the face of the stimulations it receives, sometimes willy-nilly, from these quarters. The future is in the present only as a state anticipated, but as such it joins the past in creating the present apperceptive mass with which all experience is coördinated. Or, to put it differently and more accurately, any present (datum) self is the self of a moment ago modified by the aims it had and by the stimulations it has received.[42] The unity

[38] *Philosophical Theology*, I, 92.
[39] *Ibid.*, I, 97.
[40] *Ibid.*
[41] Cf. Brightman, *An Introduction to Philosophy* (1925), Chapter VI, and *A Philosophy of Ideals* (1928), Chapter I, to which we are heavily indebted.
[42] Here we are influenced by A. N. Whitehead's discussions in the classroom and in *Process and Reality* (1929).

of consciousness has not been passed over or transferred to any present, but the present *is* the past unity modified by cognitive, emotional, and volitional processes within it, and presents a new unity in the sense that the direction or context of life is changed somewhat. Memory and continuity are possible because the present is the past plus or minus certain experiences and characteristics. (In the same way, for example, metaphysical questions aside, the body is the same body of the moment before, living because it has been able to digest what it has taken in and to adjust itself to its environment.) On this view, which *begins* with the experienced unity and order of the specious present, we can account, without references to a noumenal ego, for the unity, order, and continuity of the self.

We can also agree with Tennant in the following description. (a) The soul (which for us means the conscious self and for him the pure ego that *has* consciousness) is "an impenetrable or impervious monad with its 'own point of view': which is not to say that the soul is 'windowless' or devoid of active *rapport* with objects, or that its experience is explicable as a series of immanent states." [43] (b) Each self possesses its own unique idiosyncrasies or specific nature which will determine how it will react to the world. (c) The self "is not a blankly receptive *tabula rasa*, nor is it exclusively cognitive," [44] but, because of its own unique feelings, it is an interested agent. We should also agree that "its *known* essence is to function," but we should go further than Tennant, who holds that the self cannot be "a substance to which experience is only incidental," [45] and say that we have no ground to suppose that the self is *anything but* its experiencings (as opposed to objective experiences). The functional relation here adopted between the pure ego and its states, a pure ego which *has*, but which is neither thinking, willing, nor feeling, is completely meaningless to us. The self is a conscious complex of feeling and willing and knowing. These are not

[43] *Philosophical Theology*, I, 96.
[44] *Ibid.*
[45] *Ibid.*, I, 97.

properties of an underlying and uniform reality. Tennant himself rejects the notion of the self as "static or changeless . . . for continuity of becoming may be the law of the soul's being," [46] and he holds correctly that "substance is through and through causality." [47] But we cannot follow Tennant [48] in holding to a becoming or causality which is the basis of feeling, willing, and knowing, but not equivalent to them, for this is an abstraction of activity from specific activities, analogous to the abstraction of extension from color. We know extended colors, and we know specific activities of willing, feeling, and knowing, and these constitute the self. Tennant comes very near this position when he says that "thoughts, volitions, etc., are not accidents or adjectives" [49] of the soul; but he leaves us with them inhering in a "substratum" subject which supports them.

We may conclude this section by noting that for Tennant the pure ego just described is the first determinant of personality, which is different from subjecthood (a) in being self-conscious, (b) in being made (and not born) by interaction with the environment and other persons, and (c) in being capable of indefinite growth. To deny that the personal self can determine its conduct by ends determined in turn by itself is to deny the very essence of the ego. Accepting Tennant's view of personality thus briefly indicated, we differ by substituting for Tennant's basic pure ego what Brightman called the "minimum self." [50] This is the simplest possible conative self-consciousness that is at least vaguely aware of its objects, is to some extent reflective, and transcends time in the sense that it is a unity in time (but is not nontemporal).[51] Before turning to relevant points of Tennant's epistemology, we cannot better summarize this portion of Tennant's thought than by quoting him approvingly.

---

[46] *Philosophical Theology*, I, 97.   [48] Cf. I, 101.
[47] *Ibid.*, I, 99.   [49] *Ibid.*
[50] From a "Syllabus on the Philosophy of Religion," 1933–34.
[51] Though Brightman and Sorley have been referred to, and though the essence of their views of the self have been included, the reader must look to them for fuller details.

It is from our knowledge of self that our fundamental categories of identity, continuance, substance, causal activity, end, in terms of which we "know" — i.e., interpret — the world are derived. That of personality is in the same case; and it is our highest interpretative concept. For the theist, it is the key to the universe. . . . And inasmuch as personality is a product of the world-process, man being (save in respect of his soul or pure ego [minimum self]) organic to Nature, the world itself has made imperative the interpretation of itself in terms of this concept. If such interpretation promises anthropomorphism, it need be but in the sense in which anthropomorphism has already been represented to be the inevitable mould in which all human thought is cast, and by which it is shaped from first to last; because man, after all, is man, and must think as man if he is to understand — i.e. to assimilate to himself.[52]

E. The Theory of Natural Knowledge

For Tennant, as for Ward, the two poles of certainty are logical and mathematical truths, on the one hand, and the immediate and incommunicable qualities and relations of impressions or sensa on the other. But neither of these gives knowledge of the World, for logical propositions may or may not be true of it, and the presence of sensa and their relations would never take the individual beyond his private world. "The [psychological] object of each man is private; no man can apprehend another's,"[53] and no objects of different men are qualitatively the same. The result is that communication with others can be had only by resort to a common pattern (to use the terminology of C. I. Lewis,[54] of Harvard) which individuals find in their respective objective continua. "Thus it is relations between sensa or simple percepts in individual experience, not impressional *quale*, that can be known in common."[55] In this way, transition is made from the sun of individual experience to the conceptual Sun of common knowledge.

But our Objects are in Time and Space and related in various ways to each other, the fundamental relation between

[52] *Ibid.*, I, 127. N.B. Not man's ego or ultimate ego is organic to Nature, but only his acquired personality. Let those thinkers also take notice who refuse to consider God a person on the ground of anthropomorphism.
[53] *Ibid.*, I, 164.
[54] Cf. *Mind and the World Order* (1929).
[55] *Philosophical Theology*, I, 164.

them being causal. Tennant agrees that the subject contributes to experience, but the rationalistic conception of the a priori as independent of sense and not in any way derived from sense is rejected in all its forms. Space is not a pure Kantian intuition but an idealization of and abstraction from the extensity of sensa. Time, which is psychologically more nearly fundamental, is an abstraction from the duration, simultaneity, and succession of perceptual time. In other words, Physical Space and Time are concepts reached by abstraction from perceptual experience.

Not even the formal categories of mathematics (like unity) and of logic (like similarity) are a priori, for they are derived by reflective comparison of the sense-given and are thus objectively prompted. Though mathematical categories give intuitive certainty and universality, they do not give universal and necessary knowledge about the World. "Knowledge of a common external world involves more than objective data of individual experience and formal categories of universal Experience." [56] It involves use of the "real" or dynamic categories of substance and cause, which in turn, presuppose the "forms" of space and time, and originate in the action of a conative-cognitive subject, not (as Kant's did) in logic. We have already noted that substance and cause are "not purely subjective furniture, but analogical ejects [of the self] objectively prompted, and, consequently, derived from commerce of subjects with objective environment." [57] In their explicit form they originate in self-consciousness as developed by intercommunication with others.

Knowledge for Tennant, consequently, is not spun in logic or in fancy, but controlled by impressional data. It is inextricably permeated and indelibly stained by man's psychical make-up, which determines what his data shall mean to him as he assimilates them. Knowledge is not "mental photography of the ontal," and the dynamic categories do not "mirror ontal structure." [58] Nevertheless, it is important to realize that relations are the occasions and control of our

[56] *Philosophical Theology*, I, 174.
[57] *Ibid.*   [58] *Ibid.*, I, 176.

ejective analogy. Consequently, "it [knowledge] is not necessarily a phenomenal caricature or a garbled rendering of
the ontal, or a pretending that Reality is what it is not." [59]
The real categories are neither read in nor read off completely; "they are established by postulation that is subjectively derived but objectively evoked, and are principles of
interpretation." [60] And the fact that these postulated categories or functionings of the mind in relation to the environment have been found to be practically successful shows that,
though they do not mirror reality, they have a relevance to it.
For Tennant sense-certainty is blind, formal relations that are
read off with immediacy and necessity are empty, and percepts and concepts without interests are valueless in the
knowledge of actuality. "Our knowledge of the external
world is, from its very foundations, a matter of more or less
precarious and alogical analogy rather than of self-evidence;
of hope and venture that have been rewarded." [61]

Nor do we lose this alogical element when we come to
think about the World we have thus constructed, for thinking is neither mere observation nor logical induction, nor
deduction. In searching for a valid solution of a problem,
thinking is experimental and involves the use of alogical
imagination, insight, and association. Thinking carries on
the process of relating our impressional data to our human
demands, and is therefore teleological. We are not surprised,
therefore, to find Tennant concluding that when reasoning
means the discovering of truth about Actuality it contains an
alogical and teleological drive which differentiates reason from
logical or formal rationality. Reasonable knowledge about
the Actual is consequently never completely certain but always contains an element of faith. Kant's distinction between
the understanding and reason disregarded the teleological
element in both, while any view of reason as *sui generis* or as

---

[59] It may be said here, that, developing this line of thought, Tennant holds
that the laws of nature we formulate are relevant to and stimulated by ontal
orderly processes we interpret according to our interests. (*Ibid.*, II, Chapter I.)

[60] *Ibid.*, I, 177.

[61] *Ibid.*, I, 183.

lumen naturale overlooks the fact that "reason is made, not born," being "an outgrowth of the understanding which has a common root with sense." [62] Knowledge is rational faith; the truth is the most reasonable hypothesis. There are a priori capacities for knowledge, but there is no a priori knowledge. The rationality of the world is no a priori necessity but ascertainable only by experiment and investigation.

So far the results of Tennant's empirical approach coincide with Ward's in respect to the theory of knowledge. Tennant has succeeded, we believe, in making the necessary synthesis between rationalism and empiricism. The words of F. C. S. Schiller show the similarity between Tennant's thought and his own.

> Thus our final "knowledge" will be neither wholly *a priori* nor wholly empirical. It will be a product of the continual interplay and inter-action of the knower and his world, and will owe its character to *both*. . . . Knowledge becomes a continuously developing process to which no term need be set.[63]

We may briefly indicate the implications of this empirical theory of knowledge for metaphysics.

F.   EMPIRICISM AND PERSONALISM

We have seen that for Tennant the Common World is the thought-product of individuals sharing the communicable relations between their private experiences of objects, or worlds. The problem of metaphysics, however, centers about the nature of the metaphysical object and not the perceptual object or conceptual Object. One thing is obvious — that since only the object is known with certainty, and since in-vestigation has shown that there are no pure data unaffected by human activity, the nature of the metaphysical object is a subject for hypothetical knowledge. Realism may be imme-diately set aside because it assumes that the object and the metaphysical object are photographically identical, and be-cause it cannot explain error. The Sun is not the sun of perceptual experience, and there is no metaphysical object

[62] *Philosophical Theology*, I, 193.
[63] Muirhead, *Contemporary British Philosophy*, I, 399.

exactly corresponding to it, though there is one for which it is relevant. Rationalism, on the other hand, overlooks the alogical object and subjective, conative activity.

It is clear from what has been said that, for Tennant, knowledge is restricted to phenomena from which the nature of the noumena or metaphysical objects are inferred. Indeed, the phenomenon is "the utterance of the ontal to *us.*" We have acquaintance with the sensible, but the latter is the result of our dynamic interaction or *rapport* with the noumenal of which we have phenomenal knowledge.[64] Once more Kant must be modified. If the metaphysical object must be invoked to account for the appearance of sensa or phenomena, as he held, "it must equally be invoked, in order to account for their relations to one another," [65] and "there must be a one-to-one corespondence between phenomenon and noumenon, in respect of detail." [66] The noumenon is not totally unknowable, and our phenomenal knowledge is at least relevant to it even if its "noumenal essence" is not copied, since it is received *ad modum recipientis.* The conceptual and phenomenal World of common sense or science is the result of the criticism of private data resulting from the *rapport* of individuals with the noumenal world to which, as source of stimulation, the phenomenal world is relevant.

All this, it seems to us, must be granted to Tennant as eminently empirical and reasonable. But, concentrating on one theory of the nature of the metaphysical object, it is difficult to grant the grounds for Tennant's implicit accusation[67] that a Berkeleyan idealism cannot transcend solipsism or cannot account for the laws of nature. For even Ward admitted that occasionalism was a possible theory. If, as we held then, the view of the object as a subjective modification be abandoned, and the metaphysical object with which the mind is in *rapport* be considered the energizing of a Will, it is difficult to see how Tennant's objections hold. The laws of nature on this view become our interpretation of God's

[64] See *Philosophical Theology,* I, 247.
[65] *Ibid.,* I, 248.
[66] *Ibid.,* I, 247.
[67] Cf. *ibid.,* I, 241.

orderly stimulation, and Tennant's position in regard to the object and the Object is still tenable. The truth seems to be that Tennant cannot account for the laws of nature unless some sort of world is planted out with a certain amount of autonomy. Indeed, the reader of *Philosophical Theology* will note that, when Tennant does state his own metaphysical view, he finds Ward's most acceptable.[68] Our criticism of the latter has already been recorded. Orally, however, Tennant has stated that though Ward has shown how belief in metaphysical dualism has arisen, this is not sufficient disqualification of it. This criticism seems to overlook Ward's essential objection to those dualisms at least which do not conceive of the metaphysical object as activity (which for Ward, as for Personalists, is unintelligible except as will).

We can best indicate Tennant's present state of mind [69] on this subject by saying he is convinced that the metaphysical world must be (relatively) independent of God and man in order to explain the laws of nature. Whether those ontal beings, of which the physical things are phenomenal, are spiritual or are inert — that is, whether spiritualism or dualism is true — he finds no means of knowing and regards the solution of *this* metaphysical problem as of no real significance for theism. Ward's spiritual pluralism is possible and economically preferable, but not proved to the exclusion of dualism. But in any case, it is not, as Ward thought, indispensable to the proof of theism. Tennant knows more about the noumenal world than Kant did, in that for Tennant the relations among phenomena are noumenally grounded, but he finds it impossible to decide categorically between spiritualism or some species of (relative) dualism. For him Being need not be activity, or activity, will. In *Philosophical Theology*,[70] Tennant says that dualism does become "a more obviously dispensable theory" for theism, since inert matter

[68] Cf. *Philosophical Theology*, II, 214.
[69] That is, as recorded and approved by Tennant after a prolonged discussion of this point sometime in March 1935.
[70] *Philosophical Theology*, II, 213, 214.

has then no value and meaning in itself but is simply a medium for the interaction of finite spirits. Of the spiritualistic alternatives, Berkeleyan theism and pan-psychism, the former is specifically rejected.

G. Empiricism in Ethical Theory

We are finally ready for the consideration of those parts of Tennant's philosophy which have more direct bearing on the problems of religion; but the foregoing, if wearisome, has yet been necessary to the understanding of Tennant's theology. Many, including James Ward himself, who would grant Tennant the theory of natural knowledge outlined, would differ on theories of ethical and religious knowledge. And they falter simply because, as we have tried to show, they forsake the *ordo cognoscendi,* or empirical method at its best (since it is a more comprehensive approach to problems and takes least for granted), and become realists as regards ethical knowledge, though they are phenomenalists as regards natural knowledge. As Tennant has shown, realism overlooks the coloration or transformation of the object by human, organic, and mental idiosyncrasies and supposes that the object and the metaphysical object are photographically identical. We have tried to show how those men in Great Britain, through whom the moral argument for God stands or falls ultimately, reject ethical phenomenalism (which would insist on the creative activity of the mind in ethical knowledge) for ethical realism, essentially by making feeling simply an instrumental pathway to the cognition of value. Tennant has succeeded, we believe, in breaking down the traditional fences between cognition and conation in every realm of experience, and, to change the figure, has brought together the Siamese twins which had been cut loose by less persistently empirical philosophers. Once the vain hope for absolute knowledge is relinquished, Objective knowledge, we have seen, is still possible in the natural realm without recourse to epistemological realism. We ourselves have tried to show that Objective knowledge, under the same conditions, is possible in the moral realm also. We shall find, when we consider Tennant's theory of value,[71] further justification for our contentions against those who have turned to ethical realism to avoid the "subjectivity" of value.

Basic in Tennant's view is the contention that, just as there is continuity of development from perception through ideation to abstract thought, so "there is continuity traceable by psychology from individual feeling and desire, together with their cognitive concomitants, to aesthetic and moral sentiments, and acquisition of ethical principles." [72] Tennant, however, is able to evade the condemnation of a Martineau disciple, who might say that morality cannot be derived from the nonmoral, by holding that evolution is epigenesis rather than the mere unfolding of the preformed. Nor does Tennant disagree with Sorley that moral judgments may not be derived from "purely" existential judgments. "Moral consciousness, indeed, is not resolvable into feeling and desire, or into intellection: it may none the less be emergent from them, when they are compounded." [73] We shall find greater light as we trace the more important steps in Tennant's view.

Our philosopher begins once more with the *ordo cognoscendi*, the psychology of individual valuation, rather than with the *ordo essendi* or axiology, for he would not risk the loss of relevant information which analysis of the value-experience might yield. At any rate, Tennant's investigation reveals that feeling is not merely instrumental to the apprehension of value, but constitutive of value itself. Feeling (pleasure) evoked in the subject by an object, or the desire for an object, is the minimum that is needed to render it valuable to him. "No further objective quality [than its sensory ones], tertiary or other, requires to be postulated, nor any new feeling-induced cognitive activity to be invented *ad hoc*." [74] This theory at least is compatible with the fact that there is no accounting for tastes, as there should be if, in the experience of value-claim, feeling introduced the individual to some

[71] Tennant's theory of value is largely influenced by W. M. Urban's work: *Valuation: Its Nature and Laws*, 1909.

[72] *Philosophical Theology*, I, 139.

[73] *Ibid.*   [74] *Ibid.*, I, 141.

added (moral) quality of the continuum besides the impressional qualities and relations.

These private valuations of Objects (though of course for the individual it may be of objects) are, like the private experience of objects, the basis for over-individual valuations, and the scale of values which self-interest has prompted the individual to choose for himself will become subject to criticism and modification in terms of the experiences of others. The basis for intercommunication about the natural world was the similarity of sensory pattern, but here the ground is the fact that, though not psychologically identical, no two individuals are altogether different, that none are isolated or pure egoists, and that therefore coöperation with an over-individual end is possible.[75] But once the individual has been "baptised into the over-individual, he becomes a new creature to whom all things are new," [76] and he comes to see himself as others see him and to reflect others' approval or disapproval of his own desires.

It is in this way that "*con*science" of a jural kind arises; the recognition of duty or debt to the common good is the original "oughtness." Tennant admits, however, that "it is a far cry from such crude morality" of the "I owe" to the unconditional categorical imperative. Tennant believes, however, that "there is continuity, if logically there is disparateness," between "I owe" and "I ought." [77] He holds that the axiological level of the categorical imperative "is itself reached by idealisation and abstraction from the empirical value-judgments of social experience." [78]

Tennant is here arguing against those rationalists who assert that there is "no escape from the a priori grounding of ethics on the ultimate deliverance, both rational and immediate, of the moral consciousness that asserts the categoricalness, unconditionality, or absoluteness of its findings." [79] For

---

[75] Let it be carefully noticed that the basis for the uniformity of values is not the nature of value-objects, but the nature of the individual subjects which constitutes objects or actions valuable.

[76] *Ibid.*, I, 146.

[77] *Ibid.*, I, 146.

[78] *Ibid.*, I, 147.

[79] Cf. *ibid.*, n.

he believes that in this assertion the psychological immediacy claimed is confused with the epistemological and is really acquired. Tennant, in other words, is denying that conscience has any cognitive value *per se*, that there is any uniquely *moral* consciousness, that there is any value-object, as we have put it, the immediate, original experience of which makes it obligatory. Moral progress is not owing to the perfection of a faculty, but "what is called moral insight is largely [we do not know why Tennant does not say wholly] intellectual discernment of existential truth, determinative of conative disposition." [80] The social prophet "discovers a better than the old good, something more . . . conducive to the abiding happiness of a greater number; his criticism of *mores* does not presuppose, actually or logically, any new and unique conception such as that of absolute good or oughtness." [81] This conclusion is, of course, contrary to the contention of our other writers.

Correct as Tennant is in his rejection of the moral *consciousness*, he too has failed, we believe, to distinguish between the psychology of moral obligation and the epistemology. For he not only denies that there is knowledge of a unique moral object; he also denies the *sui generis* quality of moral obligation. His confusion leads him to identify a cognitive *verdict* of conscience with moral obligation itself, as is evident when he tries to show, against Martineau, that a "conscience that approves real altruism can be accounted for by genetic psychology," the clue being that "when conscience is thrust upon him, he [the individual] already knows sympathy." [82]

It would seem to us, on the other hand, that since Tennant grants orally and in writing [83] that the growth of the jural conscience into the feeling of absolute obligation is not completely traceable, a faithful empiricism demands that theory be restricted by known facts. Consequently, we should hold that the presence of sympathy is an important point in the rational solution of a *particular* problem of morality,

[80] *Philosophical Theology*, I, 147.   [82] *Ibid.*, I, 148.
[81] *Ibid.*   [83] *Ibid.*

altruism, but of no relevance to the problem of conscience. We need not review at length our own conclusions on this point, but may simply repeat that analytic psychology (from which the genetic must set out) reveals that the whole person feels an unconditional obligation to do the Good, an obligation the violation of which is accompanied by certain unique moral emotions like remorse. The feeling of obligation cannot be reduced to either volitional, conative, or intellectual elements, but is a new activity of the whole complex of these. In itself it sheds no light on the nature of the Good, but it holds the person obligated to do whatever he thinks is the Good, whether that be mere self-preservation and egoism or the greatest self-sacrifice (thus being consistent with change of ethical concepts and men's loyalty to unfortunate conceptions). From the obligation to goodness no psychological alchemy can get more than the unconditional feeling of ought, which is the only (psychological) absolute there is in ethics. This theory, as indicated, is consistent with the facts of moral evolution which, we should agree with Tennant, is caused by the development of insight and will. It also would account for the unique imperative which men like our writers find as *concomitant* with many valuations, this *obligation* (rather than true values) being what cannot be reduced to desire. The principle of moral alternation is living and thinking, thinking and living, a sincere venture in response to internal and external stimulations, a constant effort to render ourselves increasingly sensitive to all our environment may hold, adventurous living and adventurous thought. So much may be offered by way of addition to Tennant's view, but for the rest, Tennant's theory of value seems to account for the facts of experience. The remainder of his view may now be outlined.

"The self has a self-interest that is inalienable, though capable of transformation and indefinite refinement," [84] and as the self rises morally "the conception of a relatively more ideal self to be attained" results.[85] Instead of being imperfect translations of vaguely seen metaphysical ideals, "the succes-

[84] *Ibid.*, I, 149, 150.   [85] *Ibid.*, I, 150.

220   EMPIRICAL ARGUMENT FOR GOD

sive ideals are *imaginal or ideational constructions*, original
or suggested, reached by thinking away faults and shortcom-
ings of which the higher self has already convicted the
lower." [86]   Furthermore, Tennant finds that cultivation of
the self as an end in itself and cultivation of it as an instrumental member of society are bound to conflict, and he consequently rejects both self-realization and the social good as
"*the* highest good." There can be "no monistic ethic transcending the dualism of 'personal' and 'social' valuation,"
and "if so, the expressions '*the* highest good,' '*the* absolute
ideal,' are meaningless." [87]   For Tennant, our ideals arise as
a result of our affective-volitional attitudes in concrete situations and are relevant and valid of them. They are not absolutes reached by such abstraction from the individual desires
and the initial situation that they no longer acknowledge their
birthplace.

From the desired to the desirable, from the concrete good, that is
good for something, to the good-in-itself, from the subpersonal to the
over-individual, and from the social to what may be called the over-social
or the absolute, there is a way. But there is no deductive way back from
high abstractions, so reached, to particular moral judgments relevant to
specific Actual issues. Necessary truth, in ethics as anywhere else, is pur-
chased at the price of possible irrelevance to Actuality. . . .[88]

What then does the objectivity of value mean for Tennant? It means Objectivity. Just as we build up our common
world from private sensa, the criticism of private conative
valuations or value-claims results in Moral Judgments and
Valuations which are independent of individual tastes and
preferences, but not independent of the affective-volitional
experiences of a community of individuals. Thus, an empirical ethics rejects the extremes both of individual whim and
of absolute or unconditional values, and substitutes a rational
postulation of ethical norms valid of some "Actual or possible situation." [89]   As we have tried to put it, an empirical
ethics is based on the coherent systematization of value-

[86] *Philosophical Theology*, I, 150 (italics mine).
[87] *Ibid.*, I, 152; cf. below, pp. 237, 238.
[88] *Ibid.*, I, 153, 154.
[89] *Ibid.*, I, 156.

claims that issues in the ideal of the Good which, in turn, grows with experience and criticism. As Tennant says, such a position does not relieve man of practical absolutes. "It only denies that they [ideals] are literally and theoretically absolute, and affirms that they issue from, and are relevant to, life in the environment of Nature." [90]

H. EMPIRICISM AND RELIGIOUS KNOWLEDGE

Tennant's views on the cognitive value of religious experience have been subject to much misunderstanding, and though we are not able at present to evaluate them properly, we shall attempt to outline and clear away possible misunderstandings of his position at this point. Tennant is really challenging conclusions which he believes have been too hastily drawn, on the one hand, from the fact of religious experience by the mystics, and, on the other, by the development, modification, and addition to Schleiermacher's view, such as are found in Otto's *Das Heilige* and John Oman's *Natural and Supernatural* (a critique of both Otto and Schleiermacher). We have studied Tennant's resistance to both the thought-given realities of the rationalists and the value-given realities of those who, like the thinkers we have criticized, would find in moral experience an independent pathway to God. Our philosopher, in contrast, using the sensuous-given as a standard, rejects both the moral and the religious-given. But his position is misunderstood unless seen in the light of his careful investigation of the psychology of knowledge. Once the student realizes that for Tennant (a) "our percepts and their simpler relations are the sources of our ideas and universals, at least in the sense of being the occasions of our obtaining them," that "sense-givenness is the sole original certificate of actuality"; [91] (b) that ideas, once derived from the sense-given, may without further reference to it yield the pure sciences; (c) that value is not owing to the perception of a value-object but to feelings evoked by sensory data — he is ready to understand Tennant's reasons both for

[90] *Ibid.*, I, 159.
[91] *Philosophy of the Sciences*, p. 168.

rejecting the religious-given and for finding it not so necessary as some think for belief in God. Let us first be clearer about the position this empiricist opposes.

The view under attack maintains that there can be an independent science of theology whose task is to systematize religious data as ultimate and irreducible as sense-impressions, the immediate apprehension of which reveals a supersensible, spiritual environment. Now Tennant is quite ready to grant that there is no a priori impossibility of this; indeed for a theist such a position would be quite paradoxical. But the cautious empiricist demands that a careful analysis of known facts show this to be the most reasonable conclusion. Tennant *is not denying* that there is religious experience, but he is sceptical about maintaining that this experience, which is (phenomenal) effect, is the result of the religious *cognition* of a (noumenal) cause which alone rendered the religious experience possible. Beginning with the numinous or religious valuation, which cannot be denied, we must not infer, as hastily as has been done, (a) that there is a numen, or religious object proper, as its cause, and (b) that we have acquaintance-knowledge of it similar to that which we indubitably possess in sensory experience. So far, it seems to us, Tennant cannot be gainsaid; for, given a certain effect, the nature of the cause is a subject for investigation and not for that dogmatism which has a parallel in the identification of the object of experience with the Object or the metaphysical object. The very fact that all data are received *ad modum recipientis*, that knowledge is phenomenal (in all cases, we should say, except in the basic instance of self-experience), invites caution in deciding the nature of the noumenal. We are now ready for Tennant's main objections to this purely theological approach.

a. The first difficulty arises in connection with the nature of the numinous object. Unlike the sensory object, the numinous has no specific quality.

The numinous Real is indeterminate enough to enter equally well into a multitude of diverse mythologies and religions; it therefore seems to partake of the nature of the vague generic idea, rather than to be comparable with an underived and "perceptual" object . . . its abstractness, qualitylessness, commonness to a variety of phenomena, etc., render precarious and apparently groundless, the assertion that it is apprehended in the concrete and with immediacy.[92]

We saw that the absence of the specific *quale* was one of the reasons why Tennant rejected acquaintance-knowledge of the ego, but, whether or not one agrees with him there, when the object is the self, the denial here has greater weight. Tennant's point would be that, though Otto, for example, correctly emphasizes the direct reference to an object involved in the numinous feeling, he does not, in his analysis, realize sufficiently that the ideal and the imaginal, as well as the illusory, are also psychologically objective. Nor does he take full account of the generality which, characteristic of the numinous object, weakens its claim to direct givenness.

b. Second, if there is direct knowledge of a numinous object, it is impossible, Tennant insists, to account for error. Here it would seem to us: (a) *if* it could be shown that in the experience of the numinous, man is controlled, as in sense-impression, (b) this objection would fall away before a theory which admitted the subject-object duality, criticized numinous objects coherently, and held such knowledge to be only relevantly valid for a spiritual realm. Tennant's opponents, however, must answer at least on the first count; for, to repeat, "it would seem that the numinous object, constitutive of religious experience throughout its many stages of refinement, cannot be a quasi-perceptual datum, of the same order of underivedness as the sensory." [93]

c. The third objection, relating to the alleged immediacy of the numinous object, is that the psychologically immediate and the epistemologically immediate are confused, and what is really mediated and inferential is assumed to be self-evident.[94] Unless there is more evidence than the mere immediacy of the numinous object, the foundations for an *independent* theology tremble. For if the datum is not quasiimpressional, the only other conclusion is, as Tennant holds, that it is "rather a derived and mediated image or conception which is interpretatively read into perceptual or ideal objects, as the case may be." [95] Tennant's positive point is that we take the numinous object to be knowledge *of God* only because we previously believed in God "on less direct grounds reached by more circuitous paths," [96] rather than by this "short cut."

d. This objection may now be developed. To be sure, in religious experience there is undeniable *rapport* with the objective, and it is true that the person who believes the object of his cognition to be "the holy" issues from that experience a changed man. But nevertheless, the fact that there are certain concomitant emotions and feelings which are inspiring and lead to better living is not enough to justify the inference that there is a metaphysical reality causing the emotions. For not only does the psychologically objective include the ideal and the imaginal, but the ideal and the imaginal "when they are *believed to be actual* can evoke feelings and sentiments as profound, intense, inspiring, and practically fruitful, as those excited by perceptual or actual things." [97]

e. Whether there is an actual metaphysical counterpart to the religious experience cannot be answered by religion itself without begging the question (granted Tennant's point that the supposedly "insensible" numinous data are derived and read in rather than immediately read off). Religious experience is unique and evokes certain emotions *because* it is *interpreted* in terms of an idea of God derived from *other* sources. "Previously to the acquisition and the causal or interpretative use of this derived notion [of God], experiences such as were destined to become religious could not be religious: they could only be regarded as natural, not as supernatural, whether aesthetic, moral, or of other types." [98] In

---

[95] *Philosophy of the Sciences*, p. 174.

[96] *Philosophical Theology*, I, 311.

[97] *Philosophy of the Sciences*, p. 176; and cf. *Philosophical Theology*, I, 311 (italics mine).

[98] *Philosophy of the Sciences*, p. 177; cf. pp. 178, 179, and *Philosophical Theology*, I, 311.

favor of Tennant's view, one might ask of Otto, for example, whether, apart from the *idea* of God as Creator, we would consider the experience of "creature-feeling" as such. And the fact that interpretations of the nature of God have kept step with moral and intellectual changes, instead of surging ahead on the wave of religious experience as such, is another aspect which claimants for independent religious knowledge must cope with.

Thus does Tennant cut at the roots of a theology which, overlooking the interpretative factor that constitutes the essential uniqueness of the religious experience, would seek to establish itself by appealing to pragmatic considerations. We are no more able to obtain direct knowledge of God than we are of other persons. All of this having been noted, however, we must not conclude that Tennant disparages the moral inspiration or the "personal convincedness" of religious truth made possible by religious experience. Nor would he belittle the "hunches" which the subject might derive from it and test by their coherence with other known facts about the world and man. Tennant is simply denying that religious experience is a self-sufficient and independent pathway to public, *philosophical knowledge* about God.

What has been said about nonmystical religious experience may be applied to the mystical. Again, Tennant does not deny that the mystic may be in contact with God, but, for reasons similar to those given, he does not consider the evidence in favor of supersensuous knowledge about God forceful enough. The very fact that the mystic's experience is ineffable gives little cognitive value to his utterances, and when the mystic *is* intelligible he tells us nothing we could not know otherwise. Tennant's whole point [99] is that the psychology and epistemology of religious experience must be "atheous" (but not "atheistic") until re-expounded "on the way back," after the theistic position has been established on the grounds of more comprehensive knowledge about the world *and* man. The procedure in acquiring religious truth is not essentially different from scientific method philosoph-

[99] Cf. *Philosophical Theology*, I, 326, 328.

ically interpreted. Of the latter we must now say a few words, before passing to Tennant's teleological argument for God.

Since philosophical theology has no peculiar religious data of its own, it is restricted, along with science, to perceptual data. It might seem at first glance that, since science does its work so well, there is no need for two cooks who will "spoil the broth." But we begin to acknowledge that science does not embrace all problems as soon as we take full cognizance of the following considerations. The Nature resulting from the descriptions of the physical sciences is a skeleton from which the scientist, interested in the quantitative, has stripped the flesh of the qualitative and the purely subjective. The Fact of science is partly theory and already involves human interpretation according to real categories, while "Nature, as commonly before our minds is not natural rock, but rather a concrete in which the cement is mainly human assimilativeness." [100] There is an ultimate alogical element or surd, not reasoned but to be reasoned about, that is man's stimulating partner in the enterprise of knowledge. This surd forces knowledge to be not only a joint-product of man's active response to it, but also reasonable rather than exhaustively rational. Science pays no attention to values as such. These limitations are not defects of science or to be used in disparaging it, so long as it stays in its own realm. It is only when science tries to extend its methodology over the whole realm of experience and dictate to the epistemologist, metaphysician, ethicist, and theologian that it becomes too pretentious. "The alogical, which science increasingly ignores, and replaces by the conceptual when from experiment and verification it passes to theory, calls for the exercise of Reason, as distinct from formal rationality, for teleological explanation and 'understanding,' and evokes considerations as to value." [101] The science Tennant inveighs against is the scientific rationalism which explains away the brute facts of experience and which forgets that "its verification is pragmatic, not logical; the probability that is its guide is not mathematical but at least in part, psychological." [102] Tennant is not concerned to

[100] *Philosophical Theology*, I, 337.   [101] *Ibid.*, I, 363.   [102] *Ibid.*, I, 365.

throw stones at scientific glass houses, but he does insist that "science and theism spring from a common root" in the practical needs and intellectual curiosity of man. Therefore, he is confident that there may be peace and mutual respect once both science and religion are conscious of their respective presuppositions and true aims. Philosophical theology attempts to find the most reasonable explanation of the world as a whole. Since this includes molar and microscopic bodies, as well as life and the purposes and values of human beings,[103] the teleological explanation is the only kind that will not involve the denial of the mechanical but will welcome it *and* the nonmechanical. We are now ready for the understanding of Tennant's positive argument for God.

I.   "THE EMPIRICAL APPROACH TO THEISM: COSMIC TELEOLOGY"

Tennant has rejected a priori pathways to knowledge of the actual world and ethical truth, while the claims that there is direct acquaintance with God have been set aside as unproved and as depending on ideas of God derived from more circuitous paths and read *into* religious experiences. The teleological argument to which Tennant turns as evidence for God does not depend on particular and multiplied cases of adaptedness in the world. Rather is it built on the less precarious grounds constituted by "the conspiration of innumerable causes to produce, by their united and reciprocal action, and to maintain, a general order of nature." [104] The "gravest" objection to such an argument follows from the possibility that the knowable world is a fragment of the whole universe, and "our ordered fragment may be but a temporary and casual episode in the history of the universe, an oasis in a desert of 'chaos.' . . ." [105] To this charge Tennant replies in several ways. First, we have no right, as empiricists, to refute interpretations of the known by unknown possibilities. To say the least, a mechanical view of the total universe cannot be assumed, when the facts within our known world contradict it. Second, the "ordered oasis is not an isolable fragment.

---

[103] Cf. *ibid.*, II, 72.   [104] *Ibid.*, II, 79.   [105] *Ibid.*, II, 80.

It and the supposed desert or 'chaos' are interdependent." [106]
There is no evidence that our known ordered world, included
within the whole universe, is the result of selection out of ran-
dom variations similar to the selection within the organic
realm of our known world. "This is but conjecture or appeal
to the unknown, and, confronted with the second law of ther-
modynamics, is overwhelmingly improbable." [107] Nor does
our knowledge allow the supposition that an unlimited re-
shuffling of a cosmic atomic deck, "by mechanical forces,"
can deal out minds. Third, "the nerve" of the teleological argument is that design issues in values. "Teleology,
after all, is a value-concept; and magnitude and worth are
incommensurable." [108]

C. D. Broad, however, centering attention only on the claim
that the ordered fragment is not isolable from the rest of the
universe, holds that "this is surely insufficient," because the
question is whether this vast universe "might not be reasonably expected to contain occasional small 'pockets' in which
the rather special conditions needed for the production and
temporary flourishing of life and mind are realised, without
deliberate design. . . ." [109] Tennant, of course, would be the
first to admit that the teleological argument is not completely
demonstrable apodeictic proof, but his point is that it is to be
more "reasonably expected" that a universe, containing
pockets within which mind and value are made possible,
should be designed by a Mind than be the result of a clash
of atoms. And it seems to us that Broad's objection can be
sustained only if the design argument were restricted to the
particular adaptations which Tennant has replaced by ultimate collocations. Thus Broad writes: "If holding the five
best trumps be compared to an 'oasis' and holding anything
worse than this be compared to a 'desert,' it will be true that
my 'oasis' and the other players' 'deserts' are interdependent.
Yet the 'oasis' is not a product of design. . . ." [110] This is an
argument valid against organic adaptations within the world,
but it misses the point of the wider teleological argument. For

[106] *Philosophical Theology*, II, 80.   [107] *Ibid.*   [108] *Ibid.*
[109] *Mind*, XXXIX (1930), 479.   [110] *Ibid.*

what is to be explained is *not* simply my holding the best five trumps, *but the deck of cards which allows trumps* in this particular way. The deck of cards is so made that my having five trumps is one of the possibilities, and when I am in a universe in which I am holding trumps, the most reasonable hypothesis is that my trumps are not chance happenings produced by a universe which *by hypothesis* had no trumps (mind and value). Tennant is consequently justified in arraigning the evidence for a cosmic Designer.

Tennant's concern for a strong theistic argument leads him to evaluate certain groups of data to which some philosophers have given too much weight in arguing for theism. (a) The adaptation of thought to things, or the fact that our anthropic or real categories are relevant to the ontal reality, "does not of itself testify that the adaptedness is [necessarily] teleological," [111] for it is only when, like Descartes, we hold that ideas and percepts live in independent systems of their own that divine agency needs to be invoked to allow for the correspondence of thought and thing. Ideas are suggested by the non-ego. It is only when we consider that the world, which might have been a chaos without fixed relations and common patterns, is actually quite intelligible and penetrable by humanly developed categories that the epistemological argument becomes a strong link in the chain of evidence for a cosmic purpose.

(b) When Darwin showed that particular organic adaptations in the individual or species might well be owing to proximate causes, he undermined the argument of Paley. But he provided a broader basis for the teleological argument by transferring attention to the evolutionary process as a whole; for the proximate causes must be accounted for. "The discovery of organic evolution has caused the teleologist to shift his ground from special design in the products to directivity in the process, and plan in the primary collocations." [112] However, since the adaptiveness of an organism is not consciously purposeful, there are those who have suggested that the adaptiveness of the whole world was not the result of foresight. With this contention Tennant deals later.

[111] *Philosophical Theology*, II, 83.   [112] *Ibid.*, II, 85.

(c) The fact that an inorganic universe contained those elements which made organic life possible, even though the inorganic is in no way dependent on the organic, bespeaks a formative principle that cannot be without intelligence and foresight. Reasonableness "regards the 'probability,' that the apparent preparedness of the world to be a theatre of life is due to 'chance,' as infinitesimally small." [113] The dice seem to have been loaded for a throw resulting in this kind of organic world.

At this point Tennant considers the objection of the logician who holds that "If the world be the sole instance of its kind, or be analogous to a single throw [of dice], there can be no talk of chances or of antecedent probability in connexion with our question." [114] Tennant replies that when the teleologist talks of the improbability of the vast coincidence involved, he does not mean "a logical relation, but the alogical probability which is the guide of life and which has been found to be the ultimate basis of all scientific induction." [115] If theology parts with logic here, it does so in the good company of science. On this Broad makes several critical observations.

First, this argument would be helpless before the sceptical philosopher who could "see no more logical justification for science than for theology, but found that in practice he could not help believing the results of the former and could quite easily help believing those of the latter." [116] To this it may be replied that for Tennant a logically coercive justification for science as well as theology is impossible. But it remains for the person who, for biological reasons presumably, prefers to believe the results of science, to show why another cannot reasonably supplement his practical faith by intellectual faith in a postulated existence which introduces more order into his intellectual household than any other alternative.

Second, continues the critic: "Is there *any* sense of probability, mathematical or 'alogical,' in which a meaning can be attached to the statement that the antecedent probability

---

[113] *Philosophical Theology*, II, 87.
[114] *Ibid.*, II, 88.
[115] *Ibid.*
[116] *Mind*, XXXIX (1930), 479.

of one constitution of the world as a whole is greater than or equal to or less than that of any other? I very much doubt if there is." [117] The answer is that the logical difficulty here is the very one Tennant avoided by appealing to a nonlogical relation which he unfortunately still called "probability" but by which he meant the "venturesomeness" that guides all life. The only way in which probability is involved here is expressed in the question: The world being what it is, from our vantage point within it and the knowledge available to us, which hypothesis (not which constitution of the world) *about* the constitution of the world is more probable of those hypotheses at hand? We cannot know if there were other throws than the one which resulted in this world, and for this very reason there cannot be talk of "antecedent probability" of the constitution of the world, but only of antecedent probabilities between hypotheses. In any case, theology can no more be attacked at this point than can science. And this brings us to the third point.

Tennant holds that we have almost as much antecedent probability for believing in an intelligent Designer as we have for belief in other persons, which is based on ejective analogy (or is the most reasonable hypothesis to explain the behavior of certain bodies, and so on). Tennant admits that "there is a psychologically stronger compulsion, a nearer analogy, and a more immediate and constantly reiterated verification-process" [118] in our belief that other persons exist than there is in belief that God exists. Still Broad holds that Tennant's first comparison "seems hardly fair" for I know myself and "I can see that it is the kind of existent of which there might be many instances. . . . But I have no such grounds for assigning a finite antecedent probability to the existence of a single divine mind on which the whole world depends." [119] This, however, assumes what Tennant would not grant. Apart from my *assumed* belief in other selves, there is no *greater* antecedent logical probability for my saying simply

[117] *Ibid.*
[118] *Philosophical Theology*, II, 88, 89.
[119] *Mind*, XXXIX (1930), 480.

on the basis of knowledge of myself that there are other people like myself, as Broad seems to think. We transcend the egocentric predicament by alogical but reasonable faith, as Tennant holds. We are fortunate in finding other minds which we can understand and which we judge to be more acute and powerful than ours when we compare their "works" or manifestations. If, then, we find that the processes and contents of the universe are best explained by postulation of a Mind analogous to but greater than our own, why is the comparison unfair, especially if, as an empiricist, Tennant waits for the facts to suggest exactly how great the Mind is? We now continue with the main argument.

(d) Reflecting on the data of teleology supplied by our knowledge of man, Tennant says: "Values alone can provide guidance as to the world's meaning, structure being unable to suggest more than intelligent power. And beauty may well be *a* meaning." [120] Beauty saturates nature to such an extent (as Ward also said) that it becomes a miracle from the point of view of mere mechanism, which is in no known way dependent on beauty. The fact that Tennant defines value as constituted by feeling is no ground for supposing it to be a purely subjective creation, for the feelings are evoked in *rapport* with the noncreated ontal world; beauty is phenomenal, but is controlled by the ontal, which allows it, as well as formulated natural law, to be possible. "And the more we magnify man's part in this making, phenomenalising, and appreciating, the more motivation have we to believe that Nature comes to herself in man, has a significance for man that exists not for herself, and without man is a broken circle." [121] Nevertheless, it is "too precarious" to argue from beauty alone to the existence of God by arguing that since in human art beauty is owing to design, so all natural beauty is designed; for often, even in our experience, beauty occurs where there was no design. As Tennant says: "That natural Objects evoke aesthetic sentiment is as much a fact about them as that they obey the laws of motion. . . ." [122] And yet, though the beauty of nature

[120] *Philosophical Theology,* II, 93.
[121] *Ibid.,* II, 90.   [122] *Ibid.,* II, 92.

may help, when seen teleologically, to reveal the ultimate nature of reality, it is but a link in the chain of the more comprehensive teleological argument.

(e) Turning to moral arguments for God, Tennant argues that a posteriori arguments, like those of Balfour and Wallace, which invoke God to explain the extension of moral sentiments beyond what would be required by natural selection, overlook the fact that the human mind may proceed from intelligence and emotional sensibility, which are biologically useful, to not purely pragmatic endeavors, without the aid of a *deus ex machina* — just as bodily organs acquired for one function are found to be capable of others. A priori arguments holding that the rationality of the universe demands realization of ideals are condemned for confusing *rational* with "teleologically ordered" (which is to be proved). The only meaning for rationality we have the right, in the beginning, to assume is "analytically intelligible," [123] or "interpretableness" [124] by our regulative categories applying to the here and now. "Neither certainty nor probability that the universe will respect our aspirations can be given by moral judgments alone." And again: "The moral value-judgment, which simply predicates value and nothing else, cannot carry us a step beyond itself towards knowledge as to the existence of anything which, if Actual, would possess value." [125] By no stretch of reasoning can we argue from the present truth of value-judgments (on any theory of their nature, one might add) to what ought to be. We need not repeat corollaries following from Tennant's view of moral value, by which he is forced to reject views like Kant's, Rashdall's, Pringle-Pattison's, and Sorley's. Tennant would agree with the present writer's evaluation of the moral argument for God, and indeed, our own smouldering dissatisfaction with arguments like those criticized caught fire through the stimulation derived from *Philosophical Theology*. Tennant, denying that God is the direct source and home of human ethical ideals, nevertheless considers these ideals "an essential, and indeed the most significant part of the data to be taken into account in a

[123] *Ibid.*, II, 94.   [124] Cf. *ibid.*, II, 75.   [125] *Ibid.*, II, 95.

synoptic view and interpretation of the world. They supply the coping-stone of a cumulative teleological argument for theism." [126]

In our argument for God, man and his moral ideals are, therefore, not to be isolated from the world into which he was born. The only significant meaning Tennant can find for "man is organic to the world" is that man as phenomenal, *not* as noumenal (we have spoken of the cultured over against the ontological structure which became cultured), is organic to nature, for man's body, sociality, knowledge, and morality are " 'of a piece' with Nature." In the light of man's continuity with the rest of the organic world, which, in turn, has been fostered by Nature, it is extremely difficult to hold that the known history of Nature indicates that she "suddenly 'stumbled' or 'darkly blundered' on man, while 'churning the universe with mindless motion.' " [127] Nature, after all, has made moral beings possible by virtue of the provision not only of nonmoral data to be controlled but also of stability without which no ordered living would be possible. Such facts certainly indicate that Nature is contributing to a larger purpose. "Nature and *moral* man are not at strife, but are organically one." [128] And if such a statement seems to overlook the problem of evil, we refer the reader to our consideration of that problem in the next chapter. We are now ready for Tennant's final synthesis.

Tennant has been showing that certain data suggest teleological as well as causal and descriptive explanation. Since in each instance final causality *need* not be invoked, no one group of data is worthy to prove theism. However: "Theism no longer plants its God in the gaps between the explanatory achievements of natural science which are apt to get scientifically closed up." [129] Since causal and teleological explanation can live together happily, Tennant builds his case by showing that the different fields of fact dovetail and are interconnected as parts of a continuous series which cannot be adequately explained apart from a divine design.

[126] *Philosophical Theology*, II, 100.
[127] *Ibid.*, II, 101.
[128] *Ibid.*, II, 103 (italics mine).
[129] *Ibid.*, II, 104.

a. The order and arrangement of the universe cannot be adequately explained without reference to the activity of an intelligent God. "For cosmos-quality, or intelligibility, in our world, which conceivably might have been but a determinate 'chaos,' non-theistic philosophy can assign no reason." [130] Here Tennant joins Ward in insisting that the mysteries of pluralism are minimized if a creative God is postulated.

b. But the original adaptiveness of many existents, which is the prerequisite of the cosmos in its togetherness, merely indicates that the dice are loaded. However, "the hint becomes broader" when we analyze the knowledge-process. We then realize that "the particular species of intelligibility, in which the knowledge of common sense and science consists, is mediated by the 'real' categories" [131] whose success is contingent on the coöperation of the rest of reality.

Thus, as step by step the machinery which produces intelligibility is scientifically explored and made manifest, the richer in specialised determinateness are some of the world's constituents found to be; and therefore the more suggestive is the intricate adaptiveness, involved in the knowledge of the world by man, of pre-established harmony or immanent guidance, or both, and the less reasonable or credible becomes the alternative theory of cumulative groundless coincidence. The doctrine that man is organic to Nature can now be broadened out so as to embrace the fact that it is only in so far as he is part and parcel of Nature that he can ejectively make the knowledge-venture, and only in virtue of Nature's affinity with him that his postulatory categories receive pragmatic verification, and his assimilation-drafts are honoured.[132]

But nature's knowability is only another link in the chain of the teleologist, who adds a further connection after evaluating the nonconscious and conscious teleology in the organic and human realms, respectively.

c. The special adaptation and the emergence of new characteristics in organic life which lie at the basis of development from the amoeba to man *may* in themselves be accounted for by nonteleological causation, granted self-preservation as the law of life.

It is rather when the essential part played by the environment, physical and organic, in the progressive developement of the organic world, is

---

[130] *Ibid.*, II, 105.   [131] *Ibid.*   [132] *Ibid.*, II, 105, 106.

appreciated, that non-teleological explanation ceases to be plausible in this sphere, and, conspiration being precluded, external design begins to be indicated or strongly suggested.[133]

The individual has a certain amount of freedom, but his freedom is censored by the environment which compels (under pain of death) certain developments and decides what shall stand. The theory of "unconscious purpose" (which requires us to believe that Nature "which *ex hypothesi* is brainless" keeps her head) [134] merely restates the adaptedness of the inorganic and the organic rather than explains it. "If Nature evinces wisdom, the wisdom is Another's." [135] The coincidences to be explained are ultimately "in the determinate natures of the cosmic elements, the world's original existents and their primary collocations." [136] The adjustments of these are such that a relatively stable Nature, informed with law and variety and not only assimilable to human knowledge but also evoking values in human beings, is possible. The conclusion, then, is inexorable: "Organisms, and man in especial measure, have the world with them in their aspiringness." [137]

Furthermore, the harmony of intricate interconnection, which makes progress, as conceived by human beings, possible, may be judged by "the good" toward which progress aims.

[The moral data] enable us to advance from belief that the world is a work of art to belief that it is constructed for a purpose, and worthily specifies what the purpose is, or includes. If we decline to explain things thus, it would seem that the only alternative is to regard the self-subsistent entities, of which the world is constituted, as comparable with letters of type which shuffled themselves not only into a book or a literature but also into a reader commanding the particular tongue in which the book utters its unintentional meaning. If the inference from cumulative adaptiveness to design be non-logical, as is admitted, it at least is not unreasonable.[138]

The world's "thusness" cannot be explained, therefore, apart from a creative Being, who purposed the realization of moral values, beyond whom we need not and cannot go, but to whom we *must* go if a sufficient reason is to be given for cosmic

[133] *Philosophical Theology*, II, 107.
[134] Cf. *ibid.*, II, 108.
[135] *Ibid.*, II, 109.

[136] *Ibid.*, II, 109, 110.
[137] *Ibid.*, II, 110.
[138] *Ibid.*, II, 111.

evolution. Even Broad says that "if one *must* try to explain the ultimate and formulate the ineffable," Tennant's "type of conclusion [referring to Tennant's Theism as a whole] is perhaps the least unintelligible explanation . . . here and now." [139] In answer, Tennant might well join Ward in asserting that the *demand* for a sufficient reason is one which the world itself has raised in the highest product of its evolution. The "anthropocentrism" in Tennant's teleology does not mean that man is "the highest being under God," or that in judging the end of the universe by man we can fathom the divine purpose completely, but simply that in man, as a creature possessed of the power to think, the best-known clue is given to the nature of that purpose. In man and his values Tennant completes the curve begun by plotting the relationship between the inorganic world of law and an organic world driven by self-preservation.

It will be noticed that Tennant makes no direct use of religious experience as evidence "on the way up" to God. This is understandable in view of his contention that religious experience is atheous until *interpreted* as the presence of the God whose existence has been established by the more "circuitous" path — here the wider teleological argument. Once the existence of God has been rationally grounded, the fact of religious experience is more intelligible, and its inspiration is rationally justified. Furthermore, the religious moment now makes possible a "living awareness," an *erlebt* confirmation, of the God otherwise established. At any rate, the fact that Tennant does not use religious experience "on the way up" is to be taken solely as a minimizing of its independent evidential value.

A word may well be added at this point in regard to the nature of the moral goals man should set for himself. Tennant seems to be correct in maintaining that a monistic ethics, or an ethics contending that there is one absolute ideal and one highest good in which the demands of self-realization, on the one hand, and of social good, on the other, are compatible, always or necessarily is based on a gratuitous assumption. For

[139] *Mind*, XXXIX (1930), 484.

he points out situations in which the realization of self conflicts with social duty. Hence there is no objective standard
for deciding the issue, and the only appeal is to the conscientiousness of the individual. He contends, consequently, that
the only absolute in ethics is conscientiousness, that because
no ethicist can assume self-realization and social duty to be
compatible in all situations, the individual is thrown back,
not on any objective norm, but on what he thinks is the
most reasonable thing to do in that situation. This being so,
we would, with Tennant's approval, maintain further that,
though no ethics can reasonably assert *one* all-embracing ideal
or "complete" good wherein self-realization and social duty
are compatible, a system of formal ethics is possible in which
these two duties serve as poles of orientation, the basic
duties being reasonableness and conscientiousness.[140] We
are *obligated* to realize the best possible as moral beings,
and must accordingly search for that state of society in which
the development of the emotional, aesthetic, moral, and
intellectual capacities of the individual may be encouraged.
Keeping in mind these two goals, which Sorley has designated
by the terms the "higher life" and the "wider life," as those
which experience has shown to contain our highest good, we
may resolve conflicts between the two in particular cases only
by the most reasonable solution in that situation. Sad experience has taught that progress apart from love is not so progressive, that love apart from progress is not love. These ideals of
progressive love, of mutual dependence, and reciprocal independence between persons express the laws of adaptation to
be fulfilled for progressive spiritual happiness. They are our
generalizations from our past and present experiences, and
their presence, as well as that of physical and organic laws,
throws light on the purposes and nature of cosmic Mind. For
man has produced neither his own ultimate collocations, as
it were, nor nature's. That love for fellow man (and for God)
is an experience which sanctifies and glorifies all others is not
a mere fancy, a law we create *in toto*. It is, rather, a generaliza-

---

[140] Cf. E. S. Brightman, *Moral Laws* (1933), as the best exposition of this
viewpoint.

tion which is relevant to the created natures of individuals *in their* interrelation with others. And now, evidence for belief in a designing Mind having been adduced, we may turn our attention with Tennant to the implications of the same evidence for possible attributes of God.

J. AN EMPIRICAL DESCRIPTION OF GOD

1. THE EMPIRICAL APPROACH TO GOD'S ATTRIBUTES

The empirical approach to the problem of God's attributes requires, as Tennant says, that the philosopher will "entertain, at the outset, no such presuppositions as that the Supreme Being, to which the world may point as its principle of explanation, is infinite, perfect, immutable, supra-personal, unqualifiedly omnipotent or omniscient." [141] God's knowable attributes must be those which will adequately explain the empirical *known* facts. A basic passage may be included at this point:

> To Hume and Kant it is willingly admitted that from a finite effect we cannot infer a cause greater than is necessary to produce it. And if the empirical method can attain to knowledge of but a finite God, it is to be debated whether, when the meanings of "finite" and "infinite" are gauged by reflection rather than by sentiment, any conception of God save as a finite being can be reached with consistency. . . . God's attributes must immeasurably [by which Tennant must mean merely *not measurably*] transcend man's attributes of similar kind, but it is a further question whether there is sense in calling them infinite.[142]

Whether Tennant is successful in fulfilling the requirements of this empirical standard will be the subject of the remainder of this study.

For Tennant, it must be remembered, God is an "efficient, intelligent, ethical Being," and though our philosopher does borrow the name *God* from religion, he does not borrow any particular idea or argument from religious experience as such. Instead, he asks what the facts of the world and man (apart from his religious experience) compel us to think as regards

[141] *Philosophical Theology*, II, 79.
[142] *Ibid.*, II, 122.

the nature of the World-Ground. Religious experience may then be interpreted in terms of the conception of God arrived at by a criticism of less ineffable experience.[143]

2. GOD AND TEMPORALITY

We turn first to the problem, central to the consideration of the other attributes, of the relation of God to time. A true empiricist, Tennant for knowledge of time turns to experience. In his analysis, he finds, following Ward, that all concepts of Time, whether held by common sense or mathematics, are abstractions from the alogical perceptual time of psychologically immediate experience. Experience *is* change, or real duration, "but the presentation of change, as distinguished from change of presentation, involves awareness of perceptual time." [144] This is experience as we know it, and anything which claims to be experience, divine or human, must involve it, so far as we know (and that is all we are entitled to talk about). Duration involves succession, and God's specious present must have duration, no matter how great its span. This at least must be true if our experience is to be an index to what is not ourselves. So far the empiricist must go with Tennant.

The rest of Tennant's argument proceeds by analogy with the human self. The time we perceive, from which we extract different Times, is perceiv*ed* and experienc*ed*, and for Tennant the problem arises: What is the relation of the noumenal self which does the perceiving to the duration or time perceived? Tennant, in accordance with earlier conclusions, insists that the noumenal ego must have some relevant relation to the phenomenal self which it determines. Just as the relations in the object cannot be explained without reference to the ontal relations of the noumenal agent in natural epistemology, so Tennant consistently holds that the noumenal ego must be *functionally* related in such a way to the experience of

---

[143] This is really what is done anyway, Tennant insists, except that usually religious experience is not interpreted in terms of concepts carefully obtained by critical investigation of other realms of experience.

[144] *Philosophical Theology*, II, 130; cf. *ibid.*, I, 169.

the empirical self that the temporal relations of this phenomenal self are not complete distortions of the noumenal
agent. Tennant has not muddled the problem by introducing
the word "eternity," to indicate either the power of the self to
transcend time (when regarded as disparate moments), as
Pringle-Pattison did, or a state of conative or moral satisfaction, as Taylor does.[145] The word has its origin in attempts
to describe God, and the problem which now presents itself
is: What can eternity mean in terms of human experience?

If "eternal" means everlasting in conceptual Time, then it
means Time, and as such it introduces no new meaning if
applied to God. If it means "absolutely timeless, it is predicable only of truths or reason, which may or may not be valid
of our world, or be actualised in it, and is not predicable of
the existent"[146] and, therefore, of God. Time, however, cannot be illusory unless experience be denied. Hence, unless
eternity has some relation to time, it is meaningless. This relation Tennant holds to be functional. Eternity does not mean
timelessness, but "it denotes the noümenal, in the Kantian
sense, or the supra-temporal. . . ."[147] Temporality, on the
other hand, is not purely illusory, but the phenomenal expression of some serial but nontemporal order. The supra-
temporal order, however, must be "essentially identical with
the temporality of perceptual experience"[148] though not with
the conceptual elaborations of it, if the "determinative po-
tency," and the "functional relation" of the noumenal beings
(the soul or God) are to be at all effective. God, then, as
noumenal subject is not in time, but time is in him; as such,
God is "out of time," and he has "the world-process as an object of knowledge and a sphere of activity."[149] Tennant,
Ward, and Sorley are at one in this view.[150] The point Tennant is really stressing, of which even he does not seem to see

[145] Cf. Taylor, *Faith of a Moralist*, I, Chapter III.
[146] *Philosophical Theology*, II, 138, 139.
[147] *Ibid.*, II, 139.
[148] *Ibid.*
[149] *Ibid.*, II, 135.
[150] Cf. Ward, *Realm of Ends*, pp. 468–477. Sorley has orally observed that
God is not in time but "time is in God."

all the implications, and which, when fully developed, revo-
lutionizes thinking about God, comes out in the following
passage.

> But the most important consideration for theistic philosophy is that,
> however inadequate conceptual Time be for purposes other than those
> for which it was fashioned, perceptual time, with its alogical factors which
> the abstract concept ignores, does not seem to admit of being expunged
> from experience unless experience itself, or all that we have any right to
> bestow that name upon, vanishes with it into a contentless abstraction.[151]

What light, then, has Tennant thrown on the conception
of eternity? He has told us that it is to be applied to the
noumenal self of man and God. Yet when we come to think
of the functional relationship and describe it concretely, we
can do so only by conceiving a supratemporal realm (therefore
in some sense nontemporal as *we* know time) having a one-to-
one correspondence with the temporal. Attending first to the
relation between the noumenal and the phenomenal self
(granting the distinction), we may say: There is no reason to
suppose that anything comes between these selves to distort in
any way the reception by the phenomenal self of the noumenal
ego's functional relations — as, for example, the mind and
body of the individual mediate and affect the ontal relations
of the natural world.[152] What then does it mean, if anything,
to talk about an eternal noumenal which can be described
only by the *temporal* phenomenal? Even if the distinction
between the noumenal and the phenomenal were tenable on
other grounds, the fact that there is no evidence for a distort-
ing medium between the noumenal functional activity and the
phenomenal effect, leaves insufficient ground for holding to
any distinction between the noumenal temporal and the phenomenal temporal. And the same must be said for God's
experience. It is only because Tennant carries in his mind the
idea, influenced perhaps by the difference in words, and especially by the difference between the noumenal object and the
phenomenal *joint-product* issuing from the mind's interaction

---

[151] *Philosophical Theology*, II, 139.

[152] Indeed, Tennant himself holds, against McTaggart, that introspection
does not involve "phenomenalising or distortion." Cf. *ibid.*, II, 163.

with it in knowledge, that the noumenal self is similarly thought to be different temporally from the phenomenal. And the very fact that we can say nothing concrete about the noumenal self would demand that in a thorough empiricism this unnecessary notion, as we have tried to show, be dropped.

And along with it the whole notion of eternity.[153] For, we ask, what empirical facts does the eternity of God explain, which the correct notion of time as applied to his experience would not explain? If time and the Temporal process exist for God in a way different from its existence for us, the difference is owing to a possible extension of his time-span and a correlated different *tempo* in his experience. Yet in either case, as Tennant himself has maintained, the essence of time as we know it, succession, is present. (Whatever empirical evidence there is for a different time-span in the divine experience may be derived by applying the law of continuity beyond human experience, which, presumably, enjoys a greater time-span than does the amoeba.) Thus, though the natural Temporal process may be differently presented in God's experience than in ours, we have no right, on this account, to infer that God is mysteriously supratemporal, except from the point of view of Time, or of time as experienced by us. If his functional relation to the latter is causal (creative and immanent or recreative), then he cannot be conceived as being the changeless source of change, or the supratemporal source of time. It is truer to say that we are in time because God is in time, and the difference between the two times must be decided as is the difference between his intelligence and ours. Tennant comes very near to this view when, in a concluding sentence, he says:

It may well be that duration and succession are unique modes of ontal as well as of phenomenal being, which cannot be, as well as have not been, translated into terms of another type of serial order: that becoming, not static perfection, is the fundamental nature of all created Reality, and also of the life as distinct [unfortunately] from the "substance," of the Creator.[154]

[153] That is, if eternity means more than endless duration.
[154] *Philosophical Theology*, II, 139. Cf. the note at the end of this chapter.

3. CREATION

When we were discussing Ward's view of creation we argued that (to put the argument in a briefer and different form) the relation of God to the universe had to be either logical, as Spinoza held, or dynamic. That is, the relation must be either logical implication or a causality which brings into being something new. It is the newness, as well as the relative independence, of organic life and man, at least, which the hypothesis of creation is trying to explain; and because *newness* [155] is inexplicable apart from change and time, we insisted that creation, resulting in the production of what was not similarly existent before, was a temporal act of God at a certain point in divine history. Ward, rejecting the view that all active experience is temporal, is attempting to show that creation is not logical, *but yet not temporal*!

Tennant's position is not essentially different from Ward's. Since the Designer of the universe is responsible for its "primary collocations," he is not simply the Architect but the Creator. "In other words, the ordering of the world as a whole cannot be conceived as transcreation, or as relative creation. . . : the initial determining of specific initial interrelations, and the positing of *relata* with determinate natures, are necessarily one and the same activity." [156] Creation means "positing of other onta" [157] and implies that the creative activity is volitional, since that is the nearest analogue we have in our experience.

Yet Tennant, like Ward, is quite willing to admit "that the kernel of positive meaning in the notion of creation, viz., positing, is inexplicable," and that "the *modus operandi* of divine creativity is wholly unimaginable and inconceivable." [158] But he defends himself by holding that (a) there must be some unanalyzable and unassimilable ultimates, (b)

[155] Independence does not require time and change ordinarily, but unless ultimate plurality is admitted, it does when we are considering God's relation to man.
[156] *Philosophical Theology*, II, 123.
[157] *Ibid.*
[158] *Ibid.*, II, 125.

that theism is here not setting up a new mystery not present in any other theory. These two points Broad seems to overlook when he says: "But surely the essence of Dr Tennant's defense of Theism is that it does, and rival theories do not, give an intellectually satisfactory explanation of this mystery." [159] Theism, we should hold with Tennant, can hardly be said to be superior to other views because of its doctrine of creation, but since other cosmogonies are no more intelligible in this respect and cannot account as adequately for the *explicanda*, Theism is more acceptable. As Tennant says:

> If the alternatives [to creation] are self-subsistence, indefinite regress, emanation, and self-manifestation in a finite many, these are equally obscure or mysterious; and for the same reason. But while all these leave the particularity and diversity, the inferiority and dominance, of the various constituents of the ontal world wholly unaccounted for, and thereby decline to reduce superfluous mysteriousness, they supply no sufficient reason for the forthcomingness of this peculiarly ordered world rather than of any "possible" aggregate whatever.[160]

But Broad returns with a more formidable, though already weakened, objection. To say that the notion of creation is "not derivable from experience" [161] is "a very awkward admission" for Tennant, who is arguing by analogy with human experience and "who insists that *all* our concepts are of empirical origin. I cannot imagine whence, on Dr Tennant's view, the notion of creation can have come into the human mind." [162] This latter objection would be stronger (and unjustified) if Tennant claimed that he had a clear idea of the *modus operandi* of creation. At all events, in addition to what he has said about the necessity of alogical ultimates somewhere, Tennant might well answer that, as Ward said, there is nothing *in* experience to contradict creation and that in the experience of free will and relative creation we have suggestions of creation. He might also have suggested that the mystery involved in the notion of God's creating without preexistent data is ultimately not essentially different from the

[159] *Mind*, XXXIX (1930), 481.
[160] *Philosophical Theology*, II, 125, 126.
[161] *Ibid.*, II, 125.
[162] *Mind*, XXXIX (1930), 480.

mystery involved when one soliloquizes: "How does this other person think or do this? I can by analogy with my own experience go so far with him, but I cannot see how he goes on from there. The very fact that I am not he makes my exact knowledge of it impossible." In other words, in God's creation we have no intrinsically greater mystery than exists for us when we try to understand the creative genius who, by virtue of his genius, is different from ourselves. We can recognize the difference but we cannot define the exact operation of his extraordinary power.

Broad himself, it is interesting to note, unable to accept free will, finds it necessary to account for moral responsibility by postulating the pre-existence of persons. A person is morally responsible for an action (a) if it is intentional, (b) to the extent that it is determined by his character and disposition, and (c) as long as these in turn are products of his previous experience. "In order to reconcile (b) and (c) it seems necessary to assume that the person has existed and has been having experiences and doing actions through all past time, though there may have been periods during which he was completely quiescent and unconscious." [163] Though Broad (presumably) does not claim that all notions are derived from experience, it is difficult to see how this notion of self-subsistence and everlasting pre-existence is any more intelligible than the kind of positing involved in creation. Of course, Broad might well answer that theism employs the concept of self-subsistence and everlasting pre-existence to describe God, and that the theist in adding creation is including another mystery. To this it may be answered that the relation between self-subsistent minds and God is open to all the difficulties Ward found in pluralism; mystery is still with us.

Turning now to the details of the Creator-Designer's relation to his creation, the problem arises for Tennant, as it did for Pringle-Pattison and the others: Does purpose as ascribed to God have the characteristics especially of desire or want

---

[163] This quotation is directly from the lecture, delivered in the class on ethics, February 2, 1935, and is made possible by Dr. Broad's generosity in lending his notes for this purpose.

and *pre*conceived plan? Tennant is emphatic in holding that "the element of value, of desire and satisfaction, is not eliminable from the idea of purpose," [164] for then purpose is no different from cause, mechanism, or noncontradiction. But Tennant joins Ward in holding that "God quâ God is creator, and the creator quâ creator is God: or 'God without the world is not God.' " [165] Furthermore, it is superfluous anthropomorphism to hold that for God, as for us, presentation and will are distinct, and that for him to whom "intellective intuition" is ascribed, there needed to be a prior will to create. Creation can be conceived as "idea and deed together, and the divine transcendence as not temporal priority, but as consisting in the difference between God and His utterance." [166] We need not repeat our objections and alternative to Ward's similar views. It does seem, however, that Tennant also is neither sufficiently empirical nor coherent in overlooking the emergence of the organic world and man in the temporal order of evolution.[167]

At all events, we see no difficulty in supposing that God has a plan which he has not fully completed, and, indeed, which must wait for its fulfillment on human coöperation in the human sphere and on the effects of his own working against obstructions within his own nature.[168] Tennant himself insists that divine purposiveness must be conceived not as the working out of a preordained plan in which all is foreseen, but as one which allows some adaptation to the developments of created autonomous beings. This plan must not "involve sacrifice of ethical dignity of the individual person as an end for himself, and [consider him] no mere instrument to the future perfecting of others." [169] But there is no other factor of which the divine plan must take account.

It has been evident all along that Tennant is anxious to state theism in terms of other than "static concepts," such as abstract perfection and immutability. Consequently, in dis-

---

[164] *Philosophical Theology*, II, 116.
[165] *Ibid.*, II, 128.
[166] *Ibid.*, II, 129.
[167] Cf. Chapter III, above.
[168] For further definition of the "obstruction" see Chapter VII, below.
[169] *Philosophical Theology*, II, 118.

cussing immutability, he insists that as applied to God it can refer only to his purpose "as a whole." [170] "The divine immutability, in fact, can only be self-identity and self-consistency through change; and the divine perfection, if it include more than morality, *cannot be static completeness* but is rather self-manifestation of the Eternal in the temporal process of ethically significant history." [171] As for the word "infinite," its significance for theology is merely to repeat what creation already implies, that God is not dependent on any other self-subsistent being. The meaning of God's goodness and omnipotence will be discussed in the next chapter in relation to the problem of evil.

4. THE PERSONALITY OF GOD

The hypothesis required to explain the intelligence and ethical purposiveness of the world and man must for this very reason be a God who is a person. The nature of God may not be exhaustively described by the empiricist, but God must be "at least characterised by intelligence, valuation, and volition," [172] which constitute the essence of personality as we know it in addition to the subjecthood it presupposes. If "supra-personal" simply means the transcendence in God of those characteristics of personality which, apart from these submitted, are purely accidents of human nature in this environment, then the expression is acceptable. But if it denotes the "non-volitional, non-purposive, and non-ethical, the expression becomes a synonym for 'impersonal,' and must be rejected." God, as an hypothesis adequate to explain the data, cannot be a name for a "universal reason, ineffable being, or even for absolute morality or a tendency that makes for righteousness, but rather . . . a determinate spirit who is an artist and a lover as well as a geometriser. . . ." [173]

5. THE OMNISCIENCE OF GOD

In his treatment of the omniscience of God, Tennant once more follows the empirical approach. Accordingly, he poses

[170] *Philosophical Theology*, II, 148.
[171] *Ibid.*, II, 149 (italics mine).
[172] *Ibid.*, II, 166.
[173] *Ibid.*

the question: What aspects of knowledge in human experience are "characteristics as are known to be humanly conditioned"?[174] After analysis, he concludes that though mediating objects are involved in human knowledge of noumena, they need not be similarly posited for a personal Creator, while sense-knowledge, conditioned by the body, cannot be attributed to him.[175] To repeat, though we are limited to the phenomenal, there is no reason to suppose that God does not know the ontal "face to face" (and this is certainly true in a personalistic metaphysics where the ontal world is God's energizing, his body, as it were). Furthermore, God as Creator, "uniquely related to every part of the world and to the world as a whole, must be . . . omnipresent; and, in virtue of an unrestricted range of attention, He must be said to be omniscient as to all that is and has been, and also as to all that will be, *in so far as it is the outcome of uniform causation.*"[176]

The limitation suggested in this last clause is that God cannot foreknow the exact future, as contrasted to the general tendency, of those creatures which are also creators (and for Tennant and Ward this means the inorganic world, while for us it means simply the organic and human in various degrees, according to the amount of freedom possessed). God can neither foresee, nor experience, as *erleben*, the states and feelings of these individuals. In creating free creatures God limited his knowledge by the number of alternatives they might take.

Sorley, however, argues that (a) since God's knowledge of man's mind is not external but internal and even better than man's knowledge of himself, and (b) since "God's knowledge is not limited to a finite span of the time process," (c) therefore, "the whole course of the world's history will be seen by him in a single or immediate intuition."[177] Consequently, God knows the entire past and future and present in the same way, for example, as we know past, present, and future in the specious present. But Tennant cannot be gainsaid when he fairly retorts to such a suggestion that (a) since the difference

[174] *Ibid.*, II, 173.
[175] Cf. *ibid.*, II, 174, 175.
[176] *Ibid.*, II, 175 (italics mine).
[177] Sorley, *Moral Values*, p. 465.

between the past and future still holds for our experience, and (b) since we are notes in the symphony (contemplated by Sorley, Pringle-Pattison, and Taylor) which has not yet been *played entirely*, therefore (c) God can know the symphony only as the designing Composer, rather than as a listener who, hearing it for a second or third time, can know it as a whole. Exact knowledge of the whole is impossible unless there is "one sole composer, not many," but then "prescience becomes predetermination, and the foreseen is the intended, down to the veriest detail." [178]

6. DIVINE IMMANENCE

Obviously one's views of divine immanence will be influenced by one's metaphysical construction, but Tennant's general position, metaphysics aside, is that the creation of primary collocations is not in itself enough to account for the present world, as a deist might contend. The groundwork of Tennant's metaphysical thinking is, as already noted, a relative (created) dualism of God and the ontal world, which we conceptualize as Physical. Cartesian continuous recreation is superfluous unless we suppose, without empirical justification, that "the beings which God creates or plants out, with existence-for-self" are fleeting and need continual support. God's immanence *is* needed, however, to account for the *con*sistence of perduring elements whose "delegated spontaneity and independence," or "erratic tendencies," might well have developed into a "purpose-foiling aggregate." [179]

But if all, or even any, of the world-constituents have this relative independence as substance-causes, their conspiration to produce our cosmos, with its particular trend and purpose, can be better accounted for if we suppose their possible waywardness to be compensated by a continual directive or creative activity of God, for Whom the world, with all its differentiated detail and its ever new emergent products, is always one whole.[180]

Thus God's activity is not confined simply to the creation of primary collocations; and the interrelation of things, which was the ground for belief in God, would have been impossible

[178] *Philosophical Theology*, II, 177.
[179] *Ibid.*, II, 212.   [180] *Ibid.*, II, 212, 213.

without providential control. For Tennant, who rejects
"wholesale occasionalism" in order to allow for the "free play"
of ontal beings which become proximate causes in the evolution of the world, immanence is consequently conceived as
divine action on the substance-causes. This divine activity
consists in either "an unceasing providential guidance or in
sporadic creative activity which miracle involves when it is
conceived as the production of effects such as could not emerge
out of unassisted potencies of the world-elements." [181] God is
transcendent as Creator but immanent in his action on spontaneous individuals, so that the laws of their interaction
express their own created natures and God's providential control. Hence, the laws of nature are not a self-subsistent *prius*
to God or to created substance-causes. There is every reason
to suppose that the cosmic Ground may have more immediate
contact with monads than souls have with each other or the
dominant monad with lower monads.[182]

Our objections to pan-psychism which, if of any avail, are
all the more applicable to this view of substance-causes (provided the spiritual monad is not meant), need not be repeated.
Tennant, furthermore, would have difficulty in justifying his
accusation that the "thoroughgoing doctrine of divine immanence in the physical world" would conflict with the "fundamental assumptions on which all scientific induction has been
found to be based"; [183] for scientific induction rests not on the
existence of a "planted out" world, but on the order of phenomena which, on a personalistic metaphysics, would have as
its ontal ground the divine energizing. If it is true that on this
system "*all* possibility of coping with the problem of evil" [184]
is removed, an empirical theism must take the consequences,
and, as we shall try to indicate,[185] traditional theism will have
to be modified.

The fact that the purpose of the world is ethical imposes
limitations on the scope of God's immanent action or influence
on persons. The human mind is not "the passive mouthpiece

[181] *Ibid.*, II, 215.
[182] Cf. *ibid.*, II, 219.
[183] *Ibid.*, II, 215.
[184] *Ibid.*, II, 214.
[185] Cf. Chapter VII, below.

of God," and God's immanence is, therefore, neither to be conceived as operating in human reason as the activity of the Logos or in conscience as the voice of God. "Indeed so long as God's immanence is identified with grace, and grace in turn is conceived as quasi-physical, non-moral, or impersonal force, an occult and coercive influence upon the soul . . . ethical theism can be but hostile to the doctrine," [186] for it means overriding human personality. Furthermore, if such grace could be given without violating human personality "it would be inexcusable for not removing *en bloc* the moral infirmities of man." [187] Finally, Tennant reminds us that there *may* be intimate contacts between God and man, since (a) there cannot be less and there may well be more in the unfathomed life of man than psychology has discovered,[188] and since (b) operations not open to introspection but consistent with moral dignity may be possible. Yet *known* fact does force Tennant to deny the impartation of knowledge and moral strength over and above that made possible by the creation or transcendent, rather than immanent, activity of God.

K.   SUMMARY

We now have outlined an empirical theology which at most points avoids the errors of the other empirical arguments for God. Not only does Tennant stay closer to experience and use a method which prevents him from being easily led astray, but his analysis and conclusions are on the whole more adequate. *Philosophical Theology* and *Moral Values and the Idea of God* tower above the other works we have studied, as well as practically all the literature on our subject in Great Britain. These two works part company mainly on the status of values, or the last and very important step in the wider teleological argument. Tennant's account we take to be more empirical and more adequate. Our criticisms of his work have been at points where the empirical wedge was not driven deeply enough, where the demands of the rigorous empirical method were not quite adequately met. As we study the problem of

[186] *Philosophical Theology*, II, 222.
[187] *Ibid.*   [188] *Ibid.*

evil we shall find that Tennant (as well as the others) falters to a greater degree in the application of this method.

The following theses give too briefly the main points of this chapter:

1. The most empirical method is that which investigates the order of knowing by criticism of presumptive knowledge with the aid of genetic-analytic psychology.

2. The *core* of objective reality is sense-impression, from which ideas are derived by way of the imaginal, but for which alone they are valid; yet the mind selects and interprets its data according to its interests and derives the basic categories of cause and substance from the experience of the self and body.

3. The pure ego is an inferred Reality, and its noumenal unity, presupposed by the awareness of consciousness, makes experience possible. But we have argued that the self can have acquaintance-knowledge of itself even though there are no impression-like *qualia*, and that the noumenal self is an empty abstraction from the experienced self.

4. Knowledge, the result of interaction between the interested subject and the objective continuum, always involves alogical elements, is neither completely empirical nor a priori, and ultimately is faith in the most reasonable hypothesis.

5. Knowledge is of the phenomenal world whose relations express those of the causal noumenal world which, for Tennant, is relatively independent and may be non-spiritual. But since activity which is not will is meaningless, we follow Berkeley and Lotze, Bowne and Brightman, in holding that the noumenal inorganic world is God's will.

6. In ethical knowledge there is no unique value-object, but value is partly constituted by feeling and conation and partly by the capacity of things or of the noumenal to affect us or to cause feeling and consequently evoke valuation; ethical principles are generalizations from experiences of value and have Objective validity for

personal life in concrete situations. But moral obligation to will the best is *sui generis*, though it has no
cognitive function.

7. Religious experience is not an independent source of
   knowledge about God, for it is constituted "religious"
   and *sui generis* by being interpreted in terms of the
   idea of God or of a superhuman being — an idea derived, by idealization, from ordinary knowledge of the
   world and man.

8. Tennant's wider teleological argument is a chain whose
   links are the regularity of nature, knowledge, and
   value, which are inexplicable apart from a good God
   who created and directed the ultimate collocations of
   reality so that a universe in which moral values could
   be realized was possible.

9. For Tennant, God, not nontemporal but supratemporal, has a functional relation to Time and time. But
   a function related to time yet not temporal is an impossible abstraction like extension without color, for
   activity without change and time is meaningless. However, God's temporal experience probably has a different time-span and tempo than our own.

10. God is a Person who (a) knows the past and present
    completely but cannot know exactly the future of free
    created beings, (b) exerts a providential control over
    his nonpersonal creation, and (c) respects the moral
    dignity of persons.

ADDENDUM: TENNANT ON TIME

Dr. Tennant wrote the following addition to proposition 9. This statement is not inconsistent with what has been said and criticized, but it does bring out the temporalism in his thinking which is modified by what we have tried to show is an untenable distinction between the noumenal and the phenomenal, especially as regards time.

God is supra-temporal *not* in the sense of absolute timelessness, such as is predicable only of truths or ideas, but in the sense of noumenal. *Conceptual* Time can safely be applied only to that from which it has been abstracted, i.e., the phenomenal, or to the effects of the efficiency of noumenal beings whose acts make "filled time"; not to the noumenal beings, which are not effects nor phenomena. Also God is not supra-temporal in the sense that He has no functional relation to the temporal; the phenomenal is not the illusory, but is grounded in the noumenal.

At the same time, though I regard the noumenal, and therefore God, as not "in" conceptual Time, as is the phenomenal world, I cannot conceive of the experience of a Spiritual Being as not involving an element of the temporal kind, however differently it may need to be expressed in the case of God from the way in which it is expressed in our case; so that though I maintain we have no right to regard God as not supra-temporal I admit that He cannot be regarded as supra-*temporal*; but whether this means more than "functionally related to Time," our knowledge as to the noumenal is too limited to permit of dogmatic assertion.

CHAPTER VII

AN EMPIRICAL VIEW OF THE GOODNESS OF GOD

A. Review

OUR investigation so far has revealed a halting use of empirical method in late British thought. In the work of Tennant we have found the most faithful adherence to this procedure and the soundest use of the data available, though we have argued that his views of the noumenal ego, the nature of moral obligation, the eternity of God, nontemporal creation, and ultimate reality are insufficiently empirical and inadequate interpretations of the data. The dominant thought of this study has been that the known facts of man's experience in this physical universe must be explained, our premise being that the task of philosophy in any age is to give the most coherent account of the available data supplied by the whole of man's observation. Any idea of God, the mystic's, the scientist's, the moralist's, or the idea that there is no God, has been treated simply as an hypothesis with no more *prima facie* preference for one than another, though as the facts were organized we or our subjects tried to fit each key to the lock of coherence.

A large part of our investigation was concerned with the evaluation of moral arguments for God. We found that, with the exception of Tennant, our philosophers made a peculiar disjunction between the human and subhuman world. Man was not to be considered as nurtured solely by Mother Nature but by a non-natural realm whence his true values had their source. Therefore, though his physical sustenance came from his natural and human environment, his ethical life would have been impossible had he not been provided with a metaphysical moral environment whence he could read off moral valuations as he did physical relations in his objective continua. That is, rightly insisting against Hume that an empirical philosophy must consider the moral as well as the physical realm, they turned with Kant *away from* the natural world, including the natural man (which at most gave them — so they thought — an indifferent Intelligence), and posited a moral world as in some sense responsible for moral valuations (as the ontal world was responsible for their phenomenal world). They did not stop to ask whether the phenomenal moral world, with which they perforce had to start, could be explained by analysis of man's own developing nature in relation to Nature. They did not realize that the effects (moral valuations) might be explained by reference especially to the conative and affective life of man as stimulated by the environment, so that human valuations, like natural judgments, might be considered joint-products of man and the world in interaction. Hence, though they were not oblivious to the existence of the physical world and man's conative nature, in actual argument for God they turned to man's non-conative *cognition* of a non-natural moral realm. Without such a moral realm they found no basis for the knowledge and inspiration needed for the ethical transformation of the natural world and the conative nature of man, which was meanly conceived as desire simply for selfish ends and pleasure.

Thus, the moral and the natural realm (including man as conative) were really dichotomized, and the moral was the superinduced supplement of, rather than growth from, the natural. This dichotomy was based on the additional premise that, unless there were such a moral realm of valid ideals, ethical progress was inexplicable, and insuperable difficulties confronted attempts to establish the existence of a good God. On the views considered, however, though ideals were *not* sufficiently realized in man, the unrealized but *known* moral realm was still to be explained, and a good God was therefore postulated. Thus, the existence of such a God was based, not on the fact that this was a world in which values could be and actually had been realized and enjoyed, but really on the necessity for a source of the metaphysically objective values which were supposedly the *conditio sine qua non* of whatever values had been realized. Consequently, the argument for God's goodness rested ultimately not on a *fait accompli*, not on the progress of the universe to this point in history, but on what might be. The argument stood, and faltered, at its most critical point on a moral epistemology which, we have tried to show, is faulty.[1]

And the main ground for this error was the failure to take the conative life of man seriously enough. Indeed, Ward, Pringle-Pattison, Sorley (and Taylor) would find conation a very important factor in the selection of parts of the natural objective continuum, but, strange to say, they make it a mere spectator in the achievement of moral knowledge. In some respects they treat it as matter for the moral form, as it wére, to inform. It was Tennant only who awoke from the rationalistic slumber which not only led Kant to overlook the significance of the conative life, but through him also affected the moral epistemology of our writers. Tennant profited from the mistakes of the others and, analyzing experience more correctly, found that conation was the raw material *constituting* value-claim.

Proceeding from this point in the company of Tennant, we argued that our value-claims were the result of our determinate natures in a *given* environment. Instead of explaining progress in (true) valuation by increasing vision of a dimly conceived realm, knowledge of which in any case had to be translated into terms applicable for this human-natural realm, we found rather that man's created nature, its capacities never clearly gauged, was the ground for his ever-recurring moral unrest and strife, and that his ideals at any point were the results of his rational criticism of his value-claims. And, now proceeding alone, we also discovered that the conscience or *moral* intuition, which was the subject of much controversy, was neither a cognitive faculty with a peculiar moral object, nor something reducible to feeling, thought, or will. On the other hand, conscience though it denoted the unique experience of obligation to do what was considered the best, had no cognitive function. Thus, any value-claim may have been morally imperative; yet the Good was not the object of one moral intuition or a set of moral intuitions but the result

[1] The reader is referred to my article "An Empirical Critique of the Moral Argument for God," in the *Journal of Religion*, XVIII (1938), 275–288.

of criticism of value-claims. In this way, the absoluteness felt in moral experience was taken into account without muddling the epistemological issue, or, in other words, the most significant claims of the moral realist or intuitionist and the moral naturalist were thus reconciled.

Therefore, a realm of metaphysically objective values, personalized or not, is by no means the main source of belief in God. A personal God, however, is necessary to account for the natural and moral developments of the known and experienced universe, as Tennant's teleological argument shows. In short, the alpha and omega of Tennant's reasoning are the values grasped and realized in finite personality. And we have insisted (a) that man's discovery of the laws of spiritual well-being, the "higher life" and the "wider life," laws applicable to man in his relation to himself, his fellow men, and his environment, are not simply fancies created entirely by man, but laws expressing his created nature and its experienced values in his created environment; (b) that consequently they may be used to indicate the nature and purpose of the ultimate Source of both. Our other philosophers, however, felt constrained to base God's goodness not on the achieved but on the achievable, and, indeed, the empirical *facta* were supplemented by *cognita* in order to find more adequate ground for the goodness of God. As we have noted, each of them felt that realized value was inadequate to establish God's goodness, and Tennant's position would be criticized for resting on evidence which could indicate no more than a powerful Intelligence. What is very important, therefore, is to consider Tennant's arguments for God's goodness in the light of the facts of evil. The problem of evil, of course, is a problem for the others also, but we turn to a consideration of his treatment because it reflects the excellent work of Martineau, who affected Tennant through Ward. The main arguments of Pringle-Pattison and Sorley [2] are not essentially different from Tennant's. Hence, though important differences will be pointed out, Tennant's argument may be fairly considered as representative.

[2] Cf. Chapter V, Section I, above.

B.   The Problem of Evil

1.   MORAL EVIL

(a) Tennant makes short work of theories which would pronounce evil illusory, "for, if evil is illusion, the illusion is an evil. . . ." [3] Tennant's thesis, on the other hand, is that this is the best possible world for the creation of ethical beings who are the products of God's love. This does not mean that God was confronted with certain possibilities from which he had to choose prior to his actual creation, for the very determinateness of God's being foreclosed possibilities; and possibility, as Lotze correctly held, has meaning only in relation to actuality. In any case, for Tennant as for the others, "God without a world is a superflous abstraction. . . ." [4] The main point is that truth and goodness, for example, or any other "eternal laws," are not to be conceived as a *prius* which God had to realize, but that the constitution of this world and man reflect God's determinate nature. The creation was a Creation in Love whose very nature it is to impart itself. The world is an evolutionary one because moral goodness cannot be created as such or implanted by God in his creatures. What the theist must show is that "in and behind . . . evil there is a soul of good," that the evils are not superfluous.[5]

(1) At this point, as we stop to get our bearings, we may merely mention a minor objection. Has Tennant any right to hold that God's creation of other beings was owing to love, before he has successfully solved the problem of evil? This, however, is largely a matter of procedure in argument, and we pass to a larger issue.

(2) How frequently it occurs that theists who reject the deterministic view that the character of the finite self determines action hold a similar doctrine about God's action! Do the facts of experience, however, allow us to say: God being what he was, this evolutionary world was aimed at a

[3] *Philosophical Theology*, II, 181.
[4] *Ibid.*, II, 183.   [5] *Ibid.*, II, 185.

moral end, not because God could have done otherwise, but because he could not violate his own nature, from which this world alone could follow? Are we justified in maintaining more than the position that God is responsible for this evolutionary world, whether there was an alternative or not? It is only when God's nature is regarded as inflexibly good, working goodness mechanically or automatically, that the view cited is possible. It is difficult, in dealing with the attributes of God, to keep on the empirical trail and not reason in the manner of the ontological argument. Yet, when empirical theology abides by its method, it can grant only that this world is the one actually created (chosen or not), and concede that perfect goodness may not be a structural property of God, for conceivably it may have been subject to development. We cannot tell. All we can ask is: Has the God who made possible the history of the world *we know*, whether he was good before that or will be good a million years hence, been good in that history, and how good? A related point must be added.

(3) We have found every reason to suppose that the creation of man was an act in time for God's experience and in Time for our experience. The doctrine of the eternity (as meaning other than everlasting duration) of God solved no problems and created the problem of relating God to time and our Temporal measurements. Instead of giving God power to overcome change, God has been lifted above change (not so much by Tennant) to protect certain human aspirations against the anthropomorphic conception of time as a disintegrating factor. On the other hand, cosmic and organic evolution indicate that God "worketh" and is not overcome with labor. It is no mere first glance which results in the view that God has not finished his creation, or, if the inorganic world is identified with God, his own development. The important point, however, is that a changing God may well be consistent with the facts of experience, and, indeed, is it not difficult to think of an immanent God who worketh not? The problem is: What is the relation of that change to us, and how is it to be conceived? Is it a growth in power, wis-

dom, or goodness, or in all together, or in any two of these? We may now continue with Tennant's argument.

(b) God's goodness can be judged only in terms of *our* categories of worth. Consequently, it is important to say what kind of world would be best for moral man. "The 'best possible' world, then, or the world that is worthiest of God and man, must be . . . a theatre of moral life and love." [6] A world catering to man's pleasure, in which neither want nor effort was necessary, would not be conducive to moral character and moral progress, our highest goods.

The idea of the "best possible" forces Tennant to consider the meaning of omnipotence as applied to God. In the first place, since ultimate possibilities are limited by the determinate actualities of God's nature, it is absurd to say that he can do both the possible and the impossible when these are correlatively defined. On the other hand, to hold that the laws of thought are valid independently of God and of the world and impose themselves upon God, as upon us, with necessity is once more to hold to a validity which is not valid of something, and therefore "a mental figment." [7] For Tennant "the sum of eternal truths become modes of God's being and activity, and is neither their *prius* nor their product." [8] God is not to be considered as a *non-logical* Being becoming logical, an indeterminate Being becoming determinate by the realization of possibilities. It is the self-consistency of God's activity that is the basis of logical eternal truths and his goodness is his activity of love — if it can be maintained. God, therefore, can do all that is in his nature, his moral purpose being the product of his nature. The only modification we should make is that there is no ground for supposing (unless we use the ontological argument) that God could not have been inconsistent or evil, though his *choice* to be self-consistent and good certainly expressed his nature — a nature which, however, was *also capable* of doing otherwise.

(c) If moral character is the end to be achieved by man, freedom is necessary, and God could not therefore will a best possible world in which freedom and the possibility of evil

[6] *Philosophical Theology*, II, 186.   [7] *Ibid.*, II, 187.   [8] *Ibid.*, II, 188.

EMPIRICAL VIEW OF GOD'S GOODNESS

were excluded. Hence, God foreknew and was responsible for the possibility of evil but not for its actualization: "He permits, . . . the evil in order that there may be the good." [9] We cannot have our cake and eat it too; if we desire moral character and its basis in self-determination, we cannot fairly object to a world in which the possibility of failure is open. Hence, there may be evil incidental to the world, but if the ideal of moral character and its essence, love, are the highest values, "the process by which it is attainable is also good, despite the evil incidental to it."[10] Thus, theism has an explanation for moral evil in the discipline requisite to the achievement of moral character. "We deem the prize worth the cost, and life without moral strife and attainment to be not worth while." [11] The values we have achieved and may call our own have been worth the sweat and toil, and we approve of a universe in which we can learn to love, even though the consequence is suffering and evil.

(d) One of course might argue that the delegation of freedom to man might mean that evil will one day overcome goodness, but Tennant once more forces us to face actualities and judge possibilities by them. First, it cannot be denied that there has been moral advance in man's history though the line on the cosmic graph zigzags. We cannot regard man's development as a sheer accident likely to be permanently reversed; nor can we argue that evil will ever be completely overcome. When we were considering the empirical conservation of value we found that our universe was one in which, despite the fact that many values had been lost, others were *aufgehoben* in a universe which still made the creation of new values possible. In this very decade we find the nations more capable than ever before of destroying their respective civilizations and values, while internally, suffering, uncertainty, and fear dominate life. But in the presence of despair itself hope is still possible because Nature's breast is full, agencies for the reorganization and development of the wider life are still at work. Knowledge awaits courage. We are living on the edge of volcanoes of our own making, but we are

[9] *Ibid.*, II, 189.   [10] *Ibid.*, II, 191.   [11] *Ibid.*, II, 192.

also faced with ideas of a new order we can venturously create. If we allow another cataclysm to overtake us, it will remain for those who are left to philosophize about progress. The hope and despair which fill our hearts and minds constitute the concrete meaning of moral freedom, not only in our national and international life, but in our personal moral struggles.

What has been said is not contrary to Tennant's next contention that "there is something in goodness which promotes its own conservation, and something in evil that promises disruption — if not self-extinction, at least impotence to become supreme. And this is so, contingency and freewill notwithstanding." [12] As he continues: "Evil desires and evil purposes conflict with one another, so that evil as well as goodness resists and thwarts conspiration in evil." [13] And, as already mentioned in addition to Ward's similar argument, the very facts that evil itself cannot be successful without a modicum of good and that the strength of nations engaged in war depends to a good extent on the courage of their people and the loyalty of their allies indicate that evil is not a structural element of the universe which brought man into being.

It would seem to us, therefore, that considerations such as these adduced cannot be explained without postulating a Friend as the Designer and the Ground of the universe. The values actually achieved — and values which might have been achieved had man controlled himself to the extent of his powers — in a world that made him and them possible cannot be explained apart from the hypothesis of a God good enough and interested enough to provide them. To this extent are we forced if we are to explain our present universe and its achievements, to postulate a Spirit in the universe who conducts his own life in such a way as to make possible humanity's achieved values. Even if God were interested mainly in a universe and other creatures unknown to us, so that the whole history of man would be a by-product of the cosmic process, we could say that the process has on the whole been good to that by-product. But there is no reason for this

[12] *Philosophical Theology*, II, 194.   [13] *Ibid.*

premise if we argue empirically only from what we know. Our argument would derive its worth not from moral imperatives, not from the existence of a cognitively experienced realm of "ensouled" values, not on the supposition that "even if" a perfect deed had never occurred the existence of God would be a reasonable postulate, but on man's actually grasped and experienced values. We find no adequate grounds for Hume's statement: "The whole presents nothing but the idea of a blind Nature, impregnated by a great vivifying principle, and putting forth from her lap, without discernment or parental care, her maimed and abortive children!" [14] There is no sufficient reason for holding that the goodness of God cannot be inferred from the phenomena of the world "while there are so many ills in the universe, and while these ills might so easily have been remedied as far as human understanding can be allowed to judge on such a subject" [15] — at least so far as *moral* good and evil are considered. If we are going to evaluate what we know and not be led off by mere possibilities, we may rest reasonably confident that we have a Friend in the universe.[16] This is fundamental to our whole discussion and is presupposed by any attempt to account for natural evil.

2. NATURAL EVIL

So far our argument has been built on the actual realization and the possibility of the achievement of values allowed by a universe which brought us forth, the thesis being that the achievement of the highest value, moral character, depended on moral freedom in a relatively stable world. We have acknowledged and insisted upon the necessity of the possibility of evil for moral discipline and have held that man's progress has not been held back by the Master but by his own dullness as a pupil. The evils which befall man, however, are not always of his own brewing; as Spinoza put it,

[14] Quoted by Sorley, *Moral Values*, p. 331, from Hume's *Dialogues concerning Natural Religion* (1779).
[15] Sorley, p. 331.
[16] Cf. Chapter V, Section H, above.

man is also in bondage to nature, and he who would hold to the complete goodness of God must explain natural events which, opposing and destroying both man and his values, are therefore evil.

But it is well, before proceeding further, to understand what we mean by God's moral perfection. We have already contended that there is little reason for holding that any of God's attributes are what they are simply because they were the only ones possible, given his nature. Consequently, whatever goodness means, it does not follow from God's nature as the properties of a triangle follow from its nature. But goodness may mean either the consistent willing of a good purpose (formal goodness), or the realization of a good purpose (material goodness), or both. When the theist, including our writers, speaks of God's goodness he usually means the last, namely, the fulfilling of a consistently willed good purpose. This, at least, is the meaning we shall discuss. What this involves is that God, having set as his goal the creation of individuals who would autonomously realize themselves in accordance with the principle of love, used his otherwise unlimited power to make a world in which moral development would not be thwarted by anything external to man. A perfectly good God in this sense would create a subhuman universe in which man, by the use of his delegated powers, could achieve reasonable ends.

Now our argument thus far has established the fact that the cosmic Mind is well-disposed toward us and has made possible a balance of good over evil. However, the problem remains: Is the nonhuman environment such that (though it is not a victorious enemy, but the ground of many of our values) it is the best possible *for our moral development?*

We may now consider the essence of Tennant's arguments for the affirmative. To begin, we can do no better than to quote the main problem and the proposed solution as Tennant states it.

Much of human suffering, and many of the outrages of this present life upon our rational prudences and our most sacred affections . . . seem to be good for nothing, or to be non-essential for the realisation of goodness. If a man already has it in him to meet pain with fortitude and patience, he is not necessarily one whit the better man after actually enduring excruciating tortures; and if an all-powerful being "appointed" him such tortures, merely in order that his fortitude might pass from potentiality to actuality, such a being would be but a super-brute. However, it can be argued that the forthcomingness of our suffering is inevitably incidental to a moral order in a developing world. It . . . is a necessary outcome of a determinate cosmos of the particular kind that can sustain rational and moral life.[17]

The arguments developing and supporting this thesis are the following:

(a) Whatever the metaphysical structure of reality may be, it is essential for the achievement of moral ends that the physical order be regular. "Without such regularity in physical phenomena there could be no probability to guide us: no prediction, no prudence, no accumulation of ordered experience, no pursuit of premeditated ends, no formation of habits, no possibility of character or of culture." [18] No intellectual development would be possible, and hence no basis for moral achievement. In other words, just as Tennant held that moral freedom, which often resulted in pain and suffering, was necessary for the attainment of the highest good, so now he holds that "we cannot have the advantages of a determinate order of things without its logically or its causally necessary disadvantages." [19] God accordingly does not will particular ills antecedently, but consequently, as the necessary outcome of the more basic provision of the stability which is the *sine qua non* of moral achievement. If a moral order was to be God's, "a determinate world-plan" which automatically eliminated other goals and methods of achievement was necessary. "As Dr Martineau has put it, the cosmical equation being defined, only such results as are compatible with the values of its roots can be worked out, and these must be worked out." [20]

We cannot, therefore, have determinate substances in a determinate and calculable world, which, when about to injure sentient beings, so change their properties that no

---

[17] *Philosophical Theology*, II, 199.
[18] *Ibid.*, II, 199, 200.

[19] *Ibid.*, II, 200.
[20] *Ibid.*, II, 200, 201.

harm ensues. In a calculable world the water which cleans us, quenches our thirst, provides steam for power, and so on, cannot be expected or rationally desired to change its properties in order not to drown us. Hence, in a necessarily complex world, "physical ills follow with the same necessity of physical goods from the determinate 'world-plan' which secures that the world be a suitable stage for intelligent and ethical life." [21] And the important conclusion is that because natural evils are a necessary part of a whole order which makes the ethical order possible, they are neither superfluous nor absolute, unmitigated evils. Since Nature as a whole is good, there is no reason for supposing that God is limited either in power to accomplish the good he intended or in goodness. But there is an important modification which deserves further analysis.

As Tennant writes, "the goodness of God is vindicated if there be no reason to believe that the world-process involves more misery than Nature's uniformity entails." [22] But as he himself has already indicated, it does! Patience and fortitude would be possible without the excruciating pains man often has to bear, and the presence of imbeciles and other abortions of humanity cannot be explained by reference to their disciplinary, educative, or spiritual values. And "the hardest fact of all for human equanimity" [23] is the chaotic distribution of suffering and the lack of adjustment of anguish to particular needs, circumstances, and ability to suffer and overcome. "But the wind is not tempered to the shorn lamb; the fieriest trials often overtake those who least need torments to inspire fear, to evoke repentance, or to perfect patience. . . ." [24] In other words, if evil is for disciplinary value, God is not so efficient as the good teacher who gives the pupil only the problems for which his faculties are ripe.

(b) These facts, Tennant holds, are not disastrous, however, for a theism such as his own, which grants a limited autonomy to the created world, not only of human beings but of subhuman spiritual monads. For a theism (like personalism) which identifies the ontal world and God, however, there is

[21] *Philosophical Theology*, II, 201.
[22] *Ibid.*, II, 202.   [23] *Ibid.*, II, 203.   [24] *Ibid.*

no retreat, since all physical happenings are then directly willed by God and reveal his nature.[25] This contention, however, overlooks the fact that, on the personalistic view, also, physical evil is explicable as the necessary result of a universal regularity required for the production of a moral order. The same explanation is forthcoming, though now the laws and regularity of Nature express the activity of God.[26] If stability is the condition of the moral order, God, in order to fulfil his purpose, on this view, limits his activities to ways which scientific laws describe. Consequently, so long as God's activities are motivated by the same ends, the explanation of physical evil is not different simply because the laws are of God's activities rather than those of substance-causes, spiritualistic or otherwise. On either hypothesis, however, since God is responsible for the structure of the physical universe, the question remains: Would (or could) a good God with *none* but self-imposed limitations create a determinate universe in which certain evils had to be?

Tennant's apology rests on the delegated autonomy and proximate causation of a "planted out" world,[27] inert or not. As already stated, he prefers the pan-psychist view of reality. We turn, therefore, to a criticism of this aspect of pan-psychism, since the main contentions against it apply to an inert world or to any *relative* dualism. Tennant adopts enough of "deistic tendency" to allow "relative independence or free play to the ontal beings of which physical Nature is a phenomenal revelation . . . ,"[28] and consequently his substance-causes, though not necessarily spiritual, serve the same purpose in relation to the problem of evil as do Ward's monads.[29]

There is a seeming advantage in a pan-psychistic view of the natural world. We say *seeming* because we have tried to show that, as a metaphysical view, apart from its relation to the problem of evil, it has incurable defects. But now we

[25] Cf. *ibid.*, II, 214, 215.   [27] Cf. *ibid.*, II, 203, 204, 212–214.
[26] Cf. *ibid.*, II, 213, 214.   [28] *Ibid.*, II, 215.
[29] We shall use the word "monad" alone to avoid repetition of "monads and substance-causes," though it must not be forgotten that on Tennant's view the substance-cause need not be spiritual.

must consider the apparent advantage it derives by holding
that natural evils and, presumably, the superabundance of
evil as a disciplinary factor, are owing to the errancy of
impulsive monads. We must remember that (on Tennant's
as) on Ward's view, whatever order the natural world possesses is the joint-product of the creative and directive activity
of God and the monads, to which he has delegated sufficient
spontaneity and autonomy to place contingency at the heart
of Nature. God's relation to these monads is transcendent in
creation and immanent in the providential control which,
through direct action, guarantees the order of the universe.
God will not allow the freedom of the monad to undermine
the order necessary for the ethical life of man. Nor can God's
supervisory and compensatory immanence "be taken to include suppression of 'inerrancies' which constitute physical
evils," for "divine correction of all the latter inerrancies
would involve sacrifice of the uniformity which renders the
cosmos a theatre of moral life." [30] Thus Tennant must hold
that, though God will insist willy-nilly on a certain modicum
of order, (a) the maintenance of that determinate order necessitates certain phenomena which are evil for human beings,
and (b) the otherwise respected spontaneity of the monads
issues in physical catastrophes which cannot be blamed on
God but on their "willful" errancy. Let us evaluate each contention. The first is the more important one for Tennant and
for the other writers, but the second is the supplementation
of the first by Ward and Tennant.

The most embarrassing question Tennant may be asked is
well put by Broad. "Must *every* possible system of things with
fixed properties and subject to general laws involve so wide-
spread, so intense, so unjustly distributed, so useless, and so
morally detrimental suffering as there seems to be in the
actual world?" [31] Broad admits, as we should insist, that the
general validity of Tennant's and the traditional theist's defense must be granted, but the point is: *Must* there be the
creation of those things whose properties, ordinarily the source
of value, produce pain and useless suffering upon entering

[30] *Philosophical Theology*, p. 213, n.   [31] *Mind*, XXXIX (1930), 483.

into certain collocations with each other? The earthquake and the flood, the tornado and the lightning, bodies victimized by cancer, and other scourges which paralyze even the mind — must these, parts of a necessary, determinate system, be *necessary* parts of *any* system?

Tennant replies by shifting to the opponent the burden of proof "that there could be a determinate evolutionary world of unalloyed comfort, yet adapted by its law-abidingness to the developement of rationality and morality," and by adding that "in so far as experience in this world enables us to judge, such proof seems impossible." [32] In other words, we are told that since we cannot specify alternatives we must accept the present order as *necessarily* the most conducive on the whole to morality. Our protest is supported by several reasons.

First, it is hardly fair for the empirical theist to expect his finite opponent to provide specific details when all this opponent's knowledge is that of a created person in a world with whose ultimate collocations he cannot experiment. In any case, the theist is no better off, for he cannot prove any more than the general outline of his defense, which is admitted. His opponent, indeed, cannot show what changes can be made without losing other goods, but the empirical theist cannot reason from the *is* to the *must* be.

But, second, it seems quite improbable that a God with *none* but self-limitations, who could produce the order we do find, could not have eliminated from this or any other determinate order those concomitant aspects which result in major and humanly uncontrollable catastrophes that have no disciplinary value. If we look at the facts without a preconceived theory of God in mind, we can hardly escape the suggestion that the unsurpassed Philosopher-King did not quite succeed in persuading all the constituents in the cosmic (natural and human) state to do their own work. And it surprises us to note this fact, simply because order and justice are so predominant.

Third, the theist does court difficulty when he asserts that

[32] *Philosophical Theology*, II, 201.

God's will is limited by nothing other than his moral purpose, that God is in this sense omnipotent, since all limitations are self-limitations. The empirical theist has no right
to *assume* God's omnipotence (allowing the idea of God as
such to influence him), and then argue against other views
as if he had empirically established God's power to do all he
morally purposed. If he shows that God has limited himself
to a moral purpose, it does not follow that there are none
but self-imposed limits to the fulfillment of that purpose.[33]
In any case, he may not assert this particular quality of omnipotence before showing that the empirical facts suggest it over
and above other alternatives. It is at this point more than any
other that the uncriticized "deliverances" of religious experience are accepted without justification. Ethical theists have
accepted the notion of omnipotence and concerned themselves simply with moralizing it.

And omnipotence, as traditional theists contend, is justly
made subservient to goodness of purpose. But, if this is so,
then *we can judge God's power only by his ability to complete his purpose.* This must be our starting point, if we
would be empirical. Now the perfect moral universe, though
we cannot say exactly how it is to be realized, is one in which,
as in the ideal school, moral discipline and creativity are
made possible by stable, but not inflexible, government or
law, and by respect for the freedom of individuals generally.
That this is *not* the situation in our world is admitted by
our ethical theists, and we must say, therefore, that God *did
not* have the power to (or would not) provide a system which
would be most adequate to his purposes. If this kind of determinate system *had* to be, we still must say God was not powerful enough to complete his purposes. As empiricists, we can
only use our own standard of judgment here; consequently,
it is difficult to avoid the conclusion that there must be *some*

[33] As a matter of fact, to say that God limits himself, as theist after theist
sometimes too glibly asserts, is to *presuppose* what is not hitherto proved, that
God limits himself simply because he wants to do so, or omnipotence. The
only premise for such a conclusion is, we suggest, that there is no empirical
or reasonably speculative ground for asserting that God *would* be forced to
create human spirits.

limitation or obstruction to complete (material as well as formal) goodness. What the nature of the limitation is may well be subject to speculation, but, given the premise that a materially as well as formally good God with none but self-imposed limits to his creativity *would* create a universe in which the conditions were just right for man's moral development, any philosopher without an axe to grind must, on looking around him at the actual universe, admit *that* there is a limitation. It is of no avail to comment, as Tennant has,[34] that "the self-consistency and the 'compatibility of things' are here overlooked," for once more this assumes that the compatibility and consistency of *any* determinate system necessarily involve natural evils which serve no moral purpose. In this contention, no doubt, lies the crux of the problem, but it certainly is difficult to accept the thesis that a God with *none but self-imposed limitation*, and willing the best for man, can accomplish his will only by a system in which the compatibility of things defeats some of the ends for which it was constructed. Thus, to repeat, *that* there is some limitation which is not self-imposed is a more probable hypothesis than one which holds that for an omnipotent God (in the sense described) what *is must* be, when the *is* is not as good instrumentally as it might be. Our speculation concerning the nature of the limitation, however, must be as coherent and empirical as possible.

Can it be, then, that God does not consistently will the good, that he is not formally good, or good in the most significant sense? It is impossible to see why the cosmic Mind, having produced so much good as there is, would will the good inconsistently and consequently cause himself the moral dissatisfaction which we human beings inflict upon ourselves, largely through imperfect knowledge but partly by giving in to "the imp of the perverse"? One must be pretty hard up for a theory to suppose that, after the consistency displayed by the actual production of good, God plays tricks on himself as well as on us. To avoid cosmic insanity we must look elsewhere.

[34] A marginal note on the manuscript of this chapter.

If the consistency of God's good will be granted, we may turn our attention to his material goodness, which is dependent on the amount of power God has to render his good will effective. And, we suggest, it is the limitation not of God's love but of his power that the empirical theist must posit if he would explain the superabundance of evil, the evil which has no disciplinary value. There is no escape by appealing to human ignorance of the final outcome, for then we explain the more known by the not known at all. And if appeal is made to the supposition that what appears to us as evil is good in God's wider context, then the very ground for all human judgments of good and evil is removed. For, by the same logic, present goods may be evil in a larger context.

We may now turn to the second part of Tennant's argument, which is aimed specifically at the excess evil in the world. We have pointed out the metaphysical difficulties in the doctrine of monads, but we have also indicated that for its proponents it seemed preferable because it promised to remove the responsibility of evil from God. Speaking of Ward's bare monads, we have already said:

> Since the monad's natures are such that, though conative, they cannot learn to change their relation to their environments, and since they are not responsible for their own created natures, the responsibility falls no longer on them but on God for the statistical order or whatever physical evil there may be. Pan-psychism seems, therefore, no better off than personalism at this point.[35]

If the monads' structure is so simple and their powers so scanty, they can hardly be blamed for physical catastrophes, *and*, if anything, they would have a problem of evil of their own to be solved.

Even apart from these objections, however, another must be mentioned. Remembering our ideal of a moral cosmos, it may now be said that the pan-psychist does not solve the problem but forces it upon us in another form. For God seems to have more irons in the fire, according to pan-psychism, than he either can or should handle. God's delegation of autonomy to the monads, and then his halting regard (owing to God's

[35] Cf. Chapter IV, p. 122, above.

providential immanence) for that autonomy, allow (natural) evils to occur which conflict with his projected ideal moral development of human beings. We can judge God's material goodness only in relation to the achievement of our own values, and if God's concern for another autonomous realm either below or above us conflicts with his aim for us it must be either because he wills the conflict or because he cannot avoid it. The former possibility has already been rejected, and we are left with the latter. Thus, even if pan-psychism, or any relative dualism, were granted as a metaphysical hypothesis, it would still leave us with a God who could not for some reason create a universe in which the human moral struggle did not have to contend often with unfair and disproportionate odds. The only empirical solution to the problem of good and evil seems to reside in the statement that God, though consistently willing the good of his creatures, has not been able to overcome refractory, uncreated obstacles. *That* there is a limit to God's power which he does not impose on himself seems clear, we may now say, on *any* philosophical view which grants the reality of good and evil.

What the limitation is must be a matter of reasonable speculation. A view commendable for its clear-headed presentation of the facts and the suggestion of an attractive solution may be found in the works of E. S. Brightman.[36] We turn to an evaluation of this hypothesis, for which indeed the foregoing argument has been a preparation.

Brightman holds that the values of life, reflecting the supreme value of reasonable love, reveal God's everlasting purpose. But there are not only "light and sunshine and reason and love" but also the "blackness" of moral and natural evil. Yet, though much of this blackness may be "disguised light, as desirable discipline, or as aesthetic contrast to excess of sunshine," there is far more evil than can be fairly explained thus.[37]

[36] For a complete exposition the reader should consult Brightman: *The Problem of God* (1930), and *The Finding of God* (1931).

[37] From *The Finding of God*, p. 172, by Edgar S. Brightman (copyright, 1931), used here by permission of the Abingdon Press.

There is surplus blackness. If, now, we ascribe all the blackness to some unknown good purposes of an omnipotent Creator, we are basing more on our faith in unknown purposes than we are on our experience of known facts. We know that great bodies of experience are hostile to all the values that we know anything about; and the faith in omnipotence ignores this surplus evil in favour of an unknown good.[38]

In the physical world there is more evil than is necessary for disciplinary purposes. And the clash of empiricists, of Brightman and Tennant, in the explanation of physical evil is expressed in the next quotation.

Those who say [states Brightman], as some of my critics do by implication, that any possible expression of divinely omnipotent and benevolent power in an ordered world must necessarily contain alcohol and syphilis, insanity and arterio-sclerosis, or their equivalents, know a great deal more about what must necessarily be than is vouchsafed to me. However necessary the truths of formal logic and mathematics may be, I know nothing about what must necessarily be in the concrete world. . . .[39]

Since the obstacles which delay the fulfillment of goodness and beauty — the unnecessary suffering, our own natural ignorance,[40] and a host of physical evils which have no intelligible relation to moral progress [41] — are so great, Brightman, on the hypothesis that an omnipotent good God "could have created a race of free beings who would always choose righteously (as he himself, being also free, always chooses righteously), even though in theory they were free to sin (as he also is)," [42] concludes that there must be something in the nature of things to render such a creation impossible.

This obstacle to God's material goodness is not anything God creates, for then he would be directly responsible for evil; and since absolute metaphysical dualism creates more difficulties than it solves, Brightman is forced to conclude that in the nature of God himself there is a retarding factor, refractory to God's will, with which God must contend. This ultimate, irrational, constituent element of God's nature, which is uncreated and as eternal as God himself, Brightman

[38] *Finding of God*, p. 172.   [39] *Ibid.*, pp. 173, 174.
[40] Cf. *ibid.*, pp. 153 and 155; also pp. 115, 117, 118.
[41] Cf. *ibid.*, p. 169.   [42] *Ibid.*, p. 173.

calls *The Given*. The fact that we have so orderly a world, capable of the values realized, indicates that The Given *is controlled* by God, although it does delay the realization of his purpose. The Given must not be taken to mean that something is externally given to God, but merely that it is what God starts with, as it were, and Brightman has compared it in human experience to the impulsive and passional natures which must be rationally controlled by us. The Given is the element in the complex unity of God's nature which is a source of conflict; it does not indicate a structural bifurcation of God's being, any more than conflict in our natures threatens more than our unity of moral purpose and personality.

Hence, the superfluous evils (all those which prevent this world from being a moral paradise or training ground where moral endeavor does not meet insuperable difficulties not of man's own creation) are "mysterious by-products of God's struggle with The Given, a shower of terrible and blinding sparks from the cosmic forge." [43] God worketh and travaileth even as man does in the moral struggle. God's achievements do not always follow from the mere thought or willing of them, without the overcoming of conflicting elements. There is a Cross at the heart of the universe, the struggle of an invincible and everlasting Love which is determined to transmute evil into good and improve conditions for the development of its children. The determinate system God has been able to achieve, but the evils resulting from such a system cause anguish and distress and the persistent effort to overcome The Given. For these evils are not the necessary consequences of a determinate system but the necessary consequents of an incompletely controlled Given. On this view the slow process of evolution,[44] the destruction of species, the limitations of human body and mind exist *in spite of* God's willing the contrary, but the presence of order and the values achieved and achievable show that God controls The Given, though not yet completely.

Before we describe The Given further, we may ourselves

[43] *Ibid.*, p. 153.   [44] Cf. *ibid.*, p. 128.

now suggest that its presence makes possible the solution of a difficulty which was one of the grounds for Ward's rejection of the notion of creation as a temporal act, namely, that a good God would not have waited half an eternity without a good that ought to be. On the view here presented God waited not because he wanted to but because he had to, owing to the hindrances of the Given, an obstruction finally overcome.[45] This obstacle may now be more fully described.

"The Given, then, is the name which describes the total complex of eternal factors in the divine nature which he did not create and with which he always has to deal in the eternal activity of his perfectly good will." [46] Both "cosmic necessities" and "cosmic hindrance" are grouped under the name.[47] The following are other important characteristics of The Given:

"First, The Given is not any unconscious stuff, material substance, or mysterious entity of any sort; it is conscious experience of God." [48] There is no unconscious core in God, but all is "conscious content," [49] in the same way, we might say, as our will, emotion, and thought are. The eternal conditions (or The Given) under which God labors are parts of God's consciousness. Second, referring as it does to the uncreated and eternal nature of God, it is complex in that it includes those conditions under which God must work. These are: (a) time, for all God's creation is in time, and, because activity and change are meaningless [50] without time, because God (having work still to do and ever creating new souls) changes, Brightman insists that for God "time experience is ultimately real." [51] Again: "Indeed, the fact of temporal structure is itself part of the eternally given nature of God. Time cannot be created or begun, for creation and beginning

---

[45] Cf. Chapter IV, p. 113, above; also, Ward, *Realm of Ends*, p. 233.

[46] Brightman, *Finding of God*, p. 174.

[47] *Ibid.*, p. 173.

[48] *Ibid.*, pp. 174, 175.

[49] We remind the reader that for Brightman, as for ourselves, the self is a conscious unity, or, synonymously, a unity of thought, feeling, and will.

[50] Cf. *Finding of God*, Chapter VI, "The Patience of God," and "A Temporalist View of God," *Journal of Religion*, XXII (October 1932), 544–555.

[51] *Finding of God*, p. 133.

imply a previously existing time." [52] (b) God's "uncreated nature, The Given, plainly includes reason and moral law." [53]

It is not so plain to us, however, why the eternal nature of God contains "the eternal necessities of reason" which prohibit contradiction. If this means, as we suppose it does, that God must willy-nilly submit to them or that the laws of reason reflect God's uncreated nature from which there cannot be any divergence, we see no empirical evidence for the assertion or against it. We can understand that God is reasonable because, so far as we know from our own finite experience, he must be if there is to be order in his life and purpose, but we see no reason for holding that he *must* be reasonable whether he wants to or not. We should rather restrict The Given to the chaotic, retarding factor in God's experience and consider the laws of reason ways in which God thinks; whether he *must* think so, we cannot know. There is as much reason to suppose that they are self-imposed norms of the divine nature (which might well have allowed other alternatives as well) as to suppose that they represent immutable necessities or a logical *prius* to any activity. On a temporal view of God as developing there is more reason to suppose that the norms are self-imposed by God. For us, in other words, Process is Reality. This is true for Brightman (less so for Tennant), but for Brightman the process is dominated from the beginning by certain eternal forms, whereas it might be held consistently that God's nature allowed others in addition to such forms, though God restricted himself to these.

And the same may be said of the inclusion of moral laws or certain moral and ideal principles in The Given. Brightman himself in a passage quoted implies that God is free to choose the wrong, and, indeed, it would seem that God's goodness consists in the attitude he takes toward The Given, but which he *need not* take. God is not good simply because he cannot be bad, as the angles of an equilateral triangle must be equal; at least we have no empirical ground for saying so. And what it means to speak of The Given as including "eternal

[52] *Ibid.*, p. 134. [53] *Ibid.*, p. 175.

necessities which are simply indorsed by the divine will" [54] is more than we can understand; though one cannot help thinking of Platonic Ideas which are ensouled but, nevertheless, still static forms. We can understand what it means to say that God loves mankind with immeasurable care and tenderness and yearning, but what the uncreated ideal of love *for man* could have meant for God before man existed (or was conceived of) is more than we can say. Brightman, like our philosophers, is trying to make the validity of certain ideals eternal, but in so doing he loses the concreteness which, we agree with Tennant, must be the essence of relevant ideals for God or for man, so far as we know (a point Brightman would certainly insist on in Ethics). Briefly, we are seriously questioning the inclusion of what Brightman calls the formal aspect of The Given, as opposed to the conscious "subject-matter" with which thought and goodness have to deal "as human thought has to reckon with sense data." [55] God's goodness consists in his willing of certain alternatives which are allowed by his total nature, but to suppose that there were any one set of principles he *ought* to have willed and in conformity with which he *had* to will is to abstract willing from the act willed. Of course, we should insist that the very determinateness of God's nature excluded many so-called possibilities, but we should not conclude from this, as Tennant and Brightman seem to do, that God can act in only one way, that God's nature does not allow him other alternatives. But we do hold that it is impossible to account for the excessive evil in the world without the nonformal retarding Given.[56]

Finally, according to Brightman, The Given is controlled. For though God's mastery of The Given is not complete [and therefore he is not omnipotent] he is by no means its victim. By venturing the hypothesis that God is finite in power, Brightman does not therefore consider God to be in "knee-breeches," as some critics seem to have feared. The Given

[54] *Finding of God*, p. 187.   [55] *Ibid.*, p. 175.
[56] Brightman's *Problem of God* restricts itself to this view of The Given; *Finding of God* includes moral and logical necessities as well in The Given.

is a hindrance, a "cosmic drag," a delay to progress, but not able to thwart God or his purposes, and God's creativity goes on undefeated.[57] And if our proof of this assertion is required, we refer the reader to our treatment of the teleological argument. Indeed, the whole wider teleological argument is the colligation of the evidence in favor of God's actual control of the Given.[58]

Thus we see that a theology, even more empirical than Tennant's, makes possible reasonable confidence in the existence of a Father who loves his children, prodigal as they are. This belief is reasonable as the best interpretation of the past and present order, including the values inherent in it. It is a belief based on what *has* been experienced, on *facta* rather than *facienda*, on *cognita* rather than *cognoscenda*. The large balance of good over evil necessitates the view that God is good; if the theist cannot build his case on God's and man's past experiments, as it were, he has no rational ground for faith in the future. But once the conclusion that God is our cosmic Friend is found to be reasonable, we must ask why more values have not been achieved, why our cosmic Master has allowed nondisciplinary evils; and then, unless we are bound to prefer an a priori notion of God at all costs, we must assert *that* there is a limitation, which is not self-imposed, under which God has been working, and which he has controlled. So much, we contend, the empirical theist, loyal to facts and not to conceptions, must insist upon, whether or not he can decide what *that* limitation is. In any case, he can be confident of the goodness of God; he can rest assured that God will, so far as lies in his tremendous power, be faithful unto death. What the source of the limitation is remains a matter of speculation, but we are bound as rational beings to speculate with our feet on the ground and all our balloons tied firmly to our earthly anchorage, and Brightman's solution, with the suggested modifications, is most acceptable.

[57] Cf. *Finding of God*, pp. 115, 116.
[58] Brightman's view of values would approximate Sorley's rather than Tennant's.

We are then, in an adventurous universe, with contingency not simply at the heart of nature but at the very core of reality. A cosmic experiment has long been under way which, in the production of sentient and human life, has increased values. The great unreasonable tragedy would be that, after all the divine and human effort expended, the human spirit, at the height of its cultivation, with the body aged and weak but the mind aged and ripe, should be cut off. If death does bring the realization of our individual personalities to a sudden stop, it cannot be because such a terminus is to be preferred, but because God in his very goodness can grant no other end, even though he would. On the other hand, there is no reason to suppose that he who controlled The Given sufficiently to *create* spirits cannot *preserve* his children. Though the future life may be invoked "as further affecting the evaluation of the relativity of this world's ills" (as Tennant [59] has commented), we cannot, like most theists, invoke immortality as a partial solution of the problem of excess evil. It is arbitrary to suppose that in the land beyond the border there is a paradise for moral spirits, a kaleidoscopic change from an atmosphere in which the moral spirit at times breathes with great difficulty to one in which all the impurities are immediately removed. We seek immortality neither because we expect a promised land in which the moral life may be lived in a better environment, nor because there will be no excess evil in a future life, but because we have approved of the moral struggle here and now and of the values we have only partly realized. The problem of excess evil may be everlasting, suffering for no good purpose may be constant in the Divine and human heart, but a God bent on achieving greater value and order surely must seek to provide self-consciousness and opportunity adequate for the development of the seeds he has planted in his own human creation.

C. FINAL SUMMARY

In this study we have attempted not only an historical exposition but also an evaluation of the more significant phases

[59] Cf. *Philosophical Theology*, II, 204, 205, and 269.

of the empirical argument for God. Since our comments and suggestions have been mingled with the exposition, it seems worthwhile, at the cost of some formalism, to summarize, in closing, those contentions which have been basic to the formation of our present conclusions.

Apart from the historical exposition attempted in this study, the following main theses have been considered and defended:

1. The existence and the attributes of God must be established by reference to the criticized data of the whole of experience. Each attribute must be corroborated by fresh appeal to the facts and not by deduction from preconceived notions of God or other established attributes. But each of the philosophers considered failed, in varying degrees, to abide by this empirical procedure, especially when considering God's attributes.

2. Though we immediately experience and know the ("datum") self as the *erlebnis* of any specious present, the nature of the whole self is inferred by coherent interpretation of the present and the remembered past self-experience. The distinction of the noumenal self from the phenomenal self is (a) an abstraction similar to that of extension apart from color, (b) an incorrect analysis of the specious present in which I know that *I* know, and (c) the result of applying to the unique and basic experience of the self, in which subject and object are identical, the noumenon-phenomenon relationship involved only in the experience of the non-self.

3. The duration, continuity, and unity of the self may be explained without reference to a noumenal self provided we can conceive of the present unity of the self as the growth of an original unity of experience which at any moment is that of the past plus new influences which have been absorbed.

4. Ward's and Tennant's objections to a personalistic metaphysics are not effective for (a) science is not

dependent upon the existence of a "planted out"
world but on the regularity of Nature; (b) Ward's attempt to avoid divine intermediation does not avoid
the problem of interaction which is most intelligible
between Creator and created; (c) the monads of the
inorganic world are really nonempirical entities whose
uniqueness and individuality are no greater than that
of the mass-point rejected. But personalism is more
empirical and consistent if it grants the existence of
lesser spiritual beings in the organic world wherever
striving is in evidence.

5. The value of an object represents a dynamic (non-
logical) relation, which the object assumes over and
above existential qualities and relations, owing to its
being desired and nothing else. Therefore, values are
not "read off" but created by the desire of the individual which expresses his own determinate nature. Indeed, values, moral and otherwise, are the joint-
products of the interaction of the subject with the
personal and natural environment.

6. Failure to distinguish the problems of the psychology,
the epistemology, and the metaphysics of conscience
have led to the confusion of moral obligation with particular verdicts of conscience and to a misconception
(especially by Martineau, Pringle-Pattison, and Taylor)
of the basis for its authority.

7. Conscience does not act as human before it is felt to be
divine, for its authority rests in itself (as human) only.
But it does represent one of the whole self's experiences
which cannot be reduced to conation or thought or
volition.

8. The moral consciousness has no perception of a non-
natural value-object, or moral given which may not be
reduced to desire and its objects, but it simply represents the unconditional imperative or obligation
(which cannot be reduced to desire) to do the Good
one knows. The moral consciousness, the sense of

moral obligation, does not give any information about what the Good is; it is cognitively innocent.

9. The standard of true value is not the result of a unique moral perception or of the coherent organization of perceived, true value-objects or particular "oughts." It is the result of the coherent systematization of value-claims, or joint-products of the conative self (especially) and the environment.

10. The Good thus arrived at becomes obligatory, and particular value-claims become obligatory ("oughts"), demanding unconditional allegiance in the degree to which they are conducive to the realization of the Good.

11. There can be no obligation to inconceivable (because hitherto not actually experienced) satisfactions, and the particular moral judgment, consequently, has a reference to existence because the true value contemplated is an inductive idealization of values already experienced by the individual and others in varying degrees.

12. Validity being meaningless apart from the knowledge relation, moral values are not valid for man unless he has, to some extent, experienced them. Since, therefore, completely unrealized ideals cannot guide man, the validity of ideals refers to the applicability of coherent idealizations of man's value-experience to his whole nature, and they have "imperative reality" for man not because they already exist in a nonhuman realm, but because they are conceived by man, as a result of at least partial experience, to be the best for him. They therefore become obligatory.

13. The metaphysical objectivity of moral value is really another way of expressing God's goodness, and (a) since the concrete good *for man* cannot be intelligibly conceived as existing independently of him and as the cause of his knowing it, (b) since human moral ideals, as such, cannot be attributed to God, these ideals are Objective, as applicable to and expressing man's criti-

cized volitional activity in this environment. God's
goodness and love are, on the other hand, subject to
inference, based on human analogy, from his (purposed) relation to the world and man's moral struggle.

14. To argue for the correct knowledge of a humanly unrealized realm of moral values, independent of ourselves and valid for us, by appealing to the organicity
or affinity of man to reality is to beg the point to be
proved, the existence of such a nonhuman realm, and
to suppose that human moral dissatisfaction, instead of
being due to the *growth* of determinate individuals,
is externally provoked.

15. Moral laws are Objective and independent of individual men (but not of man), and thus their Objectivity
differs from that of physical laws (which are the result of coherent interpretation of natural phenomena)
only in the fact that they express the laws of prospective and obligatory behavior, based, as they are, on
the coherent interpretation of the affective and volitional experiences of men in relation to each other in
this natural world.

16. If the causal realm, as a necessary condition of moral
character, is, together with the actual realization and
the possibility of realizing values, insufficient proof of
God's goodness, there is no strength in arguing for
God's goodness by cognition of an independent realm
of moral perfection. For one should then be led to
doubt both the veracity of such moral cognition, and
also the relevance of that metaphysically independent
moral order to the human moral struggle.

17. The following objections are not tenable against the
wider teleological argument: (a) that *this* world, instead of being designed, may be as accidental as one
man's holding the best five trumps in a deck of cards,
for what is to be explained is not the holding of the
five trumps alone, but the deck of cards; (b) that if this
world be the sole instance of its kind there can be no
talk of antecedent probability, for the probability in-

volved here concerns the antecedent probability of only an *hypothesis about* the constitution of the world that is *given*; (c) that there is more antecedent probability for belief in other person's existence than for God's, for unless the existence of other selves is assumed, there is no more antecedent logical probability for my saying that there are others like, better, or worse, than myself.

18. Since time is at least phenomenally real and has a non-distorted one-to-one functional temporal relation to noumenal existence, there is no ground for holding that existence for the noumenal being is supratemporal (even if the distinction between the noumenal and phenomenal were otherwise tenable). If we are to reason empirically about God's attributes, time, as duration and succession, must be applicable to God's experience, even though his time-span be much greater and his tempo different from ours.

19. Though creation has no exact empirical analogue, it does not contradict any finite experience; and the inconceivability of its *modus operandi* is no greater essentially than the achievements of another more powerful human mind. But since creation must explain the newness and relative independence of man and organic life at least, it involves a dynamic relation between God and his creation which, empirically conceived, is a temporal act in God's history made more intelligible by the doctrine of "The Given."

20. Since (a) memory-less monads cannot learn and cannot be blamed for the excess evil in the physical universe, (b) since no proponent of relative metaphysical dualism can reasonably defend the omnipotence and goodness of God by holding, without empirical foundation and sufficient probability, that the excess evil which is part of this morally necessary and determinate system is a necessary part of any determinate system; and since (c) it is unreasonable to suppose that God would have more irons in the fire than the completion

of his moral purpose allowed, there seems to be no escape from the conclusion *that* there is a limitation to God's power which is not self-imposed. Brightman's view of The Given, minus the logical and moral necessities, seems to be an adequate description of the nature of the limitation.

BIBLIOGRAPHY

BIBLIOGRAPHY

[The works of the five philosophers analyzed in this book are arranged chronologically.]

CHAPTER II

Martineau, James, *Types of Ethical Theory*, 2 vols. (3d ed.; Oxford: Clarendon Press, 1889).

—— *A Study of Religion*, 2 vols. (2nd ed.; Oxford: Clarendon Press, 1889).

—— *The Seat of Authority in Religion* (London: Longmans, Green and Co., 1890).

—— *Essays, Reviews and Addresses*, 4 vols. (London: Longmans, Green and Co., 1890–91).

Taylor, Alfred E., *The Faith of a Moralist*, 2 vols. (London: Macmillan and Co., 1932).

—— *Philosophical Studies* (London: Macmillan and Co., 1934).

PAMPHLETS

(Note: all of the essays below may be found in Martineau, *Essays, Reviews and Addresses*, vol. IV.)

Martineau, James, *The Place of Mind in Nature and Intuition in Man* (London: Williams and Norgate, 1872).

—— *Religion As Affected By Modern Materialism* (London: Williams and Norgate, 1874).

—— *Modern Materialism: Its Attitude Toward Theology* (London: Williams and Norgate, 1876).

—— *Ideal Substitutes for God* (London: Williams and Norgate, 1878).

—— *Loss and Gain in Recent Theology* (London: Williams and Norgate, 1881).

—— *The Relation Between Ethics and Religion* (London: Williams and Norgate, 1881).

COMMENTARIES

Armstrong, Richard A., *Martineau's "Study of Religion": An Analysis and Appreciation* (London: James Clarke and Co., 1900).

Carpenter, J. Estlin, *James Martineau: Theologian and Teacher* (London: Philip Green, 1905).

Drummond, James, and Upton, Charles B., *The Life and Letters of James Martineau*, 2 vols. (London: James Nisbet and Co. Ltd., 1902).

Hutchinson, F. E., "The Growth of Liberal Theology," in *Cambridge History of English Literature*, XII, 279.

Jackson, A. W., *James Martineau: A Biography and Study* (London: Longmans, Green and Co., 1900).

Jones, Henry, *The Philosophy of Martineau in Relation to the Idealism of the Present Day* (London: Macmillan and Co., 1905).

Mellone, Sydney H., *Leaders of Religious Thought in the 19th Century* (London: William Blackwood and Sons Ltd., 1902).

Sorley, William R., "Philosophers," in *Cambridge History of English Literature*, XIV, 27.

Upton, Charles B., *Dr Martineau's Philosophy* (London: James Nisbet and Co., 1905).

Watson, John, "A Saint of Theism," *Hibbert Journal*, I (1902–03), 253–270.

CHAPTER III

Pringle-Pattison, Andrew Seth, *The Development from Kant to Hegel: with Chapters on the Philosophy of Religion* (London: Williams and Norgate, 1882).

—— (with R. B. Haldane), ed., *Essays in Philosophical Criticism* (London: Longmans, Green and Co., 1883). First Essay: "Philosophy as Criticism of Categories."

—— *Scottish Philosophy: A Comparison of the Scottish and German Answers to Hume* (first Balfour Lecture, London: William Blackwood and Sons Ltd., 1885).

—— *Hegelianism and Personality* (Balfour Lectures, London: William Blackwood and Sons Ltd., 1887).

—— *Two Lectures on Theism* (London: William Blackwood and Sons Ltd., 1897).

—— *Man's Place in the Cosmos: And Other Essays* (2nd ed.; London: William Blackwood and Sons Ltd., 1902).

—— *The Philosophical Radicals: And Other Essays* (London: William Blackwood and Sons Ltd., 1907).

—— "Immanence and Transcendence," in *The Spirit* (edited by B. H. Streeter; London: Macmillan and Co., 1919), pp. 1–22.

—— "The Idea of God: A Reply to Criticism," *Mind*, XXVIII (1919), 1–18. (Reply to Rashdall.)

—— *The Idea of God in the Light of Recent Philosophy* (Gifford Lectures; 2nd ed.; London: Oxford University Press, 1920).

—— *The Idea of Immortality* (Oxford: Clarendon Press, 1922).

—— *Studies in the Philosophy of Religion* (Oxford: Clarendon Press, 1930).

—— *Balfour Lectures on Realism* (delivered 1891; edited with a "Memoir" by G. F. Barbour, London: William Blackwood and Sons Ltd., 1933).

Commentaries

Baillie, J. B., "Pringle-Pattison as Philosopher," *Proceedings of the British Academy*, XVII, 461–489.

Brightman, Edgar S., *Religious Values* (New York: Abingdon Press, 1925).

Caldecott, Alfred, *The Philosophy of Religion in England and America* (London: Methuen and Co., 1901).

Capper, J. B., "Andrew Seth Pringle-Pattison," *Proceedings of the British Academy*, XVII, 447–461.

Muirhead, John H., *The Platonic Tradition in Anglo-Saxon Philosophy* (London: Allen and Unwin; New York: Macmillan and Co., 1931).

Nédoncelle, Maurice, *La Philosophie Religieuse en Grande-Bretagne de 1850 à nos jours* (Paris: Librairie Bloud et Gay, 1934).

Webb, Clement C. J., *God and Personality* (London: Allen and Unwin, 1918).

—— *Religious Thought in England from 1850* (Oxford: Clarendon Press, 1933).

CHAPTER IV

Bowne, Borden Parker, *Metaphysics* (rev. ed.; New York: American Book Co., 1910).

Brightman, Edgar S., *An Introduction To Philosophy* (New York: Henry Holt and Co., 1925).

—— *A Philosophy of Ideals* (New York: Henry Holt and Co., 1928).

Knudson, Albert C., *The Philosophy of Personalism* (New York: Abingdon Press, 1927).

Sorley, W. R., and Stout, G. F., *Essays in Philosophy* (with a "Memoir" by Ward's youngest daughter, Olwen Ward Campbell; Cambridge: University Press, 1927).

Ward, James, *Naturalism and Agnosticism*, 2 vols. (the Gifford Lectures in 1896–1898; London: Adams and Charles Black, 1899).

—— *Psychological Principles* (Cambridge: University Press, 1918).

—— *The Realm of Ends or Pluralism and Theism* (3d ed.; Cambridge: University Press, 1920).

—— *A Study of Kant* (Cambridge: University Press, 1922).

—— *Psychology Applied to Education* (edited by G. Dawes Hicks; Cambridge: University Press, 1926).

SELECTED ARTICLES

Ward, James, "The Relation of Physiology to Psychology" (London: R. Clay, Sons, and Taylor, 1875).

—— "A General Analysis of Mind"; "Objects and Their Interaction"; "Space and Time," among his "Psychological Papers" (1880).

—— (with Alexander, S., Read, C., Stout, G. F.), "The Nature of Mental Activity," *Proceedings of the Aristotelian Society*, VIII (1907–08), 215–258.

—— "Psychology," *Encyclopaedia Britannica* (11th ed.), XXII, 547–604.

—— (with Sorley, W. R., Lindsay, A. D., and Bosanquet, B.), "Purpose and Mechanism," *Proceedings of the Aristotelian Society*, XII (1911–12), 216–264.

—— (with Moore, G. E., Johnson, W. E., Hicks, G. D., and Smith, J. A.), "Are the Materials of Sense Affections of the Mind?" *Proceedings of the Aristotelian Society*, XVII (1916–17), 418–459.

—— "A Theistic Monadism," *Contemporary British Philosophy*, 2 vols. (edited by J. H. Muirhead; London: Allen and Unwin, 1924–25), II, 25–55.

—— "Bradley's Doctrine of Experience," *Mind*, XXXIV (1925), 12–38.

COMMENTARIES

Coates, Adrian, *A Sceptical Examination of Contemporary British Philosophy* (London: Brentano's Ltd., 1929). Chapter VII, "James Ward: Pluralism and Monadism."

Hicks, G. Dawes, "The Philosophy of James Ward," *Mind*, XXXIV (1925), 280–299.

Muirhead, John H., "The Last Phase of Professor Ward's Philosophy," *Mind*, XXII (1913), 321–330.

—— *Contemporary British Philosophy*, 2 vols. (London: Allen and Unwin, 1924–25).

Sorley, William R., "James Ward," *Mind*, XXXIV (1925), 273–279.

Stout, G. F., "Ward as a Psychologist" (and answers by Mrs. Ward), in *Studies in Philosophy and Psychology* (London: Macmillan and Co., 1930), pp. 123–134.

CHAPTER V

Brightman, Edgar S., *Religious Values* (New York: Abingdon Press, 1925).

Höffding, Harald, *The Philosophy of Religion*, translated by B. E. Meyer (New York: Macmillan Co., 1906).

Perry, Ralph B., *General Theory of Value* (New York: Longmans, Green and Co., 1926).

Sorley, William Ritchie, *The Ethics of Naturalism* (London: William Blackwood and Sons Ltd., 1885 and 1904).

—— *Recent Tendencies in Ethics* (London: William Blackwood and Sons Ltd., 1904).

—— *A History of English Philosophy* (Cambridge: University Press, 1920).

—— *The Moral Life and Moral Worth* (Cambridge: University Press, 1911, and 3d ed., 1920).

Sorley, William Ritchie, *Moral Values and the Idea of God* (the Gifford Lectures in 1914 and 1915; 3d ed.; Cambridge: University Press, 1930).

—— *Selections from the Literature of Theism* (edited by Alfred Caldecott and H. R. Macintosh; 3d ed.; Edinburgh: T. and J. Clark, 1931), pp. 385–416.

ARTICLES

Sorley, William Ritchie, "The Historical Method," *Essays in Philosophical Criticism* (edited by A. Seth Pringle-Pattison and R. B. Haldane; London: Longmans, Green and Co., 1883).

—— "The Two Idealisms," *Hibbert Journal*, II (1904), 703–721.

—— "The Knowledge of Good," *Hibbert Journal*, III (1904–05), 543–557.

—— "Ethical Aspects of Economics," *International Journal of Ethics*, XVII (1907), 1 ff., 317 ff., 437 ff.

—— "Evolutionary Ethics," *Quarterly Review*, April 1909.

—— "The Interpretation of Evolution," *Proceedings of the British Academy* (1909), vol. IV.

—— "The Philosophical Attitude," *International Journal of Ethics*, XX (1910), 152 ff.

—— (with Lindsay, A. D., Bosanquet, B., and Ward., J.), "Purpose and Mechanism," *Proceedings of the Aristotelian Society*, XII (1911–12), 216–264.

—— "Does Religion Need a Philosophy?" *Hibbert Journal*, XI (1913), 563–578.

—— "Time and Reality," *Mind*, XXXII, 145 ff.

—— "The Beginnings of English Philosophy," *The Cambridge History of English Literature*, vol. IV (1909).

—— "Hobbes and Contemporary Philosophy," in *ibid.*, vol. VII (1911).

—— "John Locke," in *ibid.*, vol. VIII (1912).

—— "Berkeley and Contemporary Philosophy," in *ibid.*, vol. IX (1912).

—— "Bentham and the Early Utilitarians," in *ibid.*, vol. XI (1914).

—— "Philosophers," in *ibid.*, vol. XIV (1916).

—— "The State and Morality," in *The International Crisis: The Theory of the State* (London: Oxford University Press, 1916).

—— "Value and Reality," in *Contemporary British Philosophy*, edited by J. H. Muirhead (London: Allen and Unwin, 1925), II, 247–267.

COMMENTARIES

Coates, Adrian, *A Sceptical Examination of Contemporary British Philosophy* (London: Brentano's Ltd., 1929). Chapter III, "Professor Sorley and the Category of Value," pp. 58–88.

Osborne, Harold, *Foundations of the Philosophy of Value* (Cambridge: University Press, 1931).

Taylor, Alfred E., *The Faith of a Moralist*, 2 vols. (London: Macmillan and Co., 1932).

Tennant, F. R., "William Ritchie Sorley," *Proceedings of the British Academy* (1936), vol. XXI.

CHAPTERS VI–VII

Brightman, Edgar S., *An Introduction to Philosophy* (New York: Henry Holt and Co., 1925).

—— *A Philosophy of Ideals* (New York: Henry Holt and Co., 1928).

—— *The Problem of God* (New York: Abingdon Press, 1930).

—— *The Finding of God* (New York: Abingdon Press, 1931).

—— *Moral Laws* (New York: Abingdon Press, 1933).

—— "A Temporalist View of God," *Journal of Religion*, XII (October 1932), 544–555.

Broad, Charlie D., Reviews of Tennant's *Philosophical Theology*, in *Mind*, vols. XXXVIII (1929) and XXXIX (1930).

Lewis, Clarence I., *Mind and the World Order* (New York: Charles Scribner's Sons, 1929).

Muirhead, John H., editor, *Contemporary British Philosophy*, 2 vols. (London: Unwin and Allen, 1925).

Sorley, William R., *Moral Values and the Idea of God* (3d ed.; Cambridge: University Press, 1930).

Tennant, Frederick Robert, "The Being of God, in the Light of Physical Science" (Graduate Thesis).

Tennant, Frederick Robert, *Miracle and Its Philosophical Presup-positions* (Cambridge: University Press, 1925).

—— *Philosophical Theology*, 2 vols. (Cambridge: University Press, 1929–30).

—— *Philosophy of the Sciences* (Cambridge: University Press, 1932).

Urban, Wilbur M., *Valuation: Its Nature and Laws* (New York: Macmillan Co., 1909).

Ward, James, *The Realm of Ends or Pluralism and Theism* (3d ed.; Cambridge: University Press, 1920).

Whitehead, Alfred N., *Process and Reality* (New York: Macmillan Co., 1929).

INDEX

INDEX

Absolute, the, *see* God.
Adamson, R., 134.
Aesthetic experience, underestimated, 41.
Analogy, *see* Human analogy.
Anthropomorphism, limited, 209.
A priori arguments, rejected, 3.
Aristotle, 158.
Armstrong, Richard A., on Martineau's teleology, 22.
Arnold, Matthew, 44.

Balfour, A. J., 45, 233.
Baur, Walter, 192.
Bergson, Henri, 25, 45.
Berkeley, George, 57, 102, 115, 253.
Bosanquet, Bernard, ix, 45, 47, 73, 74, 76, 83.
Bowne, Borden P., 94 *n.*, 115, 253.
Bradley, Francis H., ix, 45, 47, 51, 63, 73, 74, 76, 79, 198.
Brightman, Edgar S., 115, 194, 238 *n.*, 253, 281 *n.*, 288;
  on finite God, 275–282;
  on nature of the self, 206, 208, 278 *n.*;
  on values, 141.
Broad, Charlie D., 193, 194, 228–232, 237, 245;
  on free will, 246.
Butler, Joseph, 41.

Caird, Edward, 45;
  on creation, 17.
Caldecott, Alfred, 41, 46.
Campbell, Olwen Ward, 135.
Carlyle, Thomas, 44.
Causality, not a Kantian category, 200, 210;
  and creation, 109;
  Martineau on, 13–15, 41;
  and will, 10, 101, 102, 103.
Chance, and order, 23.
Coherence, as criterion of truth, 47, 48, 50, 63, 90, 94, 95, 153, 256.
  See also Truth.

Coleridge, Samuel, 7.
Comte, Auguste, 66, 97.
Conation, and value, *see* Moral values; Value.
Conscience, *see* Moral consciousness.
Consciousness, *see* Self; Specious present.
Contingency, and epigenesis, 51;
  as explanation of evil, 269, 270, 274, 275;
  Ward's view evaluated, 121, 122;
  metaphysics of, 87, 95 *n.*, 105, 282;
  and values, 89, 264.
Continuity, law of, 243;
  of inorganic and organic, 52, 53, 67, 68, 234;
  Ward's use of law of, 101, 103, 104, 106.
  See also Nature.
Continuum, presentational, 117–118.
Cosmological argument for God, *see* God.
Creation, 17, 18, 23, 39, 74, 187, 235, 256, 272;
  and free will, 111;
  and interaction, 123;
  personalistic view of, 115, 116;
  and time, 109–114, 260, 261, 278;
  obstacle to, 113, 278.
  See also Pringle-Pattison; Tennant; Ward.
Creation of values, 141, 163, 164, 181, 189, 263.

Darwin, Charles, 229.
Deism: Martineau's criticized, 59, 60, 61;
  rejected, 250.
Descartes, René, 21, 68, 118, 229.
Determinism, 7, 8.
  See also Will.
Dorner, A., 92.
Dualism, epistemological, 55, 56, 57, 97, 223;
  metaphysical, 16, 18, 56, 57, 103, 113.

INDEX

and matter, 102;
its place in nature, 19.
See also Self; Martineau; Pringle-Pattison; Sorley; Tennant; Ward.
Monads, *see* Pan-psychism; Pluralism.
Monism, metaphysical, 57, 58.
Moral alternation, principle of, 219.
Moral argument for God, Martineau's, 26–41;
Pringle-Pattison's, 169–174;
Sorley's, 137, 175–191;
Tennant on the, 233–239;
Ward's, 128–131; reducible to ontological, 185, 186;
summarized briefly, 256–260.
Moral character, its prerequisite, 182. *See also* Will.
Moral consciousness, its cognitive value, 26, 30–33, 34, 39, 40, 42, 67, 90;
as creative, 71, 72;
as a moral eye, 33;
its objective claim, 69;
its origin and growth, 27, 28, 29;
its preferential character, 30, 31, 39, 59;
its psychological nature, 26–30, 39;
and pleasure, 27–28, 29;
social theory of, 27, 28, 29, 30, 32, 42;
its validity, 62, 63, 66, 157;
its uniqueness, 28–30, 33, 42;
its universality, 27, 42;
its authority God, 34, 35, 42, 43, 60, 61, 66–71;
as pathway to God, 3, 26;
confusion of psychology and epistemology of, 27, 28, 29, 39, 43;
as part of the philosophical data, 136, 138;
A. E. Taylor's view of, 35, 36.
See also Moral obligation; Martineau; Pringle-Pattison; Sorley; Tennant; Ward.
Moral development, basis for, 68, 69, 70, 71, 257, 258;
as cosmic purpose, 262;
ideal of, 263;
its metaphysical prerequisites, 262, 263, 265, 267, 268, 269, 270, 271,

272, 273;
why retarded, 280, 281.
See also Pringle-Pattison; Sorley; Taylor.
Moral dissatisfaction, its cause, 159, 160, 173, 174, 176, 286;
mystery of, 158, 159.
See also Pringle-Pattison; Sorley.
Moral emotion, and moral obligation, 145, 219.
Moral error, how discovered, 69.
Moral experience, *see* Moral consciousness.
Moral intuition, *see* Value-judgment.
Moral judgment, *see* Value-judgment.
Moral knowledge, 147–152, 171, 173, 174, 175, 176, 177–178, 179, 181, 183, 184, 186, 190, 191.
See also Value-judgment; Moral consciousness; Moral values; Martineau; Pringle-Pattison; Sorley; Tennant; Ward.
Moral obligation, its authority, 83, 258, 259, 284;
cognitively innocent, 147–152, 178, 218, 219, 256, 258, 259, 284;
its origin, 216, 217, 218, 219;
its psychology, 147–148, 158, 159, 216–219;
as irreducible, 139, 144, 145, 189, 218, 219, 258, 284;
and moral emotion, 145, 219;
and free will, 80;
involves actual existence, 154, 155, 174;
involves independence, 80;
and the Good, 151, 156, 178, 186;
its immediacy misunderstood, 218;
social theory of, 128.
See also Moral consciousness; Martineau; Pringle-Pattison; Sorley; Tennant; Ward.
Moral progress, *see* Progress.
Moral values,
authority of, 34–40, 60, 61, 184, 185;
catholicity of, 140;
and cognition, 147–152, 171, 173–178, 183, 184;
and conation, 140, 150, 152, 160, 162, 216, 217;

his theory of the self, 198, 202–209, 240–243, 253;
his metaphysics, 212–215, 269;
on the evidential value of religious experience, 221–227, 237, 240, 254;
on the laws of nature, 211 n., 213, 214;
on space and time, 210;
his psychology, 197–202;
on the function and task of philosophy, 195;
his view of reason, 211, 212, 226.

Theism, and pluralism, 107, 108, 125.
See also Personalism.
Theistic monadism, see Pan-psychism.
Theology, science of, evaluated, 222, 226.

Time, its nature, 10, 17, 19, 41, 42, 84–89, 210;
and eternity, 85, 86, 241;
and God, 84–89, 91, 240–244;
and creation, 109–114;
and self, 84, 85, 86, 87, 205, 206, 208, 240, 241, 242;
and value, 51.
See also Teleology; Martineau; Pringle-Pattison; Sorley; Tennant; Ward.

Transcendence, see Immanence of God.
Trendelenburg, A., 92.
Truth, its presuppositions, 75 n.
See also Knowledge; Martineau; Pringle-Pattison; Sorley; Tennant; Ward.
Turner, William, 7.

Ulrici, H., quoted, 78.
Unity of nature, a postulate, 101.
Unity of reality, one of ethical purpose, 137, 181.
Upton, Charles B., on Martineau, 16–17, 22, 41, 61.
Urban, Wilbur M., 216 n.

Validity, of ethics, 169–172, 188, 189;
hypostatized, 127, 133, 190, 262;
of knowledge, 174–175, 201, 202, 285;
and personal realization, 160, 169, 170–172, 173, 174, 175, 259;
and reality, 146, 169, 202;

of values, 136, 144, 146, 152, 153, 156, 162, 169, 170, 174, 175, 220.
See also Moral values; Value; Value-judgment.

Value, and conation, 70, 71, 126, 140, 150–152, 160, 162, 216, 217, 221, 232, 253, 257, 258, 259, 284;
conservation of, 107, 108, 125, 162–168, 182, 190, 263, 264;
as dynamic relational quality, 70, 71, 284;
as emergent, 216;
as empirical generalization, 217, 219–221, 238, 239;
no unique object of, 216–218;
and the Good, 258–285;
the highest, 157, 259, 263, 275;
objective reference of, 126, 127, 216, 217, 232;
as Objective, 150, 159, 168, 186–189, 191, 220, 258, 259, 285, 286;
as metaphysically objective, 259;
as valid for man, 220, 285, 286;
and the natural realm, 256, 257;
source of, 175, 256, 257;
as pivot for system, 48, 50;
and time, 51;
uniformity of, 217;
as uncreated, 89.
See also Moral values; Value-judgment; Good; Martineau; Pringle-Pattison; Sorley; Tennant; Ward.

Value-claim, in relation to true value, 141, 142, 150–152, 190;
Sorley's view, 145, 150, 156;
not subjective, 151, 152.

Value-judgment, its accuracy, 62, 63, 157;
basis for authority of, 83;
criteria of, 152–160, 189;
empirical derivation of, 70, 71;
objective reference of, 67, 69, 83, 140–143, 144–158, 160, 161, 179, 190;
as involving obligation, 141, 142;
Sorley's view evaluated, 146–152, 154–160, 173–180;
uniformity of, 156, 157, 190;
universality of, 27, 28, 156;
validity of, 39, 40, 66, 67, 68.